So You Want to be a Teacher?

So You Want to be a Teacher?

Fred Sedgwick

⑤SAGE

Los Angeles • London • New Delhi • Singapore

SAGE Publications Ltd
1 Oliver's Yard
55 City Road
London EC1Y 1SP

SAGE Publications Inc
2455 Teller Road
Thousand Oaks, California 91320

SAGE Publications India Pvt Ltd
B1/I1 Mohan Cooperative Industrial Area
Mathura Road
New Delhi 110 044

SAGE Publications Asia-Pacific Pte Ltd
33 Pekin Street #02–01
Far East Square
Singapore 048763

Library of Congress Control Number: 2007936693

British Library Cataloguing in Publication Data
A catalogue record for this book is available from the British Library

ISBN-978-1-4129-4507-3
ISBN-978-1-4129-4508-0 (pbk)

Typeset by Pantek Arts Ltd, Maidstone, Kent
Printed in India by Replika Press
Printed on paper from sustainable resources

for Daniel, again

'By learning you will teach; by teaching you will learn.'
(Latin proverb, quoted in Grey, 2003)

'I touch the future. I teach.'
(Christa McAuliffe, the first civilian in space)

Acknowledgements

I am grateful to my friends for their comments: Rosa Aers, Emma Bayliss, John Fisher, Seamus Fox, Carly Gulliver, Jill Haine, David Hampson, Dorothy Hampson, Terri Morgan, Emily Roeves, Colin Sedgwick, Daniel Sedgwick and Nina Sedgwick. And especially, Helen Fairlie of SAGE. None of them is, of course, responsible for any crudities that remain.

Contents

Abbreviations

AST	Advanced Skills Teacher
BA/BSc	Bachelor of Arts/Science: the most common first degrees; some first degrees in Scotland are Master of Arts degrees (MA)
CertEd	Certificate of Education: teaching qualification before it became a graduate profession
GCSE	General Certificate of Secondary Education
GTC	General Teaching Council
GTCNI	General Teaching Council for Northern Ireland
GTP	Graduate Teacher Programme
GTTR	Graduate Teacher Training Registry
HEI	Higher Education Institute (Scotland and Wales)
ICT	Information and Communications Technology
Inset	In-service education for teachers, according to me. More usually, In-service education and training. But, as I will write later, training is about being pulled along preordained tracks, and only incidentally related to education.
LSA	Learning Support Assistant. This is problematic. They are sometimes called TAs (Teaching Assistants). I have stuck with the former because it focuses on learning and is more democratic.
M-level PGCE	Masters level Postgraduate Certificate of Education. This is new and involves gaining sixty Masters level credits.
NARIC	National Academic Recognition Initiative Centre
NQT	Newly Qualified Teacher
O levels	the old equivalent of GCSEs
Ofsted	Office for Standards in Education, Childen's Services and Skills. Tyrell Burgess (2002) offers a definition, 'organisation issuing reports which are the educational equivalent of station announcements, intrusive, vaguely menacing and unintelligible'. Disgraceful, of course. Some schools find Ofsted inspections helpful.
PGCE	Postgraduate Certificate of Education
PGDE	Postgraduate Diploma in Education (Scotland)
PPA	Preparation, Planning and Assessment – all teachers are given time within the school week for this

QTS	Qualified Teacher Status
SCITT	School-centred Initial Teacher Training
SEED	Scottish Executive Education Department
SEN	Special Educational Needs
TDA	Training and Development Agency
TES	Times Educational Supplement
TQ	Teaching Qualification (mainly used in Scotland)
UCAS	Universities and Colleges Admissions Service

Like all the superficialities of education, and unlike the basic realities, these are liable to change. SCITT, for example, in Suffolk and Norfolk is now SNITT (Suffolk and Norfolk). Keep up at the back there!

Preface: A Back-Pocket Book

During World War Two, the American military authorities issued guidebooks for servicemen (and they were, of course, mostly men) serving in the UK. These books have been reprinted in facsimile, partly because they provide insights into life at the time, but more because they click neatly into a place in the jigsaw of the nostalgia market. They sell in shops like Past Times to the over-sixties, and to children and grandchildren looking for stocking fillers to give parents and grandparents at Christmas. Much as they are the perfect size and shape for stockings now, they were the right size and shape for the back pockets of uniforms then.

The guidebooks offered advice about how American servicemen should live and work with a people, the British, who were similar to the servicemen's own but with famous differences. It is often said that the British and the Americans are a common people divided by a language. In fact the language differences are trivial, but they stare us in the face in nearly every transatlantic conversation. 'Sidewalk' and 'pavement', 'elevator' and 'lift', 'truck' and 'lorry', 'restroom' and 'lavatory' are merely the beginning.

But you could go deeper and sum up the motivation for the books by noting that American authorities saw, as a potential problem, the gap between British reserve and austerity on the one hand and American outgoingness and prosperity on the other. In other words, there is a social as well as a linguistic dimension to all this. While the locals walked to poorly-stocked grocers with their ration books, the visitors gave out Herschey bars. One day I will find out what these were. The names must have had an exotic ring to austerity-ridden Britons, especially to children and young women.

This is a back-pocket book. It is a guide for non-teachers thinking about entering the world where teachers work; where the language and social mores tally mostly, but not entirely, with the language and social mores of their own world; much as the American servicemen's world, language and social mores tallied merely mostly with the British ones.

1 'Teaching is the profession that creates all others'

The teachers' world

The teachers' world and the non-teachers' world: to be sure, the same laws of human interaction apply. Teachers are as selfless or as selfish, as kind or as unkind, as engaging or as boring, as political or as non-political, as loving or as non-loving, as abstemious or as indulgent as everyone else. If you prick them, they bleed; if you tickle them, they laugh; if you poison them, they die.

But, notwithstanding their bleeding, their laughing and their dying, teachers are members of a race (as Shylock was) apart. They work with children. This means that their everyday conversation differs from the rest of the world's conversation. Teachers' conversation is often geared to understanding experiences that children have: waking early and feeling lonely, Christmas mornings, the first day of the holidays, minor betrayals on the playground, bullying, friendship and its strength and its frailty, family breakdowns. Children's experiences are sometimes more intense than adults' experiences, even though the years they have lived are fewer. Crucially, teachers remember their own experiences of childhood. And not only remember them. They align them, somehow, with their lives as they are now. They remember disappointments, family breakdowns, even minor betrayals on the playground, and they remember them with a peculiar intensity. They *empathise*.

It is rarely noted that teachers' conversations with children don't use certain registers that are ever present in much adult conversation. Teachers exclude profanity and casual swearing, in their work, even though these registers are present (odd, this) in much children's conversation. Generally, except in particular circumstances, they exclude anything about sex, though children are interested in it and almost certainly they think and talk about it. And teachers' conversations with children, sometimes unnecessarily, are generally composed of shorter, simpler sentences than conversations among adults.

Teachers' ability to understand and empathise with children's conversation impresses many lay people to whom the business of managing a classroom is a mystery. After all, teachers are responsible for twenty-odd vulnerable humans simultaneously, all with their different personalities and learning styles. Many recognise this. 'You're a teacher?' they say, glancing sideways, as you politely eat the first course at a dinner party. 'Better you than me!' Indeed, this responsibility is a heavier one than any weighing down the shoulders of electricians, backbench MPs and Ofsted inspectors, apart from exceptional tasks such as making unsafe wiring systems safe, voting to go to war or judging a school on a three-day visit.

Occasionally, those outside the profession suggest that there is something essentially good about what teachers do. Teachers' principles for action (as with doctors, nurses, social workers and others) are largely a regard for, if not a love for, others. It is often understood that teachers have foregone choices of profession (or even left a profession) that might have made them rich. And this is often true: I have just met a London teacher who gave up a job as a legal personal assistant to train on the Graduate Teacher Programme. 'My salary was halved, but now I'm doing what I love … I'm doing something to help people have better lives'.

Others are impressed by the sheer effort teachers have made during their training and early practice to understand children. The way children think, write and draw is, teachers seem to understand, well, interesting. The things children say are worth more than the casual anecdote.

But others are not impressed. They suspect that the teacher next to them at the dinner table has chosen a world in which she can dominate people simply by being physically, mentally and spiritually bigger. Perhaps the word 'bully' hovers behind some of these people's thinking. And a teacher, for many, is someone who has avoided the rough and tumble of the business world with its highs and lows, its risks, its falls. With its poor pay but secure pension, the teaching profession is not quite the real world. I always want to tell them that teaching is the profession that creates all others.

And to many non-teachers, school is something from which you escape. Teachers have escaped and then chosen to go back. When, at that dinner table, you say you are a teacher, they look at you and simultaneously remember classrooms and the smell of chalk, the smell from the toilets, tasteless school dinners or the peeling paint on the classroom wall.

Voices from the non-teaching world

I talked to some non-teachers to put this thinking into a human context. Sometimes, people decide early in life that teaching might not be the right career for them because teachers supplied what my friend called:

bad role models ... it was a prep school, and I thought they were living in a very artificial environment, that they couldn't cope in the real world. I know that's wrong now. The teachers I know seem to be able to deal with anything ...

Another non-teacher wrote to me:

> The main reason why I didn't teach is because I did have a hard time in the last two years of secondary school (from other kids and some awful teachers!), which sapped my confidence somewhat. Perhaps I should have thought that I could have done a better job myself, but by then the damage had been done. Another reason is because I have never had or wanted children myself, so I suppose I didn't feel a natural empathy with children, which I think is a key thing for becoming a good teacher.

Here, at least in part, a bad school experience was significant.
Other people just know they don't want to teach:

> Actually I never even considered becoming a teacher, because I've never really got on that well with children ... I couldn't see myself spending my days surrounded by small people, or teenagers ...

I fear now that my questions were badly formed and made people feel that they ought to be teachers, which I didn't intend, and that therefore they were slightly defensive in their answers. Another non-teacher wrote, unconsciously perhaps, agreeing with the views of many who have become teachers:

> I thought about it for about thirty seconds, but no longer because it is too hard and I think the national curriculum is silly. The testing system seems to me self-defeating and it felt like training dogs to jump through hoops. Also, I think I do not like being an 'authority figure'. And I have too much to learn to be able to teach ...

Indeed, the best teachers could reiterate that last sentence, but they might twist it: 'I have too much to learn, so I *must* teach ...' A Latin proverb says: 'By learning you will teach; by teaching you will learn'.
Here is vocation in its raw state. It's another non-teacher:

> No, I never seriously considered becoming a teacher, largely because God stepped in first with the call to preach. My brief experience as a temporary (and unqualified) teacher convinced me, if I needed convincing, (a) that it was something I probably could do, given my stubborn and persevering, yea adamantine, nature, but (b) would take little pleasure in because of the unremitting sense of 'it's either them or me' in the classroom (it really was a blackboard jungle at — in those bad old days).

He went on to describe a city comprehensive in the seventies (later closed), and he reminded me of one of Lenny Bruce's jokes: 'I won't say our school was rough, but we had our own coroner ... We used to have to write essays on "What I will do if I grow up"'.

Teaching – a vocation?

The word 'vocation' comes from the Latin *vocare*, to call. To have a vocation is like knowing you're going to be a priest or a minister. As most of us do, I fantasised about other jobs. For me, the daydream was about being a great fast bowler or an orchestral conductor, but I had weak arms, insufficient height to bowl a bouncer, no skill and (though I loved music) a lazy ear. I was left (like millions of others) with the ability to love both cricket and music, an encyclopaedic knowledge of the former, a passable one of the latter. But I possessed skill in neither. Anyway, in the real world I wanted to teach from the age of eleven. In fact, I knew I was going to be a teacher.

But not having an obvious vocation doesn't mean you won't be a brilliant teacher. Others discover in subtler, slower ways that they want to teach. While some are converted, like me, suddenly, others find that the conversion takes time. But it is no less (or more) certain for that. It is still a vocation. I asked some teachers about this: How did they decide to become a teacher?

> I was about nine and I didn't like to go to my temporary school in Bradford. It was so different from what I was used to in Dunmow [Essex]. My grandmother taught children with Down's Syndrome in a church hall. They weren't in the education system, that didn't happen till many years later either. So whenever I could I got out of my school ('Mummy, I don't feel very well. Can I go with Grandma?') and went to the church hall.

> It's a cliché to say those children are loveable, but it's true. They gave so much, and I wanted to give back. I was only nine. Special needs chose me before teaching did. Apart from spells with evening classes, I've taught special needs all my career because of those children in Bradford.

Another friend said, rather sadly, echoing that Latin proverb: 'I wanted to teach because I wanted to keep on learning. I believed that education would change the world. I lost all that after about fifteen years.'

The calling may lead to joy, or it may lead to disillusionment. It probably will lead, of course, to something between the two.

Choosing a career – or a job?

The word 'career' is not always the right word these days. It once signified a choice that one made in one's teens, twenties or thirties, that was supposed, as *The Book of Common Prayer* puts it, 'not to be taken in hand unadvisedly', and to last, like a marriage, 'for richer or poorer, in sickness and in health', till death you and it did part. But as the hymn says, 'change and decay in all around I see': nothing, neither career nor marriage is deemed once and for all anymore. I know teachers who left the profession to go into nursing, football coaching and eventually football management, and at least one who did the latter but the other way round: managed a football club and then became a PE teacher.

I've known carpenters who have become teachers. I've known an Anglo-Catholic priest who became one, then went back to his altar. What seems certain to those who predict the future is that from now on there will to be no certainty. We will all have to be more flexible in our working lives. So choose to teach, if you want or if you are called, but don't assume you will be doing it forever.

The saloon bar and the classroom

I am not suggesting here that teachers never go into saloon bars. The phrase stands for the kind of opinions, by no means all unenlightened, routinely expressed in the non-teachers' world. Everybody has something to say about teaching, and often, in my local, views are expressed freely and loudly by two men always at the same corner of the bar.

There are two reasons for this. Firstly, everybody has been to school and therefore everybody has memories of their education. I am going to have much to say about memories in Chapter 2. Secondly, most people have children and therefore, of course, have strong opinions about how their children should be taught. Many of these opinions may be based on hearsay; they may be ill-informed; they may be based on a vested interest; they almost certainly will be out of date. But no-one will suggest that parents have no right to hold an opinion, whether those opinions are fuelled by local bitter or not. All this makes talking about teaching different from talking about, say, electrical engineering, politics or inspecting schools, of which almost all of us have no experience and therefore no opinions.

Another difference between the two worlds – the teachers' world and the non-teachers' world – is that the teachers' world is largely insulated from what I call saloon bar culture. Casual racism and sexism are either absent or suppressed in schools. This is not so in the conversations of my acquaintances in my local. And that saloon bar culture is not only found in saloon bars. I recently ate microwaved soup in a tea shop in a remote village in north Norfolk, and the proprietor invited me to agree, within five minutes of making my acquaintance, that criminals should be hanged because then 'the prisons would only be half-full'. Surely, I thought, they would be empty. In any case, even if a teacher believed it, this view simply would not be expressed (it might be suppressed) in a school staffroom.

This book's main aim is to offer guidance to four sets of readers while they decide whether teaching is for them. I like to think it will fit into the back pocket or the handbag.

Four groups of readers

Most of you reading this book will be in one of four groups:

- students reading for first degrees and considering career options, including a Postgraduate Certificate of Education (PGCE)

- graduates considering qualification through the SCITT (School-centred Initial Teacher Training) schemes run by local authorities

- men and women thinking about training as mature students while their children grow up, or as their present jobs begin to bore or distress them, who will probably be considering the Graduate Teacher Programme (GTP)

- sixth formers and students living between school and university and considering BA degrees with Qualified Teacher Status (QTS) or TQs in Scotland considering courses in HEIs.

Also interested might be your parents, partners and families. Others might be those whose work involves the notion of a calling: priests and ministers who lead school assemblies, school governors, doctors, nurses, journalists specialising in education perhaps. Some might read what follows and end up in a few years reflecting sadly that 'I believed that education (or religion, or health, or journalism) would change the world, but I lost all that ...' Others, though, and here I narrow the focus down to teachers, will find that, after forty years, children still give delight; that their world can be changed.

Another group might be Learning Support Assistants (LSAs) who find that their experience in schools nudges them towards training as teachers.

What is a teacher?

A teacher, of course, for our purposes, is an adult with certain qualifications who 'shows' children knowledge, usually in a school. I've put 'shows' in inverted commas because the Greek word for 'teach' is related to the word for 'show'.

But in a broader sense of the word, we are all teachers. In daily talk, whether we find it tedious or boring, whether we talk animatedly and listen with eyes wide, whether we yawn and wish we could go to the pub, we teach each other: we 'show' each other things. And thereby we learn, and teach. Every relationship – father–child, friend–friend, publisher–writer, inspector–teacher – is a two-way educational relationship. Marriages obviously are. Husband and wife teach with a glorious, terrifying intensity. In the immortal, desperate words of Basil Fawlty, 'Understand me', the couple seems to be saying to each other, 'understand me, before one of us dies …'

So, 'educational relationship' is a tautology.

To relate to someone = to teach + to learn. Learning, as I have already said, always travels in two directions, not one. Education is active, potent and energetic. It is on the move in unexpected, even mysterious ways. It has wonders to perform.

Schooling isn't what it's about

Nearly everyone, even the best teacher, finds this difficult to acknowledge, because 'teacher' and 'education' remind most of us of 'schooling'. Here comes a long sentence. I'd better put it in its own paragraph:

If I think of my schooling, I think of assemblies and singing 'Eternal Father strong to save', although my school was sixty miles from the sea, and 'We plough the fields and scatter', though few of us had seen a sheaf of wheat; of long playtimes when I didn't know what to do; of being put in stream 4 and then being suddenly promoted to stream 1 because I could read, the results (which most of the children *couldn't* read, but which I could) being posted on the wall; of school journeys I half wanted to go on and half didn't, that my parents couldn't afford; of being bullied and once, on a shameful occasion, of bullying; of holding Jeanette's hand during country dancing (she was the prettiest Year 6 girl); of listening to the history teacher reading notes which we had to copy down for British History; of not being caned because, unlike some of my friends, I could play the school game; of being in set 3 for maths until they invented set 4 and put it in the hapless hands of a new, very young teacher who 'couldn't keep control', while set 1 was taught by the head of maths; of being considered not worth too much because I'd settled for college of education rather than university, and, and, and …

It was schooling, obviously, but if it was education, it was only incidentally so. I learned more from Jeanette than I did from the history teacher (not, regrettably, that I learned much from her). Those teachers were *teaching* me, yes, but were they teaching me what they thought they were teaching me? The school was teaching me cynicism in the matter of the sudden invention of set 4 and the introduction of a thin, inept young man asked to face fifteen spotty youths who had already given up on maths. Were they teaching what I needed to be taught? Were they just schooling me?

Of course, that is unfair. I passed most of my 'O' levels (the equivalent of GCSEs today) and went on to the sixth form and passed an 'A' level. Someone (a maths teacher) took me in a group to hear *Messiah* at the Royal Albert Hall. Someone else took me to the cathedrals at Rochester and Canterbury. Someone else took me to see the young Judi Dench in *Henry IV Part One* at the Old Vic. And a music teacher made us sing 'Linden Lea' and 'The Vagabond' and, for multiculturalism's sake, the French National Anthem. I hope he would be pleased to know that I can still get through all three from memory.

And I developed an obsession with words: how they were formed, how they grew and what, in skilled hands, they could do. But it is significant that all these experiences, except for the singing, happened both outside the school and outside the curriculum. In those places, schooling was less obvious and less conventional than is usual. It was in the Royal Albert Hall, in the crypt at Canterbury, in a the-atre stall, in the music room singing William Barnes' and Robert Louis Stevenson's words set to Ralph Vaughan Williams' music where my life was changed; where (except for the music room) there were ordinary people, non-teachers, non-stu-dents, walking about, going about their business.

Though obviously the two words are connected, 'schooling' and 'education' do not mean the same thing. Schooling is static rather than dynamic. Its ways have no mystery at all. It's lining up on the playground and being silent in assembly while the tardier classes file mutely in. It is control and discipline. It is class lists, order and tests. Necessary, yes, but no wonder that it may ring dull notes on our bell and make us feel negative about the profession we are considering.

It shouldn't. Put schooling out of your minds. When we think about possibly becoming a teacher, we should think about learning. Of course, you'll have to school the children: make them safe, for example, and check they're present when they are, mark them absent when they're not. But schooling is not the central issue. For the same kind of reason, the word 'training' is problematic, too. Follow its metaphor: it's about being pulled along preordained tracks. However, given its predominance in education, its mention is of course unavoidable in a book like this one.

So what is teaching about?

As I've written, we are all learners and all teachers, in two senses: we are all both, and we all do both all the time. Much as it is true that we cannot talk without learn-ing, we cannot pray, meditate, or build a relationship without it either. We cannot even think (converse with ourselves, I could say) without learning. Learning the truth has been the major preoccupation of western humankind (apart from sur-vival, both of the individual and of the race) since before the times of the pre-Socratic philosophers in Greece until the present day, and the same is true of the eastern thinkers. And, in any case, survival is *learning* how to survive.

Mature men and women reflect on learning as their children grow. They can't help it, much as their babies can't help learning. They watch their babies' eyes from the moment of birth, they hear their first gurgles, then their first attempts at words, then their first words. When the children are (at last!) asleep, parents can't help but reflect, however unsystematically, on what they have seen and heard. So they understand that learning is going on all the time. They have begun the process of educating their children, simply by looking into their eyes, and respond-ing to them.

The value that their experiences as parents will bring to their teaching (should they choose to become teachers in a school) is inestimable. In the most powerful way possible, they have inducted babies into the mystery of human love and they have achieved this within seconds of their children's birth. Here are some examples:

- They have helped their children to become scientists by looking at the movement of branches in the wind or at the rhythm of waves on a beach.

- They have helped them to become readers by reading (at first) to them and (later) with them.

- On holidays, they have pointed out trees and rocks, cathedrals and palaces, the characters at Disneyland, and this has helped the children to become observers, intense lookers. And looking is a prerequisite not only for artists, but also for natural scientists, architects and critics, for plumbers, electricians and mechanics.

- They have also helped their children in the first steps in what is called 'socialisation', and this has begun the process of becoming a citizen. In that process, they will have been educated themselves, both by their children and by (not quite the same thing) their interaction with their children.

So parents who decide to teach have advantages over the rest of us.

The readers in the other groups who might become teachers, including students working towards first degrees or following PGCE, sixth formers, most (though not all) SCITT students and some GTP students, may not have had these experiences. But they will bring different advantages: youth, with its mental energy, idealism and enthusiasm, and recent access to their own studies. They too have been teachers when explaining, for example, a passion for their music, or for football, or for photography, or for computers and what they can do and what they will soon be able to do, or for the stars, or for whatever they might have an obsession for.

Here is a truth that underpins everything that teachers do. It has an unspoken presence all the time when teachers meet children. Lawrence Stenhouse sums it up in one sentence: 'The purpose of education is to make us freer and more creative' (1975). It helps us to understand that we are human beings, not cogs in a machine; that we can look back on things that we have made – an apple strudel, a repair to a plumbing system, a poem, and say, 'That's good!'

Teaching isn't about getting our class into assembly on time, or about phonemes, or even about teaching historical, scientific and geographical facts. It's not about coming top of a list. It's about the state of the world and about making it more just, about making things through a search for the truth. It is vital to recognise this at the outset and to accept that therefore it is both a huge responsibility and a huge delight. Because of that search for the truth, there is nobility in the scruffy, increasingly chancy, ill-paid profession of teaching. The search for truth is the same as the search for freedom and creativity. It is the artist in us that shows us and our masters and mistresses that we are human beings and not hired hands existing to service the economy.

The importance of education as a tool to find freedom is negatively shown by tyrants who attempt to trammel it, who know it is a threat to their regimes. Hitler wrote that 'Universal education is the most corroding and disintegrating poison that liberalism has ever constructed for its own destruction' (quoted in Grey, 2003). It has even more power to destroy reactionary values. Henry VIII knew this when he wrecked the monasteries, where knowledge was acquired and written down under candles by monks. But somewhere in England, one monk went on writing. One candle kept burning.

It is also, paradoxically, or so it might look, democratic. We are, as I have said earlier in this chapter, all teachers. So being a teacher professionally links us to every human being. But it links us in particular with all who take responsibility in a classroom. And, more to the point of this book, it links us with the tribe of children, a tribe of which every one of us has been a member, and whose present members know more than is acknowledged about the world, its trees, its waves on shores, its animals, its loves and hates. All they need is a methodology to help them understand more. That's our job.

Here is just one example from a recent trip to north-west *East* England:
I am watching nine-year-old, crop-haired, skinny Glenn. He has severe hearing loss and is normally (I am told) a disruptive boy. He is staring at the River Wear four miles above <u>Durham</u> with a clipboard in his arms and a sheet of A4 and pencil in his hand. He gazes intensely as a laser beam at the water as its bottle greens become creamy white over the rocks, as the chicks roll, tumble and right themselves. Changing him from troubled normality to such engagement is as much changing the world as I need. Helping someone to 'notice such things', if only for an hour, will do. Looking, with as much objectivity as possible, calms and sensitises the looker; it is not only pleasurable, but provides a basis for feeling and learning.

Changing the world globally is for few of us, thank goodness. We probably wouldn't do it well. But we can do this well: transform a child's life for an hour, a week, a term, a year, maybe a whole lifetime.

Education as a business

For one GTP student, the advantages of his chosen course were simply expressed: 'A 14k salary ... it was quick – 12 months to QTS status ... theory kept to a minimum'. He wrote on a questionnaire that the aim of teaching is 'to prepare children for living in a capitalist society'. He aimed, within ten years, to be either 'teaching in another country ... or running my own private tuition company ...' He added, 'There are too many areas of education "not working"!'

'I don't like what they do to the enemy', as Wellington said of his troops before the battle of Waterloo, and as I thought of these responses, 'but by G— they frighten me'.

I wasn't paying enough attention while education was changing from a calling into a business. I glimpsed the creep of the new values when I was still a head-teacher. I was beginning my second headship in 1982. Someone told us on our induction course that one responsibility was 'managing the school plant'. All I could think of, for a few nonplussed minutes, was the Swiss cheese plants, the spider plants, the cacti, the tradescantias that I always put round the school when I started on my first headship. But the Chief Education Officer and his underlings meant grounds, building, maintenance. I recoiled. I didn't want to manage them! I wanted to learn! I wanted to teach!

The questions buzzed around my head and they still do. If education is a business where what matters is profit and not people, whose interests does it serve? The company that funds a school and its shareholders? The profit motive? The parents? The teachers? The children? I remember a teacher saying, years ago, that one purpose of education is to help children to resist the blandishments of capitalism. I agreed with him then, and I do now. If children can become capable of reasoned judgements about advertising, for example, they are more likely to be able to make reasoned judgements about poetry, paintings, television programmes, music and every other artistic and media event that surrounds their lives. More importantly, a critical faculty will help them, when they see advertisements for loans that will erase poverty in two years or creams that will erase pimples within a week, to keep at the front of their minds the questions: Who is this who is lying to me? And why is he or she doing it?

City academies are the most egregious examples I've come across (so far) of the business ethic inside education. Although government lets the public believe that private concerns fund a school, they don't. Those concerns – whether they are churches, private schools or billionaire-backed businesses – pay tiny amounts. They set the school up, but the taxpayer pays the rest. The real beneficiaries are the private sponsors themselves, who revel in all the fluffy, cuddly publicity. See Francis Beckett's article on sponsored schools 'Sell 'em cheap' in the *Guardian* (2007a), and his recent book (2007b).

2 Teaching in a school

Good news

The joys of being a teacher are many and various. There is the company of colleagues. Ignore those teachers who seem to have emptied any love and joy from their lives with children. I have known them. I have drunk their powdered instant coffee, eaten their jammy dodgers and (on less prosperous days) nibbled their rich tea biscuits. I have listened to their funny stories. I have discussed last night's TV with them. They have their own chairs in the staffroom, and those chairs are an extension of their living rooms at home. And they have their lexicon: 'little herberts', 'the children round here', 'drum something into their heads'. They exude a casual, un-thought-out cynicism.

But nearly all teachers are kind and liberal, and to have lunch with them is a pleasure. If you take this step into teaching, you will enter a humane place where the inhabitants tolerate the rest of the world, not in the sense of 'allow' or 'concede', but in the sense of 'live with' and 'rejoice in'.

Here are some of the other joys. As a teacher, you can:

- watch children learn, and learn alongside them.

- help them through crises. One child wrote a note to her teacher (Sedgwick, 2001): 'You helped me when my mum and dad split up'. What a privilege it was for that teacher to have been responsible for such care, and how her eyes pricked with tears when she read that message. And how my own eyes did when she told me about it.

- be part of a community that is ignorant about most things, but ready to learn.

- enjoy their company. This should be obvious. If you don't like children, stay away from teaching. Sadly, it isn't obvious to some people. It must be your main reason for even thinking about the profession.

And remember this platinum rule, which is rarely recorded in print: children almost always behave better in school than they do in public. Embarrassing, or otherwise distressing their parents in the supermarket by demanding chocolate bars and Bacardi Breezers NOW is not typical of their behaviour with teachers. When they squabble loudly with their siblings on the top deck of the bus you have taken to get home from college, you have to remember that they are not like this in school.

Children in schools are almost always honest. Sometimes they are embarrassingly so. On my first day in my last headship, I sat with a group of eight having lunch, determined to make a good impression on the school with my firm but fair discipline, my enlightened approach to the curriculum, my closeness to the children at all times and the benign sun-like warmth of my heart. A nine-year-old boy said,

'Did you know that your ears move up and down when you eat?' I checked this in the mirror as soon as I got home. He was right.

You can enjoy, in teaching, the camaraderie of a staffroom. There's also respect from the public. If you don't believe this, wait till you see glances when you lead a group of children in York or Bristol, or wherever you go on your first school trip. The looks of bus drivers, pedestrians and shoppers will tell you: They're brave. They're doing that well. I couldn't do that. I wouldn't have the patience.

It's a good world, the school world. There's much schooling in it despite all I've said earlier. You have to make sure the children are safe and you have to encourage them to behave properly. You have to keep records. You have to play the school game; you have to get them into assembly on time; you have to write statements about them. You have to sail, with your colleagues, through the seas of the occasional Ofsted inspection. But, high above all that, you have to help them to learn. And you have to learn alongside them, as anyone does who talks to their friend about architecture, or science, or poetry, or the way clouds move.

And teaching is a successful profession. You'd never know about the many successes in schools if you relied on news stories on television and feature articles in the media, or on Ofsted reports, which tend to emphasise failure. Much teaching is both successful and aristocratic in its altruism. Teachers, within the limits imposed on them, do what they believe to be right.

On the blank page overleaf, make a list of any lessons you can remember being taught which you felt were particularly successful. Reflect on what made them so successful.

Here is an example. It's an account from a sixth-former at a local school:

> I remember a lesson when the teacher asked us to underline all the words in Keats' poem *Ode to a Nightingale* that were concerned with drink, drugs, illness, death and sleepiness. I remember that the list interested us. Even if we hadn't experimented with them, we were all interested in drugs and boozing ... I'd been bored by the poem so far. But we scurried through it again, in groups, and found: 'aches', 'pains', 'fade', 'groan', 'palsy', 'pale', 'dies', 'death', 'die', 'cease', 'drowsy', 'dull brain', 'hemlock', 'opiate', 'vintage', 'beaded bubbles', 'purple stained mouth', 'wine'.
>
> The teacher explained 'Lethe', 'hemlock', 'Hippocrene' and 'Bacchus'.
>
> This lesson was successful because it made me read the poem again with greater attention. The 'keywords' were ones that interested us. It made me look at all the words in the poem with greater attention; it hit the centre of the poem. The teacher explained to me later that she had aimed at the pupils getting the keywords.

Make a list of successful lessons you have been taught.

Do you remember?

The example above is a recorded memory of a lesson. But, rather than lessons, methods, schemes, techniques and the like, everyone who thinks back to their schooling remembers the teachers. Dig deep into the mine of your memories. Think hard for a moment about someone who taught you at primary or secondary school, or at university or college. Make sure that it's someone whom you remember with, at the very least, respect and possibly affection – or even love. Write down quickly three or four things this teacher said. Share these memories with colleagues.

Now think of another teacher. By contrast, this one should be someone you remember with little respect or affection. Forget the love. I hope hate's not there, but if it is, own up. Write down some things this teacher said. Again, share these memories with colleagues.

Write, or summarise, your notes on the following page. Again, share these notes with colleagues.

Add both sides up, the positive and the negative. In my memories: 'Don't bother with maths, Sedgwick, stick to your English, you're good at that'; 'Come out here with your hand out, boy'; 'Take down these notes'; 'Write this down fifty times, "Lesson time is not the time for general conversation"'; and 'Sedgwick – again!'. These and similar remarks, all casually made, easily beat lovely things, like something scribbled in my autograph book by my Year 6 teacher when I left primary school, 'Goodbye, Freddie, and never lose that smile!' and another lovely sentence: 'Here's a book of poems I'd like you to have …' The latter was on my final day at grammar school, and the book he was handing me, *A Pageant of Modern Verse* (Parker, 1940), was about to become the seed of my library. I have that book on my desk now.

How do the negative and the positive weigh up in your notes?

A non-teacher sent me these memories. Everything she writes is a lesson for anyone thinking about becoming a teacher:

> It's difficult remembering exactly what teachers have said in the past (it was about 30 years ago), but I had a lovely English teacher in the first two years at my secondary school, who often said my writing was 'beautiful' and that I was a good influence on my friend I sat next to, as I helped her with her handwriting (she was left-handed) and helped her keep her books tidier! Little words of encouragement like this went a long way, as we used to bounce ideas off each other in lessons and with homework.

> Contrast this with a truly awful English teacher in the 4th and 5th years, whose hobby seemed to be mastering the art of the sarcastic put-down, which was not encouraging in the slightest!

Positive	Negative

We had a fantastic maths teacher. She was a bit wild and threw blackboard rubbers, chalk and books at kids who played up in class. She did not suffer fools! On the other hand, she was really encouraging and said that anyone who was prepared to put themselves out if they were having difficulties understanding, she would give extra tuition to in the lunch breaks, which I took advantage of.

A lot of my teachers commented that I needed to overcome shyness, which was difficult because some of them were a bit scary so I was afraid to speak up in class. I also suffered from depression from the ages of 13 to 15, and they were not at all helpful. I did miss quite a bit of school during this time.

So you see, even the smallest bit of encouragement went a long way, especially if you were as shy as I once was, it was a shame that a lot of the teachers I came across were not able to provide this!

There are obvious lessons to be learned here, but I am not ashamed of repeating them because so many teachers either have not learned them, or have forgotten them, or simply ignore them because of cynicism:

- Don't use sarcasm, that bitter, witless inversion of the truth. This is a great temptation for teachers, especially if they mourn (even sub-consciously) more physical means of punishment. It's tempting for any of us who are more fluent with language than most. But it always alienates and humiliates. It avoids having to address the pupil as a person: he or she is merely a target of a teacher's sour tongue. It's a form of bullying.

- Always encourage, always. Notice what my friend says: 'What "even the smallest bit of encouragement" can do'. Pass on good news. Do this to the pupil directly. Do it indirectly: if a colleague praises a pupil's work in another lesson, pass it on to the pupil.

- Avoid contradictions, in your behaviour as much as in words. I've noticed a contradiction in my own work. I ask children, as nearly all teachers do, time and time again, to 'find a better word than "nice"' – and then five minutes later hear myself saying, 'That's a nice piece of work'. And how can a pupil be less shy when the teachers are scary?

- Eccentricity is not always bad. Indeed, a natural teacher behaves as he or she does in any social setting, and if that behaviour is innocently odd, there is no reason why it should not be odd in the classroom. Not that you would (or should) get away with throwing anything at your children today …

Now, go back to your notes and underline in blue the remarks that you remember that were about learning, and in red those that were casual in nature and probably about nothing to do with learning.

Most, I'll bet, were casual remarks. How much power teachers possess, and how often it is used without thinking! When we try to recall things our teachers said to us, we rarely remember big moments of teaching. We remember the casual, the trivial and, quite likely, the negative.

Mind-map your old school

Draw a mind map of the school you remember best. Geographical accuracy is not necessary: make it a mind map, if that is what seems right, or an emotional map, if, on the other hand, that seems right. Or, more likely, make it a mixture of the two. Make the rooms, playing fields or playgrounds that you have most to think about (or feel about) larger than rooms or areas which mean less to you. Draw little pictures (stick figures will do) of yourselves and your friends doing what you used to do there. And write. In the hall, for example, depending on your experiences as remembered, you might write: 'Here we played ball games with benches as goals and I remember the thump of the ball on the bench ... here we sat in assemblies and sang "Last night I had the strangest dream" ... here I was frightened of the gate vault and couldn't climb a rope, and was even more frightened of the other boys and the PE teacher ... This is the school field, which I didn't see for my first three weeks because of the rumours of what happened to first years on that field ...' Put a drawing in each area, the name of a teacher and a sentence about him or her.

Carly wrote on her map, and produced a microcosm of primary schools in the late eighties and early nineties:

> We helped dig the pond at the weekend ... I was the only girl allowed to play football. (I never scored) ... Embarrassing 'spit-wash' from mum at gates ... Behind the wall where people said I kissed Sam – I didn't ... Office – home of the terrifying Mrs Gray ... Miss Musslewhite brought in injured hedgehogs ... The 'corner' where my friend Jake spent most of his time ... Somebody had to hold the aerial to tune in the assembly programme ... Movable partition – had to be quickly closed when very angry mum turned up ... 1st and only computer!

Carly's mind/emotional map is shown opposite.

Rape Seed Field ↑

The only time I was in trouble with the headteacher was for climbing over the fence to hide in the Rape Seed.

Nature Area: We helped dig the pond at the weekend. (I never did).

My Primary School

Stories + lunch under the tree in summer.

Office - home of the terrifying Mrs Gray.

The 'corner' Where my friend Jake spent most of his time.

Library

Reception, Yr 1 + Yr 2.

Miss Musslewhite brought in injured hedgehogs.

Hall

Somebody had to hold the aerial to tune in the assembly programme.

Kitchen - lunch reheated from school dinnies away. I had sandwiches.

Yr 3, 4, 5 + 6. Mrs Carson - my favourite teacher ever.

Moveable partition - had to be closed quickly when mum turned up. My mum turned up.

1st and only computer.

I was the only girl allowed to play football (I never scored).

Behind the wall where people said I kissed Sam - I didn't.

The summer fête bunting was left up when my sister was born. Embarrassing 'spit wash' from mum at gates.

P.E. shed

The steps → Run up + jump off as fast as possible!

Ask your own children, or the children of friends, to make a mind map of their school.

Visiting a school

We *can* remember. We *can* tell stories. But memory presents an obvious problem: it is about the past. A parent of a child in a primary school told her son (who told his friend in my hearing as we walked in a crocodile along the River Wear in Durham): 'When mum was at the comp, and the children were naughty, the English teacher used to bang his hands on the desk and say 'Brats!'

This is one story among thousands that tell us that schools have changed. On the face of it, children are treated with greater courtesy than they were. Abuse now usually takes official forms: continual testing and preparation for those tests; anxiety about homework; the generalised worry that often comes from a competitive, rather than a co-operative environment. However recently we were at school, we will need to get up to date. So while you are contemplating a way into teaching, visit a school.

As a preliminary to this task, I suggest that you look at the school's website, assuming that it has one. But remember: you will only find out here what the head and governors want you to know.

Then, ask a local school if you can loiter in it. Don't use that word, of course. You can think of something more respectable, though that is what you will be doing. If you are under the supervision of a teacher, you will not need clearance from the Criminal Research Bureau. That will come later, if and when you are in charge of a group of children.

As a writer, I would suggest starting a journal devoted entirely to your visit and what you find out. You may prefer to keep your impressions in your head, though I'd bet that such an approach will lose you valuable data and be less useful in the long run, because writing not only records your learning, but drives it and keeps it purposeful and reflective.

In either case, note the following:

The neighbourhood

- You'll already know whether the school has a rural or an urban setting. Note the presence or absence of everyday facilities: shops, post offices, pubs, green spaces where the children can play (and, come to that, green spaces marked NO BALLS GAMES TO BE PLAYED HERE). Think about what the presence or absence of these implies for the children's lives and their education.

- Look at the roads. Are they busy? What type of traffic do they mostly seem to serve?

- What is the housing like? Do the houses have gardens? Do they seem to be private or council? Do not jump to conclusions about what the children will be like on the basis of this.

- If the setting is in a town, are there such buildings as sports centres, swimming pools, public libraries and the like?

- What seem to be the main cultures (ethnic and religious) in the area?

- Note the age of the area's buildings. In other words, have they had years to bed down? Has the neighbourhood set down roots? Or is it a modern new town, or a new town development on the edge of an old town? If it is part of a city, look at the public buildings. Watch out for buildings that tell you much about a society: a dedicated mosque, for example, or expensive antique shops, branches of Cash Converters or an art gallery.

- Since the Dunblane massacre, getting into the school isn't as easy as it used to be. How did you find the security system? Was it efficient, or did you have to wait to get in? Reflect on what impression this system gives you, and what impression it might give prospective parents, or parents who have come to make a comment about their child's schooling, or visiting inspectors. Is this system as welcoming as it could be? Or is it positively forbidding?

The school

- Check the age of the building and its condition. Note how schools built at different times speak clearly of different views of children. Victorian buildings, with their brickwork and prominent gables, for example, have higher windows. This was presumably, at least in part, to prevent children being distracted from their learning. How have such schools adapted such buildings to a modern view? That view is evident in buildings of the sixties and later, made mostly of pre-stressed concrete, with windows low to the ground. These buildings suggest that children are not distracted from learning by seeing out, but actually encouraged in it.

- Has the school got more than one storey? How does this impact on children moving from class to class, especially very young children? How do the children get out to the playground? Does each class have its own access? How big are the classrooms? Are they separate units or open-plan?

- Has the school got any grass, or just tarmac? Think about how this affects the children's learning – their fitness, for example, and their knowledge of nature: birds, trees and foxes, rabbits and squirrels.

- Look at the classroom's walls. Is there, for example, a list, with varying numbers of stars or ticks, telling the world (or whoever is interested) who has learned which tables (and, thereby of course, who has not learned those tables); who has arrived on book 3 in the reading scheme (and who hasn't); who has been sent to see the headteacher for misbehaviour most times (and who hasn't)?

- Are the displays composed of children's work? If so, what does this work tell you about the teaching? Can you find evidence of learning? Or is the work mere decoration, as it was in the copies of Holbein's portraits of Henry VIII and his wives? What is there in the displays that suggests that the children might usually:
ignore them
study them
glance briefly at them?

On the other hand, are the walls covered by commercial products – posters from publishers, or teachers' magazines? The walls speak to you about the children's learning. Look hard at them.

Children's work	Children's work where I can find evidence of learning	Commercial products

How many times did I see children looking at the displays? Did they talk to anyone else about them?

- Watch, and listen to, the children at play as they gossip, throw or kick balls, as they dance, as they squabble. Watch them in assembly as they wait for other classes to arrive, as they sing, as they listen. You are going to be responsible for these people.

- How are the children arranged in their classrooms? Check for ability-grouping. Are the children deemed best at language, for example, separated from the children deemed weaker? If they are separated, are they in different rooms, or just different groups within a room?

- Watch the children in class. Who is paying attention? Who talks to neighbours? Eavesdrop – what is the talk about? Assuming the children are allowed to sit where they like, who seems to be the centre of a group? Who seems to be an outsider? Note whether the boys and girls mix. Be a listener. Keep your own contributions to a minimum.

- Note the way the children work. If they are working individually on a piece of writing, say, who attacks the task writing immediately, careless, at least at first, of mistakes? Who, by contrast, seems to plan and think first? Who seems to worry? Who, before starting, spends time writing down the date and the learning objective? Who is obsessive about rubbing out? Have the children, consciously or unconsciously, developed activities designed to put off the awkward moment of starting, as most adults do? I make coffee, clean the sink, do the crossword, empty the rubbish, rather than sit at the desk and face the screen. What are the children's equivalents of these? If the task involves collaboration, who takes the lead in a group? Who follows? Who opts out?

- Always keep your own memories, your own stories, in the back of your mind. Your schooldays have much to teach you about teaching, and they are a resource that is as close as possible – in your head. Think about the way you used to work in school, whether in groups or individually. Were you a planner, or were you a get-something-down-quick person? I was, and am, of the latter kind. Does that make me a poorer teacher of the first kind of learner? I reflect on a rarely noted problem: as individual teachers, we are called to teach children who are not only at a very different point in life from us, and of varying intelligences and temperaments; also, they are different kinds of learners. But our teaching style will inevitably reflect our learning style. Will the studious, planned, careful style of a given child jar with my more butterfly-minded, hit-and-miss style?

The staff

- Observe the staff, both at work in the classroom and also while they sit (relaxing or still working?) in the staffroom. Does the headteacher ever sit in there? Observe how teachers relate to each other. Note especially whether they treat the other staff – Learning Support Assistants, secretaries, cleaners, mid-day supervisors, caretakers – as equals.

- Watch how the teachers look at the children and control them. Do not take these looks, these ways of controlling, as exemplary: there are other ways of doing things from theirs. Be critical. Make provisional judgements in your notebooks or in your heads. Keep them to yourself.

- Note the jobs that the Learning Support Assistants are given. Are they tasks such as trimming paper and putting up displays that detach them from the children, or are they working head-to-head and heart-to-heart with children? And, if they are working with individual children or children in groups, do they work separated from the rest of the class, or do they work alongside the teacher and the other children in the room? LSA's jobs vary from school to school. Try to assess the value of their work with the children you watch.

- Try to find out everything you can. Look at the notice board in the staffroom, for example. It will tell you much about how the different members of the staff communicate with each other. Ten minutes' study will give you hints about whether the Senior Management Team rules by diktat through memos, or whether there is a kind of participatory democracy working.

Comparing schools

Is this the environment in which you want to spend a large part, if not all, of your working life? If you have had a previous career and are planning to follow the GTP, you will notice differences between teachers and the people you have worked with before, and you will notice similarities, too. Note them down.

Find another school. Follow the same strategy there and note the similarities and the differences between the two schools.

Note them down on the following page.

If you have time, it would be useful for you to write a case study of one of the schools, using the notes you have made.

School One

School Two

3 Getting into teaching

Having examined two schools, ask yourself, do you still want to teach? If those experiences have put you off, remember that 'schooling' is not education …

Politicians make a fetish of choice. And certainly 'choice' sounds more like a 'hurrah' rather than a 'boo' word. In everyday life, I would like to choose my own dinner, rather than, as in hospital, a hostel, a prison or an old persons' home, have something set before me. One of the great pleasures of civilised life is the calm perusal of a menu in a good restaurant. Every winter, choosing my summer holiday has always been another pleasure.

But does choice mean anything if the fridge is empty, or if we are taken ill? All we want at such times are meat and vegetables, milk and fruit, and an efficient hospital nearby that will diagnose us quickly and make us well. And a pleasant place (wherever!) to go afterwards to get better.

And what does choice mean in secondary schooling, when the local schools are specialist academies? How does my eleven-year-old know for certain that she wants to be a business woman (the predominant choice in city academies), a geographer or a sports scientist, and therefore to go to a school with those specialisms? Maybe she wants to be a painter or an actor. I don't want any choice. I want, and she needs, good all-round education, and within walking distance.

There has certainly been an expansion of choice in my subject here: routes into teaching. There used to be two main routes in England, thirty-five years ago: a Certificate in Education and a Postgraduate Certificate in Education. And, realistically, this wasn't much of a choice anyway, because if you'd achieved poor 'A' levels you followed the former, and if you'd achieved good ones you followed the latter. There was also another route. A decent degree from a decent university could set you a decent job, should you so wish, in the decent prep or public school of your choice. This choice need not detain us here.

And then the BEd (Bachelor of Education) degree bowled up, partly bridging the gap between the two. Now the choice is wide. Whatever you choose there are some basic prerequisites.

Qualifications you need whatever route you follow

On paper, standards are much higher than they used to be. I crept in (though it didn't feel like that then) with six 'O' levels (GCSE equivalents); without mathematics, without a science, and with one 'A' level. Whichever route you walk, some things are non-negotiable today. This list goes for almost everyone. You must have, or you must get:

- GCSE English Grade C

- GCSE mathematics Grade C

- GCSE in a science subject if you want to teach ages 7–14, and if you were born on or after 1 September 1979.

Routes into teaching in England

SCITT

Both the SCITT and the GTP are intended for students who have some experience of life, in a family of their own making, perhaps, and/or in the workplace.

These courses are for graduates who want to train in local schools and colleges. Most students, but not all, who follow this route will be in their early or mid-twenties. Such courses are designed by experienced teachers.

Now, that word 'experienced' is a two-edged sword. Most such teachers have had ten, fifteen, twenty, thirty years experience, during which time they have become wider, broader and more intense in their feeling for, and enjoyment of, their chosen profession. They will have taught in a variety of schools: sometimes on deprived estates on the edges of towns, sometimes in villages, sometimes perhaps in church schools, sometimes in inner cities, sometimes in private schools. However, some experienced teachers have not had thirty years experience at all, but 'one year's experience thirty times' (see Carr, 1972), and others have become cynical. They thought that education would change the world, but now they know it won't. However, it is very unlikely that cynical teachers will be designing SCITT courses!

A SCITT course usually leads to an award of a Postgraduate Certificate of Education (PGCE) validated by a Higher Education Institute. It takes one year, usually running from September to June. There are groups of schools running such courses all over England – none at present in Wales – and you will be based in one school from the 'consortium', or group of schools. That school will be termed 'the lead school'.

SCITT is the course followed by a significant minority of trainee teachers, and that number is growing. You should have a good degree (upper second in some authorities: lower second in most) before applying. If you are going to teach Key Stage 1 or 2, the subject should be one of the core subjects of the national curriculum – English, maths or science. Otherwise, you may have to do a preparatory training course.

The advantages and disadvantages are ones of scale. You are likely to be part of a small group, all well-known to each other and to the tutors. PGCE and BA (QTS) students frequently complain to me about the anonymity they feel in big institutions. A SCITT course is likely to provide more friendly support.

On the other hand, a SCITT course may not offer you the advantage of easy access to a large library. And you will not have the social life a university campus offers. This latter won't be a problem, though, because you will have had enough of that in your degree course and will have developed a network of friends, some of whom (a good thing!) won't be teachers or student-teachers.

In SCITT schemes, you will be supported financially. You will collect a bursary (i.e., not taxable). You may even be eligible for a 'golden hello' after you complete your induction period.

You will enter the profession immersed in school and its ways. Or, at least, in one school and its ways.

It has been difficult to persuade SCITT institutions to let me know about what their students think about their courses, and even students who have completed questionnaires have not returned them. But at the last moment a SCITT-trained teacher told me:

One year was a whistle-stop tour. There was one day for teaching history, one day for teaching geography, one day for foundation stage. That became a problem, because I taught foundation stage in my first job, still am. There were ten days each for teaching maths and literacy. We had great chunks of Piaget and Skinner for our theory ...

As the assignment load was spread out, I didn't feel the workload was too much. About the same as a university, where I'd done my first degree in literature and music ... I was used to assignments. I felt it wasn't as easy for graduates who had done science and maths, who weren't so used to doing assignments ...

There were mentors in school, and tutors who were mostly, I think, advisory teachers. They were excellent.

As far as theory was concerned, things changed as soon as I had some experience ...

Visit the graduate teacher training registry (GTTR) to apply. See their website: www.gttr.ac.uk.

GTP

The Graduate Teacher Programme is for prospective teachers who have worked in another job for some years and are determined to make a career change. They are usually older than SCITT students. There is no bursary, but an income – taxable, of course – of about double what is available on the SCITT scheme.

GTP is a common choice for Learning Support Assistants (LSAs) who have gained a degree through the Open University or some other route. They have decided, after the valuable experience that work as a LSA gives, that they want to be teachers.

GTP students work in a school, at first typically only observing. Over the year, they teach more and more. The students I spoke to were teaching three quarters of their time in school by the end of the year. They were spending one day a week on more theoretical aspects of the profession, though no doubt bringing to their study of theory much of what they had learned in practice as much as the other way around.

You may do this course in any school that is prepared to employ you as an unqualified teacher, except for two categories of school. First, schools in 'special measures', that is, schools that Ofsted has deemed are 'failing' schools, may not employ GTP students. You will learn, whatever route you follow, that the phrase 'special measures' has the same kind of resonance in education as 'doomed to relegation' has in football, or 'we need you in for a few tests' has in medicine. It is the knell (as Macbeth might have said) that summons thee to hell.

And, second, you may not follow a GTP course in a Pupil Referral Unit either, where pupils with behavioural problems have been placed because either they can't cope with their mainstream school, or it can't cope with them. Arguably, you might learn more about the realities of education in both these kinds of school, but there it is.

Here's a note from a GTP teacher. Please note the parts I have italicised:

Previously I had worked as a chartered accountant and decided to change career when my own children started school; a decision I do not regret. I chose to apply for a part-time place on the GTP and was pleasantly surprised to be offered a place …

Some problems were in my control. So, for example, I managed to change my working days from the end of the week to the start of the week so that I could be present at staff meetings on a Monday. No one had suggested this, but with hindsight it seems an obvious piece of advice.

The teacher whose class I adopted for the duration of the course taught the class on the days I was not at school. She had had the same class for at least fifteen years and *found relinquishing the class to me difficult*. I often felt that she would have preferred to run things along the same lines as normal, but the headteacher had decided that a GTP student was *an extra pair of hands* in a very small school (50 pupils) where PPA time [Preparation, Planning and Assessment] and falling numbers were becoming a problem. On a few afternoons all Key Stage 2 children were taught by one teacher due to funding issues, so my teaching practice was a welcome addition to the timetable. The school had previously had a very positive experience with an LSA who was a trained Montessori teacher, so had plenty of teaching experience, and for her the GTP was the certificate to prove her status. I, on the other hand, had no experience at all and often felt that the support I may have had in a larger school was missing.

Having said all this, I am glad I trained this way. I think given my home commitments, I needed the motivation of being a 'real teacher' in the classroom. I spent a year with the same group of children, following their progress and taking part in events in the school calendar from the Christmas play through to sports day. I also built up a relationship with the parents and other members of staff from teaching assistants to cleaners, gaining a deeper understanding of the school and the children's environment.

I don't feel that the authority have done their best to realise the potential of their investment in me and other GTP students I have spoken to who agree with me. We were warned that the statistics show a large percentage of teachers leaving the profession in their NQT year, but still *[my authority] have not protected their investment in us by following our progress in our first year of teaching*.

Whether you're following SCITT, GTP or BA (QTS), it's likely that you'll work on a placement with a teacher who *found relinquishing the class to me difficult*. It's always been that way, a bit like treading on eggshells. You have to gain the experience you need with a class. That is, after all, the point of being there. But you have to understand the teacher's possessiveness.

An extra pair of hands – the school will almost certainly see you like this. But it will not help you unless you are more than that. Use all your power and tact in resisting being typecast in this way.

[My authority] have not protected their investment in us by following our progress in our first year of teaching. This is a serious charge. There is of course nothing you can do about it. But reflect: whatever you see your failings to be, those above you fail as well.

All these points are relevant to the account of teaching placements in Chapter 5.

Above all, in that student's response to my questionnaire, there is that scornful sideswipe at 'theory'. Theory always tends towards the subversive, because it involves teachers thinking for themselves and working with academics to innovate and develop teaching ideas. No wonder that those entirely wrapped in the business ethic will worry about it.

The relationship between theory and practice is more complex than is commonly thought. Crudely put, on a BA (QTS) course you will be fed theory, which you will then apply on a teaching practice; on a SCITT or a GTP, you will emphasise practice at the expense of theory. In fact, the best theory is at least partly generated by practice. If you examine your teaching, if possible with a colleague and perhaps guided by academics, you will develop frameworks for thinking about it.

BA/BSc (QTS)

First, find the right university for you. The *Guardian* and other newspapers supply, in May usually, lists of the universities and how they rate in various tables. These lists may also offer information about specialist subjects, students' comments on social life and on the quality of tuition, as well as information about the university's host town or city. Read this stuff, and be wary of it. Look at the websites of a short-list of universities. Your local bookshop will have books, written from various points of view, about the merits of all the universities. One example is *The Guardian University Guide*, which is updated every year.

Like all other undergraduate courses, the BA or BSc scheme with qualified teacher status (QTS) carries no financial benefits. It is probably the course you will follow if, like me, teaching is what you knew you wanted to do when you were 12 or 15 years of age and if you wanted to spend three (or possibly four) years at a university.

With BA (QTS) you can study for a degree and to become a teacher at the same time. It will take three or four years full-time, or four to six years part-time. You apply for a course through the University and Colleges Admissions Service (UCAS). As nearly all courses begin in the autumn, you can apply between the preceding September and January. You could begin by visiting two websites: UCAS: www.ucas.com; and the National Recognition Information Centre for the United Kingdom (UK NARIC): www.naric.org.uk.

With a BA (QTS) it is arguable that you will receive a better grounding in the theories of education, if by theory we mean the work of thinkers like Maria Montessori, John Dewey, John Holt and others. Here please note what I have said above about generating your own theory from your practice. In any case, this 'grounding in theory' is a double-edged sword. A disadvantage of BA (QTS) was, one student told me, 'sitting in two-hour lectures about theory ... I listened for ten minutes, and then doodled ... there was a contradiction ... for example, we were told that children have an attention span of about ten minutes, while we had to listen for two hours ... '

There is a value, in BA (QTS) courses, of having three experiences in schools rather than the one that PGCE and other students would have. 'The schools all expected different things; you had to be flexible,' said my graduate friend. This is a keyword in all teaching. Schools have many things in common: biscuits in the staffroom and those piles of books about flower arranging and royalty on horseback; the national curriculum; assemblies; playtime. But in other ways they differ unnervingly: for example, in attitudes to punishment, to decision-making, to policy-making and to the curriculum. One school will follow the literacy and numeracy hours to the letter, while another will have severely adapted or even ditched them long ago.

Some say that the QTS course is useless if you decide you don't want to teach at the end of it. But, as one student pointed out, 'It's no more useless that a history degree is. At least you can teach for a while, but if you've got a humanities degree, all you can do is teach that subject in university or school ... '

PGCE

If you read for a first degree, you will perhaps be someone who has a vocation and whose degree is going to help you fulfil it. You study vet surgery, for example, because you want to be a vet, or theology because you want to be a priest or minister, or law because you want to be a lawyer.

But many of us do not know what our chosen job or career is going to be at 18, 19 or 20. Some who want a degree course want it for the fulfilment that three years reading something you want to read gives you. Study at 'A' level, or private reading before that, or something in the family has led us to follow a course. This is probably, in the pound-noteish atmosphere of today, ridiculously romantic.

But you may do a degree because you feel you want to be a teacher, but you are not completely sure. Then, PGCE is for you.

I interviewed a PGCE-trained teacher in her second year of teaching:

I was doing classical civilisations for my degree ... I only decided that I wanted to be a teacher when I was about halfway through the course. Yeah, it's been useful when I've been teaching the Greeks or the Romans ...

The pressure on time was terrific. I was preparing assignments for university during holidays, at weekends, all evening every evening, then going into school with all my short-term, mid-term, long-term plans, and my evaluations prepared ... At my university we had to plan these Teaching Standards Activities, in case the school – the teaching practice – didn't cover them. I spent the entire Christmas holidays preparing my English portfolio for uni ...

> You had to speak to so many people at school … like the SEN teacher about any of her children who were in my class. It was difficult finding time for that, time when we both could do it, she was busy, of course … and there were other people …

> Schools are so different! … In one, everyone was a perfectionist … the teacher was good, but so stressed, we had to cover everything in the curriculum, the head got involved … In the second school I never saw the head. It was much more free. I just got on with it.

> I wasn't introduced to people in either school. The parents at the school gate didn't know who I was. Nobody had told them. But in one school it was nice to be asked out to the 'do' when they got together in the pub. In the other I wasn't.

> The PGCE was definitely harder than my degree … None of the assignments fed into my practice. I've forgotten them, I can't remember what they were about. My friend who'd done a psychology degree, she talked about things we were doing, scaffolding, language acquisition … I remember it a bit …

> At my university they had this idea that we should teach lessons to the other students as if we were teaching children, modelling the classroom situation, but it was alien once I got in the classroom. Nothing can prepare you for your first practice.

> Some of the QTS people were bitter about us, they felt we were getting it all in a year, and they had three, and we had a bursary …

Another PGCE student said that it was less stressful because the award wasn't graded. It was just pass or fail. She had been determined to get upper second on her degree, which she had, and she felt that 'just passing' meant less pressure. When asked about theory and practice, she put it bluntly:

> Uni tells you what you ought to do, in school they tell you what you've *got* to do. The teaching during the PGCE was based on a perfect class all understanding you, whereas school based it all on a reality. Uni talked about lesson plans, short-term, medium-term, long-term, but the school damped all this down …

Your PGCE will be a very different experience from your bachelor's degree. You may be familiar with a degree of freedom that won't be so evident.

Teach first

This is a specialised scheme for men and women with good degrees (2.1 and above) who want to teach in challenging secondary schools in London and Manchester. It takes two years, and you will receive food and accommodation during the Summer Training. You will receive Point 3 unqualified teaching scale during the first year, and normal NQT (Newly Qualified Teacher) salary during the second year of the programme. Application forms come from the website www.teachfirst.org.uk.

QTS only

This is another minority-oriented scheme. It is administered by Gloucester University and applies to those who have experience in a school already as an instructor or unqualified teacher, or have taught in an independent school or a college of further education. Contact the university for further information or see their website: www.glos.ac.uk.

Registered Teacher Programme

The Registered Teacher Programme caters for non-qualified teachers who have, nevertheless, had significant experience teaching in private schools or working in other student-related environments.

Routes into teaching in Scotland, Wales and Northern Ireland

Scotland

Before I write about routes into teaching in Scotland, Northern Ireland and Wales, I want to say this: everything important in this book applies wherever you want to teach. The issues of the centrality of teaching as a career in any society, of relevant skills, of respect for children, of memory are applicable everywhere. Across the three countries of the UK there are differences in the courses.

The Scots have a justifiable pride in their education system and have had for many decades. Their prominence over centuries in the fields of philosophy and engineering, and today in providing Labour politicians, may or may not speak volumes about their system. Teaching in Scotland has been independent of England and Wales for a long time, and the routes are different, too. There is a comprehensive website to help here: www.teachinginscotland.co.uk. The basic need is a TQ (Teaching Qualification), and you can get it through a Professional Graduate Diploma in Education (PGDE). You will study at one of the HEIs (Higher Educational Institutes) at one of the following universities: Aberdeen, Dundee, Edinburgh, Glasgow, Paisley or Strathclyde. Nearly all the courses are full-time, and consist of 36 weeks, half of which are spent in schools and half in the university. This leads to your TQ.

Entry requirements are similar to those in England. See the Scottish Executive Education Department's (SEED) website: www.teachinginscotland.co.uk. Or you can get a free brochure on 0845 345 4745.

You don't have to do Skills tests (see page 39)!

Wales

Higher Education Institutions in Wales offer a range of courses leading to QTS. The ability to speak Welsh is not a requirement for teaching there, but note that there is a revival in the Welsh language and a particular demand for Welsh speakers, both to teach the language itself and to teach other subjects in Welsh.

From my own limited experience working as an Inset provider and visiting poet in Wales, I have to predict that the national pride in the language will grow over the next few decades.

For further information, phone the Teacher Information line on 0845 6000 991 or look at the website: www.learning.wales.gov.uk.

A GTP programme is also available in Wales.

Northern Ireland

To teach in Northern Ireland, you need a teaching degree awarded in the UK. If your degree was gained outside Northern Ireland but inside the rest of the UK, and you want to know if your award is valid, you must contact the Miscellaneous Enquiries Section of the Department of Education in writing giving the following information: your name and address, National Insurance number, birth certificate and proof of all educational qualifications with original documents.

Contact details are as follows:

Miscellaneous enquiries section
Department of Education
Teachers' Branch
Waterside House
75 Duke Street
LONDONDERRY BT47 6FP

Telephone: 028 7131 9000
Email: miscellaneous.enquiries@deni.gov.uk
Website: www.deni.gov.uk

You must be registered with the General Teaching Council for Northern Ireland (GTCNI). See their website: www.gtcni.org.uk.

The entry requirements for all three countries vary little from those given on page 30.

Skills tests

You will be offered the chance to do these tests at university. Do them as soon as you can and get them out of the way. Otherwise, you will spend a worrying time in the summer, between the end of your course and taking up your first job, finding centres where you can do them. The tests are done on computers at recognised test centres (of which there are about 50 across the country), and you must achieve a pass mark of over 60 per cent in each test.

I summarise their contents:

- numeracy: some mental arithmetic, questions about interpreting and using statistical information, and using and applying general arithmetic

- literacy: spelling, punctuation, grammar and comprehension

- ICT: word processing, presentation packages, databases, spreadsheets, e-mail and web browsers.

One student, who cheerily labelled himself 'backward in ICT', told me that this test was 'not worth worrying about'. He said that 'anyone can pass it if I can'. Other students have told me similar things. Teachers I have interviewed in their second year of teaching can't remember anything about them.

In the literacy test, you have to show efficiency in spelling, punctuation, analysing 'texts teachers encounter in their professional reading' and to be able recognise lapses from Standard English. That bit about 'professional reading' disturbs me: it means being good at reading what descends from London, Edinburgh, Cardiff or Belfast, and your local authority, and which gathers like dust in your pigeon holes. If you become too efficient at analysing that kind of language, it will destroy your ability to read Emily Brontë, Shakespeare, Harold Pinter and the new Kazuo Ishiguro. I know which prowess I'd rather have. And there is nothing in the literacy skills test about purposeful writing. The compilers of the tests might say that there isn't time to do that, that it would be too difficult. But that makes an important point: teaching by targets (in this case, pass this test) favours low-level, trivial learning.

The same kind of criticism may be made of the other tests.

For full information, check the TDA website: www.tda.gov.uk.

Note that in Scotland there are no skills tests.

Standards required for QTS

The official guidelines document outlining teaching standards, *Professional Standards for Teachers: Qualified Teacher Status* (PST(QTS)), is available from your institution or school, or the TDA website. The TDA site explains that: 'The standards are a rigorous set of statements formally setting out what a trainee teacher is expected to know, understand and be able do in order to be awarded qualified teacher status and succeed as an effective teacher'.

It is tempting to see the standards document as a checklist. Certainly, you have to demonstrate that you are equipped to be a professional teacher. But in fact, it is better seen as a codification of what good practice will be throughout your career. It is a framework and is common sense, and, unlike much that is written about teaching and learning today, will never date.

'Throughout your career': indeed, you will have to show the characteristics in PST(QTS) right from the award of your QTS status and subsequently in movement through main scale, upper pay scale (Post Threshold (P)), Excellent Teacher status (E) and Advanced Skills Teacher status (ASTs).

The standards are divided into three interrelated sections: each one beginning with 'Professional':

- Professional attributes

- professional knowledge and understanding

- professional skills.

Professional attributes

The trick with appreciating the helpfulness of the document is to isolate keywords. The standards in this section include, firstly, expectations of pupils and effective communication. It is wise to emphasise the first of these, because in some staffrooms, it is possible for a new teacher's expectations to drop because experienced teachers have become cynical. It is a golden rule that if you expect the excellent you will at least always get the very good.

Communicating effectively is obviously an indispensable condition for being a teacher. Other keywords in this section include 'fair', 'respectful', 'trusting', 'supportive' and 'constructive'. It is impossible to conceive of anyone advising teachers to be the opposite of these things: 'unfair', 'disrespectful', 'untrusting', 'destructive' and so on. Almost certainly, you will have these right qualities when you enter the profession, and probably even earlier.

One well-made point is that teachers should show respect for parents and carers and their contribution to the development and well-being of children. This is sometimes forgotten in the profession. These groups may sometimes seem to be impediments to your work, as they use up time or are too busy to come to parents' evenings, but they always know more about their children than you do, and they have been teaching them (as I said earlier) since they were born, whether they knew it or not. The final keyword, 'collaboration' does not apply only to fellow-professionals but to parents and carers too.

PST(QTS) insists that you identify priorities for your early professional development. Be aware that, just as you wouldn't trust GPs who didn't keep up with developments in their field, so a parent won't trust you if they think you don't.

Professional knowledge and understanding

The keyword here in part two of the document is 'range'. This suggests, rightly, that it would be a mistake to become limited in the choice of what you do and how you do it. You need to know about, and implement, a range of teaching, learning and behaviour management strategies. It is not enough to believe that all children learn to read through phonics, for example, or that all children respond to 'strong discipline'. You need to have access to a range of techniques.

This section acknowledges range in terms of the children: you will, for example, have to provide personalised provision for those for whom English is an additional language and those who have special educational needs or disabilities.

You need to know, and implement, a range of approaches to assessment, and recognise the importance of formative assessment. This form of assessment, usually rather more useful than its opposite, summative assessment, runs alongside the child's learning rather than coming at the end.

Professional skills

The keyword in the skills section is 'planning', though 'range' is prominent as well. You must plan for progression across the age and ability range for which you are trained, design effective learning sequences within lessons, and across series of lessons, and demonstrate secure subject/curriculum knowledge.

You must show skills in planning classroom work and homework. You must show, rather obviously, teaching skills and skills in assessment, monitoring and feedback.

The short summary of the document I have written here is intended to take the stress out of preparing to meet the standards and to remove any cause for anxiety. The key thing to remember is that the standards are essentially about being a professional teacher.

Money matters

You (or your parents) must not shy away from the financial aspect of taking a teacher training course. For some years students at university in this country, including those (like myself) pursuing courses leading to the award of a Certificate of Education, basked in an unquestioned sunlight. This was the certainty that everyone was entitled to education to the highest level from which they could benefit, and that that education was free. I lived in a country house owned by my college for three years, rent-free; the government paid my tuition fees (a phrase uniquely Thatcherite and post-Thatcherite); I was fed three cooked meals a day; and, on top of all this, I had a grant. Of course, someone was paying – the taxpayer – but we took everything for granted.

Today's students on QTS courses work, not only in the holidays, but also during term time: waitressing, barwork, nannying, shopwork. One student I know was Saturday manager in a store in his university town during much of his course. But even more disturbing financially is the cloud which hangs over students, knowing that they will soon, while teaching, be paying back their loan and struggling to settle an overdraft. At a point in their lives when their parents were thinking about a first mortgage, these students are likely to be living in a small flat with a rent they can't afford, or (ever more common these days) still living with their parents. It will fall on deaf ears, I know, but you should try to be frugal, to spend wisely on nutritious food, to drink less than you feel inclined to drink, and to stay away from any drugs at all.

Students, or most of them, have always been hard up. Inevitably, you will meet Gideon and Gussie whose Daddy has bought them a flat, which he will put on the rental market when they've finished their course. They are the only students you'll meet who can live the lifestyle advocated in the *Sunday Times Magazine* rather than the one you live, which is that of a modern-day Dickensian pauper.

There is one certain way to avoid financial problems, both during the course and after you have completed it. Here is an eight-point plan. Brace yourself. Think secular monk, secular nun.

- Eat less meat. Contrary to what appears to be conventional wisdom, a meal can still be a real meal without steak.

- Cook vegetables every day occasionally varied with cheap cheese for protein. Eat salad. Buy fruit and vegetables late on Saturday nights from supermarkets when they're being sold off cheaply.

- Buy the following and use them: *More Grub on Less Grant*, by Cas Clarke (1999), and *First Steps in Vegetarian Cooking* by Kathy Silk. Although Kathy Silk's book is now out of print, used copies are still available. My copies of these are broken-backed and oil- and wine-stained, with clipped recipes from newspapers and magazines falling out of them. You can't pay a cookery book a higher compliment than that. Forget your Jamie Oliver fantasies for a while and go for the basics.

- Give up drink. Or if you must drink, stick (in the pub, if you must go) to cheap local bitter and, at home, bottles of paint stripper table wine from the local offie. Avoid alcopops and serious liquors.

- Be in bed by eleven every night.

- Drop all interest in music. Going to concerts and buying CDs are off the agenda for three years. Don't even think about going near HMV or Virgin for the duration. Instead, listen to Radio 1 on the set that your worried parents will have supplied you with.

- Dress yourself entirely from charity shops. Try to forget your trainer obsession for a while. Start a trend. Become the Oxfam Shop Kid.

- Save up all dirty washing till your parents come. Then get them to take it to the laundrette and, more importantly, pay for it.

I have known students who have followed that regime, and they are rich! Rich! Rich! But oh, are they boring.

Living in a student house

For at least part of your course, you will be living in a shared house or flat off campus. University towns and cities like Durham breed middle-class folk who learn quickly that the canny way to make money without doing anything is to buy houses with enough room for three and rent them out to six students.

You must prepare yourself for squalor. I mean dead vodka bottles, the cheapest brand, lying in the hallway. Old copies of *Hello* magazine and the *Daily Mirror* left crumpled or open (sometimes both – how do they manage that?) all over the bathroom floor. A vague (or sometimes not so vague) smell of the giraffe house at London Zoo, or, if you are lucky, a milking shed. The flat inevitably deteriorates to the standards of the slobbiest, because the relatively tidy student eventually shrugs and leaves his or her dirty plate on the table (or more likely next to the armchair) like everyone else does. A chipboard feel to the furniture because the landlord or landlady has chosen the cheapest materials to furnish the house. This is important because the landlord, or landlady, is making a lot of money out of you, or rather out of your parents, and has a dozen of those properties in the university town.

Even if you are a fastidious person you must be ready to be shocked by what your fellow-students are like. Your parents (and their parents) will arrive, having driven a hundred, two hundred, three hundred miles, gasping for a cup of tea and a pee. They will come back from the lavatory quickly, slightly ashen, shaking the water from their hands (that towel has done dubious service for so long, to so many people, they didn't want to chance it) and they say, 'Let's go out to a cafe for a cup of tea', and you end up at Starbucks. They may have doubts about globalisation, but they like clean cups.

Even if you are on your own, and you fancy a cup of tea, the first task is not to put the kettle on. That comes much later. By the time you have finished all the preliminary work, the water will have gone tepid and then cold. First, you must search under beds until you find a dirty cup. Then you must find washing up liquid. Then you must clear the sink sufficiently to find a space under the tap to wash the cup. Then you must locate the tea bags, the sugar and the milk. You must give the milk a good sniff ...

A digression? You're going to do a BA (QTS)? You wait.

Study can be boring, too. But not necessarily. Let's have a look at it.

4 How to study

You've decided to become a teacher, or you wouldn't have read this far. You've given the matter, no doubt, much thought. You have also talked with parents, partners, friends, workmates and, if possible (and you should have made it possible), teachers in local schools.

All this thought and all this talk is valuable data, and you will have filed it away in your mind, or, if you're super-organised, in cardboard folders or on your PC. You will find yourself going through your mind and your heart or through the files, on buses or as you walk, drive or begin to sleep.

Or perhaps you're responding to an old call that you heard dimly, through fantasies about being a footballer, a model or a rock star when you were very young. If that is so, talk has made little difference. It didn't with me. Teaching is what I'd wanted to do and, by the time I was in my late teens, it was what I'd wanted to do for what seemed like a long time.

You have decided which of the following routes you will take. You might:

- go to university and do a BA/BSc (QTS)

- go to university, get a degree and then do a PGCE

- follow the SCITT line if you already have a degree

- follow the GTP route if you have lived part of a working life already

- go into teaching through Teach First if you are part of the elite that can apply

- go to the University of Gloucester if you are in a very small minority who have found this route an amenable option

- follow the Open University PGCE course.

In Scotland, Wales and Northern Ireland there are of course different routes.

I can't emphasise this next point enough: from where I stand, as a teacher who's never regretted for a moment choosing this profession, you've made a good decision. It is often said that, as a teacher, you will forge children's minds. In fact, they will forge their own minds for themselves. But if you are a good teacher, you will show, not *the* way, but *many* ways for them to go ahead to find some kind of truth. And, if you are a really good teacher, you will find that the children will, if not forge, at least change your mind as you teach. You will learn from their learning styles, their obsessions, their personalities. One acid test for judging a teacher (I don't recommend trying it unless you know the teacher really well and you like each other) is to suggest that they learn from children. If they give way to a great raspberry or a guffaw, or say, 'What? The kids round here?' and drift off telling colleagues in so many words what a sentimental old thing you are, make your judgement.

But now, before you take responsibility for a classroom, you have to study. It's going to be difficult, but you have to remember that, through all the murk that will surround you, you are searching for and being guided towards a kind of truth.

This involves reading, thinking, writing and discussion. Much of what follows will seem obvious to many, and the first sentence more than most. But I have to write it: Studying involves reading books. When it gets extra tiresome, remember that it is a search for the truth and all that studying will one day cast a light across your path.

At the end of every term at my grammar school, the headmaster used to read the last three verses of the Book of Ecclesiastes in the Old Testament of the Bible. The first says, in part: '... my son, be admonished ... much study is a weariness of the flesh'. Most of the boys in that hall were probably contemplating football in the park or at Crystal Palace or Chelsea, or idling through Easter, Christmas or the summer, or girls (or, as I now appreciate, boys). The five out of the five hundred boys who were paying attention murmured, 'You can say that again, Sir.' Well, they probably didn't murmur 'Sir'.

Read the papers

Well, much study certainly is a weariness of the flesh. But the first reading I am going to recommend is easy and takes up very little time. Make yourself familiar with the education section of a daily newspaper. I would recommend the *Guardian*'s section on Tuesday, the *Independent*'s on Thursday and the *Daily Telegraph*'s on Saturday. They will enable you to get painlessly abreast, and then to keep painlessly abreast, of what is being said about education. I say 'painlessly' because, whatever else they do, writers in these papers write clear prose. You can read newspapers free in the university library, or cheaply on the bus or train as you travel to and from your place of study. You don't even need to set time apart for it.

A while ago, all the talk in primary schools seemed to be about 'synthetic phonics'. That is, how teachers need to reinforce the teaching of reading with emphasis on the sounds individual letters make. It's nonsense, of course. There are twenty-six letters in the English alphabet and forty-odd sounds, and, as Michael Rosen has said, if the theory held any water it would be spelt 'sinthetic fonix' (though 'th' still presents a problem because there exists no letter for that sound). In this paragraph alone there are problems with 'while', 'talk', 'schools', 'wrong' and 'flavour'. Phonetically, they should be 'wile', 'tork', 'skools', 'rong' and 'flaver'. 'Paragraph' is 'paragraf' in the north of England, but 'paragrarf' in the south.

The talk in secondary schools was about city academies. By the time this book is published there will be other issues. Twenty minutes a week will keep you informed.

Read books

Reading books is a more demanding matter and you can't escape it. There are books which are easy-going reading, but which provide an underpinning to more serious study, and many of these are listed at the back of this book. Look at memoirs about teaching – Edward Blishen's book (1980), especially – and novels, like J.D. Carr's *The Harpole Report* (1972). There's *Molesworth* (1999), by Geoffrey Willans and Ronald Searle, which, though it is much more than the laugh it looks, is worth the cover price for that laugh.

There are plays, too. Alan Bennett's *The History Boys* (2004) is a piece which no one who is serious about teaching will avoid. It has been filmed so is easily available on DVD, and it raises central and timeless issues about the nature of education. There is a tension between, on the one hand, a dubious eccentricity and, on the other, a systematic need for results and correctness. The eccentric teacher believes that 'all knowledge is precious whether it serves the slightest human use'. His teaching reveals a flawed passion, glimpsed when he calls a boy a 'foul, festering grubby-minded little trollop'. On the other hand, there is the teacher who is determined to see his boys through to Oxford, by any means, including encouraging them to say the opposite of received wisdom.

But you also have to read books about education. Now these, like all academic books, can be forbidding things. Tyrell Burgess (2002) goes so far as to define 'University Press' as a 'publisher of books which nobody would dream of reading'. Indeed, there will be few lively sentences like the ones I've quoted from Bennett, few jokes like those in Willans, few human moments like the one you will find in Blishen. Here, certainly, and infamously, study is a weariness of the flesh. It's even more a weariness of the mind and the spirit.

Approaching education books

When you get an assignment topic, you'll go to the library or to the bookshop, and you'll be faced with an alarming row of titles. Looking at my shelves now, I see such unseductive spines as: *Reflective Teaching in the Primary School*, *The Disappearing Dais* (eh?), *Pedagogy of the Oppressed*. I am, to one degree or another, familiar with these books and know that there is value in the study of them. But my first reaction, when I came across them, was almost certainly puzzlement. 'Dais'? 'Pedagogy'? This wasn't so much because I was ignorant, but because the writers of these books seemed to use a language not only that I didn't know, but more importantly, and worse, that only they knew. It seemed to be a language that distanced the writers from everybody else. It seemed to enable them to establish a platform from which they could write without much fear of debate, let alone contradiction, among readers.

This is unfair about those titles, but it's just about right for many examples of the genre. Now face the first fact: only two or three of such books will be of any use to you. So let's be practical, and not cynical. Find something that your tutor has already recommended and ignore everything else – at least for the time being. Don't worry about that peculiar lexicon. 'Reflective', 'dais' and 'pedagogy' will all become clear at some point insofar as they are necessary to you.

The second fact is: you don't have to read these books all the way through. Well, I do read whole books, of course, and so do you. I read a novel through from beginning to end much as I follow *The Bill*, or any film I see on television, at the cinema or on DVD. I suspect that everyone who reads a novel or watches a TV programme or a film does this, too (though I sometimes, like everyone else, with a sense of failure for which I blame myself rather than the writer, give up on one). I want to know what happens, like I do on *The Bill*.

I also want to appreciate (at least on second reading – all decent novels are read more than once and all great novels three, four or five times, or many more times) how this writer is doing what he or she is doing. Even with novels that I've read before, I read them through from beginning to end. I missed that clue to the murder, or to someone's character, or to a surprising, quick turn in the plot late on, the first time of reading, or to something (or things) that the untrustworthy narrator is unconsciously giving away as he or she tells the story, or his or her version of the story. But I get it the second, the third or the fourth reading. I want to know how suspense is built, how red herrings are dropped and clues planted, how glimpses of a character come from they way that character speaks. I want to know how a book works.

Have a closer look at the education book that you have chosen. Now consider for a moment: how do you normally read a book? And for what purposes? James

Boswell (1791) quotes Samuel Johnson saying incredulously to someone called Elphinstone, 'Sir, do you read books through?' First truth: you don't have to. Indeed, you probably shouldn't.

I have never, not once, unless I have had to review it, read an academic book about education all through, and I don't believe many have, or that anyone will gain much from doing so. They are mostly forbidding blocks of ruined trees. Often written with no craft, let alone elegance, many (though not the ones noted above or in my bibliography) are hack works, word-processed out of a sense of duty. Someone has written them because the author's university demands a number of published articles in what are called 'refereed journals', magazines where articles are sent for consideration to 'experts' in the same field and for which no money is paid. Their sole purpose is to enhance reputations, that of the university in the eyes of the government and that of the authors in their peers' eyes. Slowly these articles will grow in number, like a neglected compost heap. And the author will present them, yoked uncomfortably together, as a book. Of the making of such books, there is no end.

When presented with such a book for reasons of study or review, I look at it sulkily for quite a long time and then ask myself certain questions:

- What is the first sentence like? Does it invite me in? Or does it discourage me with its length, its verbosity, its bad grammar, its sense of hidden knowledge that the writer possesses? I'd love to quote some bad sentences here, but I've given the books away to enemies.

- Who wrote it, and why did they write it? Perhaps, as I've hinted, they are university teachers collecting articles from journals that they have had to write in order to meet their university's quota of referenced articles. A scary thought. Written from the soul? Written with love? Hardly.

- Why am I being asked to read this book? Is it to help me with an essay? If so, study your essay title and then scan the contents, hard.

'Scan the contents, hard'. That sentence introduces the theme of attention. This is so central to education that I need to address it and here is one good place. The French philosopher Simone Weil told school students at a *lycée* (the equivalent of our high, or secondary schools) in Paris, who were studying subjects that didn't interest them, that 'Even if our efforts of attention seem for years to be producing no results, one day a light that is in exact proportion to them will flood the soul' (Panichas, 1977). That is a truly glorious sentence, and if it applied to the studies of young people in Paris in the thirties, it also applies to us in our studies. Much grief in the study of anything will be avoided by quiet, intense thought. That thought will repay itself as Weil says it will. And all the thought that is required here is about what you can see on the contents page.

Then gut the book. This process goes something like this. After you've examined the contents page, look at the index. Has it got stuff in there that interests you (or which is supposed to interest you) and is relevant to your current project?

Then look at the references. If your tutor's name appears there, think about it, and don't necessarily be suspicious. Are the other names ones that concern you and what you are writing about?

Now, if you have bought the book, go through the bits that seem relevant to your current project and cruelly deface it with biro marks. These will be underlinings that you can pillage for your assignment and comments in the margin. Perhaps you can paraphrase these. Perhaps you can quote them whole and put them in your references (more about that later). Think, hard, about what the writer is saying. If you have borrowed the book from the university library, or from a friend, you'll have to make those notes, these defacings, in a notebook. It is far easier, of course, if you own the book.

Do not treat books about education as if they were holy relics. The best they are is part of a search for an elusive truth. I have written a few in my time and I am delighted when I see a copy garnished with notes and post-its. They are to be pillaged, defaced, abused, raped even. I love it when I see a margin with scribbles in it: 'What the hell is he on about?', 'What rubbish' and the like. Those scribbles are part of the search for that truth.

Often academic books have subtitles within chapters. Scan the book briefly, keeping alert for words in these subtitles that are relevant to your current interest. Notice that certain words – 'assessment' for example – have a different resonance in some books compared with others. Sometimes the word applies to testing. The sentence will probably betray no scepticism about the subject. We are, it implies, teachers, and assessing children is a large part of what we do. Other books (Drummond, 1994, for example) will have in the text facsimiles of children's responses to tests and will be critical of the whole testing system. This kind of book places children at its centre. The two kinds of book will have different arguments to make, and you don't have to read the whole of either to make an early judgement of what these arguments are.

Now, read a whole section of the book. This will tell you whether the rest is worthwhile, at first for your present purposes, and later generally. Then follow the same process with another book. As a character in a film once said, copying from one book is plagiarism; copying from two is research.

Thinking

Lawrence Stenhouse (1967, 1975) said and wrote many marvellous things about education. There's that sentence about the purpose of education that I've already quoted (see page 10), about freedom and creativity. And there's this: 'The only thing I am objective about is my own subjectivity'. There is no objectivity. You can easily demonstrate this by staging a happening in a classroom. With another adult, prepare and act in front of the class a quarrel. Make it physical (though not dangerous) as well as verbal. Then ask the class to write an account of what they have seen. No-one will produce an account exactly like the same as another pupil's. No-one will discover an objective truth.

Another Stenhouse insight, more everyday but rarely observed, is this: students are too keen to read and not keen enough to think. When you hear or read something during your course that seems important, or is given to you as if it is important (not necessarily, of course, the same thing), ask yourself, how does this stand up to my own experience? Think about it. You are not a passive recipient of theory. You bring your experience to the situation. Think about your own schooling and what you have read in the education section of that week's paper. Think about what you know about children today, how they behave when you see them in the streets, the park, on buses. Or you may have your own children. Think about them and their behaviour.

The same point applies in classrooms. Did you, on your visit to schools, observe much lesson time when children were asked to think and, more to the point, given time to do it? Did you observe any lessons when children were asked to be silent, unless it was for administrative reasons ('Please be quiet while I do the register!') and the like? Note that the lessons that encouraged the poems to be written (see pages 73–78) could not have worked without the children having time to think.

Writing

And then you must write. But first, I have to say that the distinction between thinking and writing is not clear, because many of us find that writing, rather than being merely a record of our thinking, is an aid to thinking or even a way of thinking. As W.H. Auden once said (quoted in Bagnall, 1973) 'How can I tell what I think till I see what I say?' In other words, the process of writing is pedagogical: writing is a teacher. Even as I compose this paragraph, I can sense my mind trying to understand the writing/thinking relationship. I learn even as I write a shopping list, about what we eat in the house, for example! How much more do I learn, and how much more powerfully do I learn it, when I write about something more important: a relationship, learning itself.

Making notes

This is a good example of writing as learning. It should be a pleasure. It's best of course to own copies of books and to write notes in margins and on the endpapers. But you could keep a notebook for book-notes when you can't scribble in the books themselves.

Making notes during lectures is for some a problem. We nearly all know that dispiriting experience when a neatly dated and titled page of A4 deteriorates into tired doodling half way down and is an anarchic mess, redolent of frustration, worth nothing by the end. It is best to keep lecture notes to brief headings, mere reminders of what the lecturer was saying, rather than make any attempt at analysis. That analysis can wait for a moment of tranquillity.

Researching, planning and writing an essay

If you are thinking about the SCITT or the GTC programme, or if you are following the PGCE route, you will already know how to write an essay. You have already got a degree. Crisp writing, the Harvard referencing system, clarity ... all that will be mother's milk to you. I have read widely about higher education and some commentators say that this isn't true; that some graduates have problems with writing essays. But I am not such a cynic and know that you will skip the following; though some GTP students may appreciate some freshening up of their knowledge. So, whether or not you feel the need, here is one approach to writing an essay.

Read the question as though it was a letter, an email or a text from a lover with whom you are having problems, a difficult poem or a label on a picture in a gallery which you like but do not understand. In other words, read it over and over again, quickly at first then more and more slowly. Read it with attention. What the question is demanding will become clearer with each reading, much like the email or the letter or the poem or the label. In other words, bear in mind that you will approach solving any problem with sustained reflection. On the third reading, start to scribble down some headings for your answer.

Now, divide the question, or title, into clauses and make a provisional decision to arrange your essay in sections, one for each clause of the question. Make sure you know which is the main clause and attack that first, and return to it in your summary. This returning to how you opened is a habit of feature writers: the re-emergence of the main theme in the last paragraph provides a satisfying feeling in the reader.

Use your computer to its fullest extent, especially in this way: cut and paste allows you to change the order of your paragraphs. It is astonishing how word-processing has changed our way of writing and thereby thinking, simply by making the re-marshalling of arguments not a tiresome business of Tippex and redrafting everything in a new order, but merely a simple matter of clicking a mouse.

Also, bear in mind some simple advice: open with a paragraph that says what you are going to say, like this:

> This assignment will address the links between a child's sense of well-being and his or her ability to learn in school.

Then say it:

> It can be hard, surely, to watch television, to play outdoors or to read a book when worried about events beyond our control. The thought of a times-tables test is not a pleasant one, especially if one perceives oneself, or one is perceived by teachers' to be weak

at the subject. Thinking about it will seep into every waking act. It can also seep into sleeping acts. Worry can invade every aspect of a person's life depending on its severity, the extremity of which is depression…

And then say what you've said:

> From the evidence and observation given above, it will be seen that there are indeed many connections between a child's sense of well-being and his or her ability to learn in school … [if you must use the passive mode – according to me, it would be better to write 'we can see that …'].

As long as you know your stuff or have ready access to it, are not too tired and are working in decent conditions, this should be a fail-safe approach. Quiet and tidiness are my pre-requisites, though for one student I know, a CD by a band called Extreme Noise Terror and the remains of last night's drinking are absolute necessities for writing essays.

Write clear prose. Draw on George Orwell's peerless advice. It's adapted in Sedgwick, 2006, where I frame the advice like this:

> Don't use clichés – any figure of speech that has been used countless times before … Even if your cliches aren't recognised as such by the reader, and they probably won't all be, they have a deadening effect overall. Use the short word, not the long one. 'Tries', for example, not 'attempts'. 'Uses', not 'utilizes'. Where one word will do, don't use two. 'Before' rather than 'prior to' or 'ahead of'. Don't write too many long sentences – they tire, or irritate readers, who may find themselves running out of breath, and who don't like having to go back to the beginning of a sentence to see how it started.

I might have added here, in the context of long words and redundant words, do not assume that wordiness is eloquence. Verbiage is a complaint suffered by the insecure. Think of politicians on the Today programme faced by the might and, more to the point, the concise sentences of an interviewer: 'Will the government support this bill?' asks the interviewer. It doesn't seem a hard question to answer. But: 'Look, John' replies the politician. 'This whole issue has to be visualised in an increasingly complex scenario where we are rolling out a whole raft of measures that will have an incremental effect on the context of these reforms …' The minister's job is to blow smoke across a truth that John is trying to get at.

Be aware that this kind of language can infect your writing, and you mustn't let it. I have seen it in essays. Be crisp. Be clear. Study the spoken and written prose style of politicians, and do the opposite.

Clive James is a modern master of clear, witty prose. I can't imagine a cliché in one of his books. He says 'the more abstruse a topic, the clearer you should be.

(The converse holds: if you are reading deliberately obscure prose, it has almost certainly been written about nothing)' (2006).

My precis of Orwell continues:

> Check whether any of your words are redundant. 'Very' almost always is, for example … 'Television is a very powerful influence on young minds'. If you can cut a word out, do. Use the active mode rather than the passive.

In fact, almost all adjectives and adverbs are redundant. 'Viciously dump quickly the unnecessary and redundant adverbs and adjectives' will be better written as 'Dump most adverbs and adjectives'.

There are different attitudes to essay writing among university teachers. There is what is called the 'academic style'. Using this style, you never use the first person ('I …'), even when writing about what you have experienced. So, rather than write (about something happening in a classroom, for example) 'I saw …' (and you don't write the simple word 'saw' either), you write 'It was observed that …' In other words, you use the passive mode and the longer word. The idea is that you should in some way be distanced from what you are writing about. But it is a phoney distance. It doesn't exist, and the words are a pretence. And the passive mode invites irritated questions on the part of the reader, '*Who* saw' it? Why be so coy? Why be so verbose?'

An example (a):

> When the children were grouped in the vicinity of the sandtray, it was observed that they interacted socially in the following ways …

By writing in a convoluted way, you are pretending to be an objective observer. But you are not. You were there. You influenced what went on. If you didn't, you weren't being a teacher, but either a robot or a god.

You may need to write like this. A few weeks at your university will tell you what is the preferred style among your teachers: the formal, passive mode academic style or the crisper, active mode style. I would ask, what is the point of those long words where short ones will do, and those redundant words? 'In the vicinity of' instead of 'around', 'interacted socially', instead of 'talked and listened to each other', 'in the following ways' instead of 'like this'. Recast sentence (a):

> (b) When I'd grouped the children round the sandtray, they talked and listened to each other, and they said:

Someone might argue (I nearly wrote 'It will be argued that' – this style is as catching as impetigo) that the children didn't just 'talk and listen', and that their body language was significant. But you could bring this out later. 'I noticed how Barry held himself back from the others and that Chantelle dominated much of the conversation, effectively preventing other contributions with her loud voice ...' Tutors always tell novel-writing students on creative writing courses, 'Show, don't tell'. The same is true for those of us writing accounts of classroom behaviour.

Don't pad: it's an ugly word for an ugly thing. You have been instructed to write 2000 words, and you only have 1789. Just imagine for a moment: by padding, you are wilfully making points you don't think are valid, justified or relevant. It is far better to take one point and think harder about it, and it is certain that something valid, justified and relevant will emerge. I have found that, if you change the order of your paragraphs, the new order will generate new material, a new paragraph.

Tell the truth. The poet, Wendy Cope (quoted in Curtis, 1997) said once on Radio 4 about the writing of poetry, 'When a poem doesn't work, the first question to ask yourself is, "Am I telling the truth?"' The same is true, though less intensely, with all but the most trivial prose (i.e., advertising and political slogans). Don't sentimentalise, over-dramatise or over-simplify. If you are tempted to do any of this, you are probably tired, so stop work for a while and pick it up later.

How to reference an essay

You must avoid potential problems revolving round plagiarism, an issue growing in importance with the expansion of the Internet's influence. I don't mean, never lift stuff from anywhere and pass it off as your own. That is obvious. But avoid unconscious stealing, too. One chore that helps with this is to compile your references as you work, making complete notes about every book to which you refer. Include all these elements:

- author's name, including initials

- year of publication in brackets

- title – this should be in italics if it is a book, in inverted commas if it is an article

- for journal articles, name of journal and volume number

- place of publication and publisher

- the page(s) from which you have taken the quotations.

This applies to journal articles and to websites.

The Harvard referencing system is straightforward to use. Here is an example from a journal article:

As Roeves (2003) writes, 'Love in an unsentimental sense is everything in teaching, as it is in the rest of life'.

Then, at the end of the essay, you write in your alphabetically arranged list of references:

Roeves, E. (2003) 'Love and teaching: a systematic study', *Journal of Education*, 26: 34–48.

Or, if you are referring to a book, you write:

Roeves, E. (2003) *Love and teaching: a systematic study*. *Colinsford*: Colinsford University Press.

But there are many other systems for referencing across different subject areas, such as the Modern Humanities Research Association (MHRA) and the Chicago styles. You will need to find out, when you arrive, which style the faculty of Education at your university favours.

Talking in groups

Read the papers; look at books both fictional and factual about life in schools; approach academic books with caution and don't be intimidated; think hard and methodically; write as clearly as possible. Until you get into a classroom of your own, these are the main ways to learn about education. But there is another resource, often neglected by writers about education, and that is the conversations you have informally in the pub and also formally in the tutorial group. Listening and talking in groups are skills that can be developed.

Traditionally, educational talk is almost all teacher talk. In our tradition until relatively recently, education was a matter of teachers – the knowledgeable ones – imparting their knowledge to students – the ignorant ones. Teachers told you things, often in a dull, though sometimes in an impressive way.

But if you remember the best teachers from your own secondary school, you will probably remember that they didn't always stand at the front of the class telling you things, but moved among you and said things like:

- 'What do you think about this?'

- 'Can you tell me how you respond to this?'

- 'Can you see how this works?'

- 'How can we make this work?'

- 'Does this remind you of anything?'

- 'Can we trust what he is saying here?'

- 'How can we get from here to here?'

That kind of teaching flourishes from a tradition older than Christianity and Islam. Plato and Socrates taught through questions and persuaded their students to think. We must value talk in groups. The teacher says, 'This is so, isn't it? What do you think?'

We glimpse the truth as we talk. This is probably why some people talk to themselves as they walk along country lanes or city streets. They are not mad, but trying to give slippery thoughts some kind of shape. They may even, of course, be praying. Their talk, or their prayer, is, as the American poet Robert Frost said of poetry, 'a temporary stay against confusion'.

Methodical, purposeful thinking is difficult, and only, I suspect, the most saint-like philosophers do it for more than ten minutes. When I think, and I, like you, do it all my waking time, I do it in a random way. I say to someone when they phone out of the blue, 'I was thinking of you just now', or 'I was thinking about that pro-gramme I just saw', or even, 'I was thinking about that lesson I just taught ...' Ambrose Bierce was right in 1911 when he defined the brain like this: 'An appara-tus with which we think that we think' (quoted in Grey, 2003). Most thought is random. That is, in part, why a large part of education is talk. We glimpse as we talk, sure, but we will glimpse more of it as we listen and relate our talk to what we hear. Talk gives thought a temporary shape. But what everyone else says helps us get closer to a kind of truth.

So at university, group discussion is a way of learning. We learn through listen-ing to tutors, to other students and through our own talking. We think before, and while contributing we think again. This seems so obvious, but often in groups we sound off with views we've brought into the room without any reference to other views expressed. Merely stating an opinion without backing it up with evidence is not argument at all but a limited version of trivial autobiography. It invites the irritated response, 'You think that? So what?'

Partly, of course, this is simply a matter of respecting the other learners in your group. But, possibly more importantly, it is good educational practice. So, when you are working in groups:

- prepare notes beforehand on your opinions and on possible counter-opinions on the subject for discussion

- get evidence for your point of view

- listen hard to what others are saying

- keep eye contact with each speaker

- make sure that your contributions take account of what has been said.

One of the truths about education is that everyone has a view, and everyone deserves to be listened to as long as they can back it up with evidence. Try the following exercise with a group of fellow trainees if you can.

Discuss the pros and cons of arranging children in groups according to their ability. Make both cases in your own mind.

The case for setting:

- It enables abler children to push ahead.

- It enables less able children to get the attention they need.

- It enables trained SEN teachers to concentrate on what they do best.

Evidence for these views might come from your own children's schools or from memories of your school. Less anecdotal evidence might be available in the form of statistics.

The case against setting:

- It reinforces the power of dubious labels like 'less able'.

- Who gave the children this label anyway? Who has that right?

- It stops children from learning from the whole range of ability.

- It is, all too often, social class that is the deciding factor on where children are placed.

Spend some time sharing opinions in your group. Have any of you changed your views as a result of the discussion?

The next stage is to go into a classroom and, for some of the time, to have complete control of a class. Education only begins when you are with the children, in awe of their innocence, of their eagerness to learn, and in awe of what (if you will only listen to them) they have already learned before they met you.

Though, as we shall see, it doesn't always work out like that.

5 In the thick of it

Two teaching placements

These two accounts were written by a newly-qualified teacher. By the time he wrote these accounts he was in his second year's teaching, so they are memories rather than reports from the front. One practice was in his first year at university, the other in his second. I leave them as they are, with minimal comment. They are relevant to whatever route you are following, and, wherever you are in England, Scotland, Wales or Ireland. These accounts of a raw experience in school are indeed relevant to teaching anywhere.

He writes about his first practice:

Teaching practice is a tense affair for most people who are involved. At my university's Education Department, there were nearly 1000 students. Finding out where you are placed is the first clue. Hundreds of students scrummaged towards a notice board to a very long, minutely-printed list. Everyone had something to say about every school you mention (despite there being 200). 'Oh, heard you get no support there' or 'Apparently the mentor's horrible'. Whether people invented some of these stories is unclear.

The first morning of teaching practice. Not living with other students, I trudged the length of the High Street to college alone and at a time (6.15a.m.) I am more used to seeing after a late night.

There was the mayhem of finding the right minibus from the fleet. Frustrated bus drivers turned you away: 'Look mate, you're pushing it time-wise, sort it out, I don't bloody know'. On the bus we sat, knowing we would have to travel the whole length of the county.

During the whole of the first placement we had to travel 46 miles through extensive roadworks on the motorway. Some days we were in the minibus three hours in the morning and another three hours in the evening. I'd been placed in a reception class – much to my annoyance, my aim being to teach Years 5 and 6 – in an infant school.

I was the only male there. Women walked in to use the men's toilets. Each day I received dirty looks, arriving late at school looking big and clumsy, creeping into sit down on a tiny chair. This was the first major test.

Not that this lateness really mattered. The children were rehearsing three hours a day for a Christmas production with sickeningly jaunty music. There was not much opportunity for teaching.

During the minimal time spent in the classroom, my 'placement partner' and I were initially made to feel unwelcome. The teacher saw us as another problem she had to deal with. Every classroom had its own many unwritten rules: children only being allowed in certain areas in certain times, for example. In the teacher's eyes it seemed that not knowing all of this meant we were unravelling her work on discipline, and that we too needed a sharp word or an irritated look to sort us out.

We could never speak with the teacher before or after school because we were late and had to be picked up at 3.00p.m. During the first week we looked to college for support, but arriving back at 6.30 most nights, the rooms of the tutors were empty.

I just got on with it, doing whatever was asked with a smile on my face for the remainder of the four weeks. Each day on the bus I hoped it would break down. The roadside, waiting for the AA, listening to local radio would be far preferable to a day in school.

A big night out at the end for all the students, big hangovers, I was glad 'Number 1' was over but already slightly worried about next time. We talked about our experiences. Some people have had a wonderful time, others haven't.

More than 40 people dropped out of the BA (QTS) teaching course during their practice.

About the second practice, he writes:

My second teaching placement began far more positively than the first. While I was standing at the board looking for my surname, a classmate looked over my shoulder and commented on the pleasant time her friend had had at that school last year. Also, the journey to — is less than half that to —, and I was placed in Year 4, closer to where I was happy to be. There were other positive signs; several friends on the bus, a jolly Gooner-supporting driver [an Arsenal supporter] …

And there were other male staff at the school.

On the first morning I was introduced to the headteacher. She said more to me in ten minutes than my previous head had in four weeks. She'd trained in a school known to me in my home town and seemed thoroughly decent. I worked with a teacher younger than me who had just finished her NQT year, and she allowed me to try ideas and gave me positive opinions about what I was doing. By lunchtime on the second day, I knew 'Number 2' was going to be OK.

I knew from my conversations with other students that I was being allowed to teach more than many others. Looking back I was pleased, and realised that I had done no teaching at all during my first placement. I was supported kindly throughout my time in the second school. It seemed to do the basic things well. The staffroom was a happy place and I was made to feel welcome: two basic requirements of a place where people can learn.

On the buses, the same horror stories were being told. I hadn't believed them until my first teaching practice. Now I sympathised, as I told about my relatively comfortable placement almost apologetically. A similar number of students left the course as they had the previous year. I have no doubt that all the buses saw tears, but not, this time, mine.

How little teaching goes on in that first practice! But as any experienced observer and worker in schools will tell you, much less teaching goes on in schools than might be supposed by the public. See it from the point of view of the children.

In the playground you play or gossip or quarrel, or just hang around. The whistle goes. You stand still. You wait for the second whistle. You stand still again. Another whistle. You file into the classroom. You listen to the register and answer to your name, 'Yes, Miss' or, 'Good Morning, Miss' or, in schools where the surface of French is being scraped, 'Bonjour, M —' You file into the hall and wait in lines, sitting on your bums – for how long? – while the other classes file in …

At Christmas in many schools you sit in the hall waiting to be called on to rehearse your roles as trees, shepherds or angels, while the principals go through the more complicated parts as the innkeeper, Mary and Joseph.

In art and writing lessons, you wait while the paper is given out by the monitors so you can write or draw. Sometimes, in what are called 'literacy lessons', you wait patiently for the delivery of paper and pencil. And should you fill a side, you wait with your hand up for permission to get another sheet …

Not much teaching is going on here. Much conversation in classrooms is initiated by the teacher and much is administrative rather that educational. Many years ago, a researcher called Douglas Barnes formulated the 'rule of two thirds'. It went something like this: in any given classroom, for two thirds of the time, talk is going on. Two thirds of that talk is teacher-talk; and two thirds of *that* talk is administrative rather than educational in character. And yet teachers are already expert in talk, while the children are still learning it …

The student's stories show how important a welcome is in a school. And this welcome is not only important for student teachers, but for everyone: visiting poets and artists; inspectors; prospective parents and parents in the school now; tradesmen bringing new furniture for the library or catering goods; repairers of computers and lighting systems; psychologists and authorities on phonetics (even them!); and obscure people who pile books on the staffroom coffee table about new recipes and royalty on horseback. As a writer, my most angrily remembered welcome was, 'Are you the writer? What do you want to do? … We haven't much idea about it … can't find out who booked you …'

A welcome is a 'basic requirement of a place where people can learn.' It is everyone's responsibility, including the student teacher's. And it is a kind of right, notwithstanding Dunblane, that nearly everyone visiting a school should feel welcome. Often all of us are greeted by an impenetrable security system.

I like this student teacher's stoicism: 'I just got on with it, doing whatever was asked with a smile on my face …' I hope that he learned that one bad experience in a school is intensely educational.

How to prepare for a placement

- Follow the advice given above (see page 22) in the section about looking at a school. Check the website, check the neighbourhood, check what you can see of the buildings from the street.

- Sleep as much as possible: the placement will be exhausting whether you teach, observe, or just hang around.

- Cut down on the booze. Eat well.

- Find out what you will be teaching, if anything (many students are disappointed by how little responsibility they are given).

- Write a list of broad aims for your teaching.

- Collect, from the resources centre, your own collection or from friends, materials that will be useful: books, posters, DVDs, etc.

- In school on your preliminary visit make a note of everybody's names. People appreciate being remembered, and you will score points with the school simply by being able to greet the caretaker on the first morning.

- Remember all your parents' advice about good manners and the like and, especially if you are of a subversive or even rebellious disposition, implement that advice with extra emphasis.

- If the school is a religious school, bear that in mind in your plans. Anglican and Roman Catholic schools vary enormously. There are some that only serve the children of the local faith community and some that admit children of all faiths. I read recently of a Jewish school in a multicultural community that admitted Muslim children, among others. Find out what kind of school your faith school is.

- Find out early who you can go to for help about teaching, about school meals, accidents, phoning if you are ill, where to get stock.

What you might expect from the school staff will vary from school to school. Ideally, you should expect a mentor, among others, to watch you teach and to offer advice, both on your teaching and on your attitude towards children and colleagues. You should expect this mentor to be constantly positive, but not afraid to point out things that you could do better. Your mentor will believe that you have a thick skin, are ready, or rather eager, to improve your work, and will stand your ground when you are doing something you believe in.

You should expect the headteacher to keep an eye on your work, because the school has taken on some of the responsibility, for your preparation to be a teacher.

Some basic issues to consider when on a placement.

Some basic issues to consider when on a placement

Planning

Mentors and tutors will expect one thing before all others: an organised file. Start as you mean to go on. Get this right, and much else will fall into place. A looser approach to planning is more likely to be tolerated if your file is in good order.

Never confuse creativity with messiness. The greatest artists – look, if you can, at photographs of Francis Bacon's studio – may believe that the order of art comes from the chaos of life, but I wouldn't trust in that until you are a great artist. Most of us need order to begin with.

Life presents tensions between what we plan and what we experience. We go to the beach having planned a day in the sun and the water. We will seal it off with meat pies, bitter ale and ice cream. But a summer downpour drenches us and we spend an hour in the amusement arcade or the cinema, watching whatever happens to be showing. It was important that we had made plans, but it was equally important that we changed them. Again, a football team plans to defend the goal to achieve a 0–0 draw; but it goes 0–1 down in the last quarter of an hour so changes its plans and attacks.

So it is in education. There is a tension between, on the one hand, planning a lesson and following that plan and, on the other, being flexible. Certainly, you need a clear, if broad, idea of what you hope the children will learn, but you must also be alive to the fact that they may learn some things that you haven't planned. You must keep your eyes on your aims, but you must be alert to all kinds of changes.

Some will be in the environment, such as the weather. Some will be in the mood of the class: what has obsessed them as they came to school this morning? A television programme? A football match? Some will be in your own feelings, even in your inspiration.

Teaching without a plan is, as Robert Frost said of free verse, like playing tennis without a net. But being rigid in keeping to a plan is like playing a game that involves no skill, like Ludo.

But here's how you plan. Or at least this is how one education department tells its students to do it. It is probably a basic if you are to satisfy tutors and mentors. You have to make notes inside a framework like this.

The template on the following page, useful as it is at the beginning of training, bears a similar relationship to a real lesson as the Green Cross Code bears to how we actually cross the road. Of course, it is important for children to know the code, but you have to bear in mind, too, that when they grow up, they will dash across an empty road without going through the code; that they will (as you do) use native wit, intelligence and road sense as well as the code. And they will be safe, because the code has implanted itself inside their road sense, their intelligence.

Classrooms, like the British weather or a football match, are rarely predictable, and outside classrooms things will happen – a thunderstorm, for example – which will, if you are a creative or indeed a sensible teacher, lead you to abandon the letter of your plans. It will even, in extreme examples, lead you to abandon the spirit of them too. Specified goals may make the teacher, if not the learner as well, inattentive

Class:	Time:

Subject:

National curriculum reference:

Learning objectives:

Possible misconceptions/difficulties:

The lesson:
Introduction:
Development:
Plenary:

to the unforeseen. If you do not abandon your plan to teach, say, adverbs when the sky is darkened by a summer thunderstorm and heaven is split with lightning, you would be like Dr Spock in Star Trek, more a robot than a human being. And you would be selling the children short.

There are many further problems. The first is in the phrase, seemingly so innocent, 'learning objectives'. If you plan a lesson in which you can predict what the pupils will learn, you are planning, at best, a dull lesson. It is much easier to make objectives for trivial learning than it is for important learning, and the very measurability that outcomes need implies a dehumanising quality.

If you teach entirely in terms of targets (the more recent term for objectives) you are not treating the children as they are when you teach them but as they will be when they have hit those targets. You teach in order to create a child for tomorrow. What about that child today? Thank goodness that children surprise us with unexpected learning, that they constantly insist on their existence now, that they refuse, with their words, to be reduced to the subjects of targets. Children are unpredictable, and you don't have the tiniest glimmer in your mind, however serious your planning has been, of what they're going to teach you next.

If you are interested in an exhaustive critique of the objectives, or targets model, look up Stenhouse, 1975, Chapter 6. More briefly, a cynic might say, and Burgess (2002) does say it, that 'aims and objectives [is a] ... method of planning based on the assumption that if you say where you want to go you can plan your route without knowing where you are starting from'. I wish I'd written that ...

I would sum up the problems I associate with planning to rigid targets by saying that it misses what Louis MacNeice (2007) calls 'the drunkenness of things being various'. A sudden storm, the arrival of someone's new baby brother or sister, the local team winning the league: all of these should be celebrated in a classroom with writing, art, congratulation cards, celebratory songs, etc.

Tests are, of course, the inevitable companion to targets. The idea that they are counter-productive is not in the ownership of the left. Alan Smithers, who is Professor of Education at the University of Buckingham, says that the government has done 'quite a lot of harm' to children by subjecting them to repeated tests. He suggests that children's self-esteem and long-term development is being undermined by the target-driven culture. He questions 'delivery' through targets. 'Schools have been reduced to almost factories for producing test and exam scores. But schools are not the product of education ... schools are there to benefit the children in them' (Paton, 2007).

This is a report in the *Daily Telegraph* (1/05/07). The source is interesting and so is the University where Smithers is professor. Neither is known as a fount of progressive ideas.

The same point goes for the word 'development'. It is fine, indeed necessary, to have a broad idea about where the lesson is going, much as you may have a broad idea about the way the day at the seaside will go, or a manager will have a broad idea how the match will go. But haven't the children the right to have a say in this matter? Isn't it possible that they will offer something that will, even if only for a few moments, make you change your direction?

To be sure, at the beginning of your time with children, structures like the template above will help your confidence and make the children feel secure, but as you become more experienced as a teacher, it will become possible, and indeed advisable, to reduce those anticipations of what the children are going to learn. There is no doubt that in the past, before the mid-1970s, there was insufficient careful planning. Now, I am sure, we have gone too far the other way. Education is in danger of being planned to death.

Opposite is a lesson planning template that I think is more creative, that honours you as a professional more and that is more faithful to the children as learners.

Try to appear confident in front of the children.

Class:	Time:
Subject(s):	
What you hope the children might learn:	
What processes are the children going to go through that might help them learn?	
What difficulties do you anticipate?	
The lesson:	
Introduction:	
Development: How will I ensure that the children contribute to the development?	
Plenary: Assessment: How did the children contribute to the development? What difficulties arose? Were the processes the children went through of high quality? How did any other adult in the room evaluate the lesson (teacher-colleague, Learning Support Assistant, parent)?	

Skills

To be a successful teacher you must be passionate and committed. You must want to do it. You must feel a desire for learning, for both the children's sake and for yours. And because of those ideas, passion, commitment, desire and learning, the notion of skills (as the notion of schooling did earlier) strikes a dull bell with me. It reduces the reality, the passion and so on, to the business of riding a bike, of changing a light bulb. To take this to the extreme, one can imagine a hierarchy of skills for prayer or philosophy, where target one is 'places hands accurately together' or 'sits with eyes closed with fist on brow in the manner of Rodin's *The Thinker*'.

But mentors and tutors will expect evidence of skills in communicating with children and, more important, evidence that you can develop these skills and gain new ones. You are born with some of them; you can learn others. Some say the first is mostly true, some the second. The second opinion is the more optimistic and I try to cling to it because I believe in the primacy of learning: not just the children's but yours too.

However, most of a lifetime's experience in teaching tells me that there are some things that many human beings can't do, and won't be able to do, however hard they are nagged about them, however well they are trained, however carefully they watch other teachers, however hard they work at them. Clarity in speech, for example, doesn't come readily to everyone. Some speak nervously, in a convoluted way, covering their mouths as if they are no longer sure of what they want to say, because they have such difficult things to say or because they haven't thought out what they are going to say, or because they haven't anything to say. Now clarity in speech is an indispensable condition for a teacher.

So is the ability, which is natural in some but has to be learned by others, to sustain eye contact with a large group. So is the ability to take up a stance in a classroom as the children enter from the playground on your first day that speaks, not of a nervousness that will break you down any minute into a gibbering orang utan, but of kindly, firm authority. Some have this naturally. Others have to learn it. The old cliché about children is true: 'They can tell ...'

Be crisp.

Be clear.

Be like the sentences in those tiny paragraphs and like the sentences in this one:

The children like to know where they stand. They like to know where they might be going. 'For the next hour we are going to learn about the movement of the earth round the sun. We are going to do that by looking at these atlases'. That is a start. Make these statements with confidence. Make them crisp. Such statements will reassure. Say them making eye contact with everybody and with a special smile for the one you think will have more difficulty than the others. That will help them to feel more confident.

If, on the other hand, as I am about to do, you ramble on saying things like 'I hope today, children, that after my lesson you will understand something about the way the earth moves round the sun – not everyone thought that was true once, but we'll come to that later – it was Copernicus who …', you'll teach nothing to some of the children and next to nothing to the others.

Children are always learning

I could have put this with the good news that I proclaimed earlier (see page 13) but I felt it had a better place here, to lighten the darkness between the minor mechanics of planning and display.

Education is part of life. Nothing is ever definitively in order, and children will learn things that you haven't planned. Look at these poems, for example.

The teacher's objective was to get the children to think about fire; to explore their feelings about it; and to write about it. Look at what these two children have done. The first is ten years old, the second nine:

1. I am an artist,

    A cook and a magician;

    A burning god

    Or a captured slave;

    I am the craftsman,

    The watchman,

    The raging warrior

    And the quiet decoration.

    I am the caring father

    And the indifferent youth;

    I am fire,

    Ignis.

2. Dancing in a fire

    Dancing in a fire

    The blue purple god

    We're not happy

We're not sad

Dancing in a fire

Dancing in a fire

The bird in the cage

Dances when the baby sings

And the song goes

The bird will dance

Inside the cage

The cat will dance as well

Tralala

The baby sits

Inside the pram

Watching the bird

dance around

Dancing in a fire

Dancing in a fire

Arguably, the teacher's objective was met. They did, indeed, explore their feelings about fire and they did write about those feelings. But both these children have travelled far beyond the teacher's targets. I can't see, not with confidence anyway, why, in the first poem, fire is both a 'caring father' and 'an indifferent youth', and in the second poem, why the god is 'blue and purple'. I can't see why the bird only dances when the baby sings.

And yet these phrases ring true. An objective along the lines of 'the children will write with vivid, if not completely translucent, simile and metaphor and surprise me as the teacher' would have been absurd. But be alert: children can learn, at any moment of the day, much more than you can anticipate. They can surprise you. The capacity to learn is at its greatest in the earliest years.

We should not underestimate the potential for learning in labelled children nor their possible needs. Labelling is always problematic, in life in general as well as in schools. That is why it is wrong to say someone is, for example, 'an epileptic'. Such a label defines someone in terms of a medical condition. It is not 'political correctness gone mad' to say we should prefer to say such a person 'has epilepsy'. This formulation, unlike the first, leaves space for all the other things that person may be: a writer, a bird-watcher, a member of the Conservative Party. In education, examples of labelling are: 'more able children', 'difficult children', 'children with special educational needs'. Once, as I walked into his classroom, a teacher nodded in the direction of a boy and said, 'You won't get much out him. He's uncreative'. The teacher had labelled that boy.

'He's uncreative'? I was so angry that I aimed my lesson especially at that child. I asked the class to write riddles. I said that each riddle should be spoken, as it were, by its answer and suggested that, if possible, each riddle should contain a pun. The uncreative boy's riddle, to which the answer was 'lion', began, 'My head is manely gold'. I was impressed, and I sent him to the teacher with his riddle. I watched the teacher nod in casual indifference. You are the uncreative one, I thought.

The boy who made the drawing below (it measures approximately 40 cm x 34 cm) was in an Area Special Class. He hardly spoke at all, not to anyone. He wouldn't tell me his name. Looking intensely at the child opposite, he made this simple drawing with a black felt tip pen. It reminds me of the African heads that influenced Picasso. It has large, sad expressive eyes and almost no mouth or ears at all. I reflected that his difficulties in communication and his frustrated desire to communicate were both depicted and (in the latter case) temporarily alleviated in the act of drawing.

And what about the possibility, or rather the certainty, that children learn without our presence? Does that offend our sense of our importance? Does it cause us, even, to question what our profession is for? After the death of his grandmother, my twelve-year-old son wrote this in his bedroom in a notebook I had given him. Providing him with that book, I reflect now, was the full extent of my teaching. He did the rest himself:

I saw in her eyes

a smile

I was sure she was

trying her best

her right hand puffed

out of size

her right was dead

her left hand

gripped my right

And at that moment

I saw what she had

been trying to do

a huge toothy grin

her teeth were out of line

It was one of the happiest

moments of my life

but it was also one of the saddest.

17 days later she died.

Watch children playing in a rock pool. They are learning. They don't need you.

I want to suggest here that you undertake a writing activity of your own. Most people don't read poetry and even fewer write it. But those who do know that it supplies insights that nothing else can offer. Poems can speak of the power of language to teach us and to evoke the truth. Here's a poem that I wrote one bright autumn afternoon, when the classroom seemed too much like a cage in which the children were protected from life. I watched them, and then wrote this (Sedgwick, 1991):

The Basic Skills

There are two silver birches in our school.

One's pollarded, and hangs like a willow

over a courtyard where children run

between work and play, between morning and afternoon.

You'd imagine the courtyard a pool

and children free to splash there

and shout and fight and innocuously laugh

and play the fool.

Instead, their feet dry,

they sit in classrooms as the day

like a bright green-skirted angel

drifts through light and stirred shadows,

drifts through light and stirred shadows

with aeon-perfect rhythm.

And Sir their ingenuous heads fills

with reading schemes, sums, and the basic skills.

Try out for yourself the possibilities of poetry as a search for the truth. Write a poem from or about any classroom experience, either from your memory or from your new experiences in schools. Include one example of alliteration, the repetition of consonantal sounds, or assonance, the repetition of vowel sounds. The thought that these techniques requires at the front of the mind may set the truth free that is at the back of it.

- Make it short.

- Include something visual.

- Include something from one of the other senses.

- Get a list in.

- Include one simile or one metaphor. ' … the day / like a bright green-skirted angel' is a simile: the word 'like' signals that. If I had written 'the day / is a bright green-skirted angel', it would have been a metaphor.

Have a go. And remember that writing, especially writing poetry, is an attempt at learning. But so is drawing. You could make sketches on sight, or later from memory.

Display

Display is low these days on a teacher's duties. You are supposed to depute it all to an LSA. But the look of a classroom is important. What follows is a brief history of its importance …

Until some time around the early sixties, display was simply a matter of a few maps, globes, alphabets and the like. The influence of behaviourism, which emphasised the quality of outward stimuli and therefore the impact of the environment, probably had a role in brightening walls in classrooms. So had the return from World War 2 of idealistic young men and women, determined to make the world a better place for the next generation than it was for them. In Oxfordshire, especially, and in other counties – Hertfordshire and Essex were two I experienced – teachers made the idea of the quality of life central. They valued, for example, topic work and art; children making their own notebooks; italic handwriting. The belief that the best display – the only display even – should be the children's own work, honoured with careful mounting and arrangement, took root.

At its best display makes pupils feel when they come into a room that it is their room; that what they did yesterday has been found good; that it is valued; that, therefore, they can do equally good, or even better things today.

At its daftest, display honoured what was on the walls and the way the teacher had put it there more than the work itself. As a young teacher in the early seventies, I spent hours after school putting up children's paintings and drawings, carefully mounted in what the advisers called 'pleasing' arrangements. In the morning, I looked with pride on what I had displayed. Did the children show any evidence of noticing it, let alone learning from it? Or the parents? No. The headteacher did, as did the advisers if they happened to visit. Much of that display was simply that, display, and pedagogically useless.

There is a test to find out whether the children have noticed your display. Put up the dear old 'Blue display' – you know the kind of thing: books with blue covers, reproductions of blue period Picasso, a few blue balloons, a photograph of a pale blue sky, a blue football shirt, some children's paintings restricted to colours in the blue spectrum. And then label it, 'Here is our display of red things.' See how many of your children, visitors and the rest notice.

Or put up those pictures of Henry VIII and his wives, but jumble the names.

All too often nowadays displays consist of alphabets, number lines and maps pinned to the wall twelve feet high, so that even the visiting poet (who happens to be fond of maps), never mind the children, can't glean anything from them. And there are commercial products everywhere, celebrating publishers – see-through plans of the pyramids or contemporary portraits of Henry VIII and his wives – none of which teaches anything at all. I have never seen a child studying such material, even when it is displayed at a sensible height.

The following are some rules for display:

- Always remember that there are more important concerns in education: above all, your interaction with both the children and each individual child.

- Keep it simple.

- Pin up work brick-style, in other words with spaces between work that are regular and which make up straight lines. Think Roman city design. Don't do jaunty angles, at least not until the National Gallery starts to display its pictures as anything but a right angle to the floor.

- Remember, the display should be the children's and therefore composed of their own work and other images that will draw them into looking at it.

- Don't drape old curtains round displays. They distract from the work, they trip people up and they look dated and precious.

- Be bold. As Peter Dixon says in his book on the subject (undated) your model should be the front page of the *Sun*: a headline or label that demands attention, a few clear images logically arranged, well-chosen captions.

- Use the simplest fonts on the computer printed large to make lettering easy and effective.

Display goes beyond the decoration of the classroom. Indeed, if display is mere decoration it isn't doing its job, which is to contribute to learning. But, to take this further, a school with a reputation for good display should have pleasant toilets, possibly decorated by the children; a dining hall that invites civilised behaviour; cloakrooms and other teaching areas that are well presented. And those teaching areas should contain children's work.

Learning support assistants = hired hands

The government has enhanced the role of learning support assistants (LSAs) over the past ten years. There are more of them, and they're not just in Key Stage 1, as they used to be, but are present in Key Stage 2 classrooms as well and beyond. Their increased presence means that they can support each other and therefore learn from each other, and they can even hold more power. They constitute a significant presence in any school today. They are mostly attractive young people, sometimes on their way into teaching, or at other times simply committed to the welfare of the community and, in particular, to the children in the community's school. It's often a school their children attend and a school that they attended themselves. These people are committed to their work. They want to make things better.

Why, then, do visitors so often find the LSA in the classroom isolated from children, teacher and that visitor? She (usually she) glues, slices, staples, mounts, cuts … does anything but work with the children. And when she does work with them, she works with them in a little room apart. She's 'hearing children read', that massively pointless activity that's so unlike anything that happens in real life, a kind of Green Cross Code for real reading (reading *with* someone is another matter). And when they do arrange displays, think how much value the children would get from the kind of purposeful conversation working together entails. They could talk with the children about which picture should go where, what colour mount goes best with a picture, how they can make this display dramatic so that people will notice it.

When you are a newly qualified teacher, liberate your LSA, give her real work! I emailed one LSA asking about what she loved and hated about her work. She replied crisply.

I love:

- working with the kids directly, i.e. small groups, one to one.

- knowing that you are actively making a difference to their education.

- developing close bonds with the kids.

- sharing their pride when a child 'gets it'.

- watching them grow up into young adults, especially when they go on to secondary school, but still come back specifically to see me.

I hate:

- the paper work!
- patronising teaching staff
- child protection issues (heart-breaking)
- endless, pointless courses.

This LSA later added to this second list:

- the worst course when I was being trained in phonics, then being trained *again* in phonics (I mean, how many times can a person be taught to sound out c-a-t?)
- teachers wasting your time by making you put up displays, when you could be in class helping the kids.

I asked this LSA to enlarge on the word 'patronised':

By being patronised, I mean: being told you have to attend Inset days, then being talked down to by some teaching staff; being sent out in the rain to collect the kids, a parent approaches you to ask a question and a teacher will come pushing past you, saying in a very loud voice, 'you're just a LSA, don't talk to the parents'.

And she went on:

I hate being treated like a servant, like working with a teacher who knocked over a plant in the classroom and being told to clean it up! And being told, I'm thirsty, make me some tea. And being left on your own with the class while the teacher goes to use the phone or have a chat.

I present all this in its raw state. It helps us to see us, and our profession, as others do, those others not quite in the country of the teacher, but not far outside its boundaries.

Discipline: 'Your eyes are your Number One weapon'

My friend David, whom I usually, though not always, trust, tells me that one training college lecturer, in the late 1960s, used to advise students preparing to teach in secondary schools, 'Pick the biggest boy out, and knock him down'.

I had, and still have, two left hands. A woodwork teacher once hit me on my right palm with a steel ruler. He did it, I suppose, to make humiliation as much of the punishment as pain ('Stop what you're doing, boys') in front of the rest of the class. Oh Thursday afternoons and the woodwork lesson! I walked home with my palms in my armpits. I had drilled a brace-and-bit through the balsa wood ship I had spokeshaved into shape, stern and bow. I was supposed to be making a hole in it for the little dowelling mast. Note how this memory means so much to me now.

And: Come out here, says the PE teacher, flexing a plimsoll with facetious glee masking low-level sadism ...

But: I had a French teacher at the same school who could intimidate (I wrote 'terrify' at first) all the boys at once, and each of us individually, into doing what he wanted us to do and into not doing what he didn't want us to do. He did this partly by the implied threat of physical punishment, true, but more by sheer force of personality. A steel-like presence ... a tone of voice ... a way with words in which none was wasted ... I am trying to pinpoint where his frightening authority came from. But it didn't come primarily from violence.

We still need discipline. Thankfully, the fist, the steel ruler and the slipper can no longer be wielded. It is strange to think that corporal punishment was outlawed only in 1986 and finally, for certain private schools, in 1998. It is always a form of child abuse and as such it was absent in primary schools, thanks in large part to the Plowden Report (1967), from the late sixties onwards.

But we need that force of personality, not just when the children are doing bad things, but all the time. We need it, of course, without the fear that the French teacher instilled. We have our eyes.

Edward Blishen, in his book about becoming a teacher (1980), quotes the fierce Mr Jeffs who lectured at his training college: 'You can pin 'em to the desks with the right sort of glare ... your eyes are your Number One weapon'. Whether this skill is inborn or whether you have to learn it, it's crucial to your practice as a teacher. You have to be able to control not so much the children, because you also have to free them, but the setting.

Blishen's experience dates from 1945. But he is a truthful writer about education, and he is recalling a remark that has much truth in it, and, which in my experience, is rarely referred to. Watch a couple of actors on *The Bill* confronting each other. Note the way his eyes tell truths about him and what he is thinking, feeling or hiding. She looks away on certain words, and we suspect she is lying. He can somehow convey with his eyes that he doesn't believe something. She makes her eyes launch-pads for daggers when she is angry. When you confront a child who has bullied another, you need those daggers. You need that dubious look that suggests that you don't believe something. You never need that shifty, uncertain look.

More frequently, I hope, you need an intelligent use of your eyes when you talk to the whole class. It is not difficult to make eye contact with everyone every few seconds. The children may not, and probably will not, consciously notice that you are doing this, but your eyes will convey the impression that you have seen them and that you'll know them next time.

When I want the children to be quiet, my method is to explain at the beginning of my relationship with them, whether it's an hour long or a year long, that if I raise my right arm I expect everyone to raise theirs. Then, if anyone sees anyone else, whether teacher, LSA or child, with their right arm in the air, they are expected to raise their own right arm and go silent. I only do this when I am teaching groups of sixty or more (this often happens to me, don't ask why), but it will work well with one class. Some teachers, to make this more democratic, insist that children have the same privilege, and if they think the room is getting too noisy, they too may raise their right arms to bring calm.

One inexperienced teacher I know claps his hands in the familiar football rhythm da, da, da-da-da and expects the children to do the same and then to go silent. But it doesn't work. They don't go silent. They are louder than they were before. The teacher has given them a loud noise. They make it louder. They compete with it. Other teachers shoosh them: a bad habit to get into. When I hear myself doing it, I cringe inwardly and know I am doing something wrong. The worst option of all is bellowing. Children will always be louder than you are. Whenever I come across a class that is too noisy, I teach more quietly, sometimes getting to such a low pitch that the children have to strain to hear.

Fox (2007) has a framework on the disciplinary management of the classroom that I find useful. I have adapted it here:

- You should agree clear, simple rules with the class early in the school year. Thus the children have ownership, at least in part, of the rules.

- Always praise, always encourage, especially when a child has been negative in some way and then suddenly does what is expected. I know this sounds patronising, but on the rare occasions when a child has simply not started to write, when he or she does, I always make a point of finding something, *anything*, to praise in the first line.

- Use the first person – 'I would like you to …' – and 'Please' statements ('Please would you …') rather than orders ('Do this …'). I make a point of using politeness that some teachers feel is exaggerated. Children appreciate courtesy.

- Ignore low-level disruption. The modern craze for 'zero tolerance' is more like a manic attention to the negative and will eventually drive us all mad.

In the staffroom

Even if you are naturally a polite person, be, for the first term or so, even more polite than you usually are. If you have a dominant personality, rein it in. Listen rather than talk. As Grey (2003) suggests, 'Look around the staffroom before sitting in a seat … literally … and metaphorically'. Think twice about all jokes, be they long stories or one-liners. As Lear says in Shakespeare's *King Lear*, 'Mend your speech a little, lest you may mar your fortunes', or as the Fool says in the same play, 'Speak less than thou knowest'.

What distinguishes teachers from the rest of the population? There are, according to me, five keywords: empathy, professionalism, structure, skills and patience.

- They have an *empathy* with their own childhood. This enables them, in turn, to empathise with children today. Their childhoods are not (in Larkin's phrase, 1988) 'forgotten boredom[s]', but rich first-hand sources for their work. They will share, profitably, for both themselves and their children, memories of their childhoods with children.

- They have what is called a *professionalism* in the school.

- They have a *structure* in their teaching. Teachers, uncomfortably, work inside two structures simultaneously: firstly, their own conscience, which is made up of what they believe is right and what they have learned and are continually learning through experience; and, secondly, the massive machine of the national curriculum and its attendant bits and pieces. In the best teachers, these two structures are in a constant and sometimes uncomfortable (if not painful) tension.

- They possess, or are in a position to acquire, both certain intuitive and certain learned *skills*.

- They have *patience*. Non-teachers often mention this quality to me, often at those dinner parties I referred to earlier. 'I wouldn't have the patience with the children', they say, meaning, I suspect, that they would want to 'give 'em the back of my hand', to use a phrase remembered from my childhood.

There are many other ways of classifying teachers. Once you've arrived in a school, study the teachers and see which of these categories provide the closest fit, then decide what sort of teacher you are going to be.

The first type is the 'hired hand'. Like an unemployed docker pulled into work when there is a crisis, these teachers (as they might well put it themselves) 'get on with it'. They simply 'do the job'. Because the curriculum and even the methodology of teaching are largely prescribed by their elders and betters – government, inspectors, headteachers – these teachers turn up at school and do what is expected of them, no questions asked. They don't understand why other teachers murmur in corners, or rail loudly against prevailing orthodoxies. Why waste energy (thinks the hired hand) on matters you can do nothing about? They also don't understand why other teachers try to change things, especially in the curriculum and how it is taught. This kind of teacher has also been defined as a 'limited professional'.

The second type is the teacher who does the job as a 'craft'. While, as above, the curriculum is prescribed, these teachers have some control over the methodology and take a certain discernable pride in 'delivering the curriculum' in the most effective way. They are like skilled carpenters who make useful and possibly even elegant chairs to someone else's design. This kind of teacher is less limited in his or her professionalism.

The third type is the scientist. These, less limited than the second type, work comfortably inside a framework of words concerned with measurement, assessment, learning objectives and the like. Their teaching is tightly structured and they accept the barrage of statistics – league tables, Sats results and the like – as though it tells essential truths about education. It doesn't. It's a way of presenting an image of success to readers of the *Daily Mail*.

The fourth type is the artist. Whether consciously or not, teachers in this group teach as if the act of teaching is a work of art; in other words, the teaching should be as elegant as possible and, above all, like all art, part of a huge human search for the truth. The process through which these teachers go, alongside rather than in front of the children, is as important as the product. They have perfected their craft, or rather are constantly in the process of perfecting it; they take what might be relevant from the scientist's repertoire. But they have nothing in common with the hired hand. They are extended professionals.

You have power

This is more good news. As a young, or not so old, or at least as an inexperienced teacher, you face a delightful and encouraging truth: you have power.

First, there is the power you have over children. You make the emotional weather in the classroom. You can wound or heal; deflate or inspire; fan flames of anger or drench them. You can help them to heal fractured friendships. You can make them laugh and you can make them cry. They will greet you (and eventually say goodbye to you) like friends.

If you talk playground slang it may seem a bit odd to the children, but it won't sound as odd as when the 'old' teachers do it. And you have energy, not just physical but emotional and intellectual. The children sense it.

The power you have over children is the power to set them free.

But you also have power in the staffroom. This may seem silly, because around you, both while on placement and in your first appointment, are experienced teachers. In contrast, you are the lowest paid teacher on the staff. You arrive at school every morning in your Dad's old Toyota Corolla, which has done 130,000 miles and which he had been driving for four years before he bequeathed it to you when you went to university. You have, in all likelihood, a shoe lace from an old trainer making sure the back windscreen wiper doesn't fall off, and when you put it through an overdue service last month, it was a financial crisis.

You don't feel powerful. You are not on the senior management team. You think you count for nothing. But, as far as the teachers are concerned, you have come recently from a fount of wisdom. I don't mean this satirically. Whatever your university seemed like to you while you were there, the tutors were reading. They were keeping up to date. And you have thought, read, listened and talked with both tutors and fellow-students. While much of that thought, reading, listening and talking has seemed airy-fairy, much of it wasn't, and it will have seeped into your blood. You know things that you can apply to your work.

And the professional teacher will welcome you and listen to you.

There are also your personal qualities: a willingness to work hard, decent manners, kindness, an eagerness to learn and a belief that you are in that school to enrich lives, both the children's and yours. As a teacher, you are a special person. Be extraordinary and, if only for a moment, change children's lives. Change the world.

How to get a job

Getting a job in teaching has much in common with getting a job in any other profession. You should present yourself well first in your phone call asking for forms and details, and then in your application letter (or, no doubt soon, in your email):

- Write clearly and unpretentiously, and keep sentences short or medium in length – remember George Orwell.

- Be conventional in presentation:

  - Type your address top right and the addressee's under it to the left.

  - Date the letter.

- Sign it 'Yours faithfully' if you don't know the addressee, 'Yours sincerely' if you do.

- Make several drafts. Read your letter to a critical friend after each draft.

- Photocopy your form and your letter for future use (adapted, of course).

When you are preparing for the interview, remember health. Go for the five-a-day fruit-and-veg option. That all applies, with minor changes, for applications in any profession. In teaching, prepare by reading the educational press carefully for the two or three weeks before the interview. What is the buzzword at the moment? The newspapers I've already mentioned in How to Study (see Chapter 4) will tell you, and will enlarge on it.

Do what you can to research the school and its neighbourhood (see Chapter 2) . Ask if you may visit the school.

Talk about teaching to anyone who will listen. Not your pub landlord or the waiter in Pizza Express, but a colleague, a parent or a child. If you are already working in a school, arrange for colleagues to put you through a dummy interview. Whether asking fellow-students to perform this service will help, I am not sure. Read and re-read *Professional Standards for Teachers (QTS)*, covering it with notes.

Re-read your form and letter immediately before going to the interview. Once you are in the interview, take a deep breath before every answer and make eye contact with your questioner (though not so much as to intimidate him or her). Decide before the interview (or at the latest during it) whether you are going to accept the job. In teaching, to turn down a job once it is offered might get you the beginnings of a reputation.

Present yourself well in person at the interview. Look good (though good for the workplace, not for the nightclub). Believe in yourself.

Afterword

My friend David read a draft of this chapter. He said that it was 'a touch cynical'. So I am on my guard!

But a cynic, according the *Shorter Oxford English Dictionary* (*SOED*), is 'churlish', a 'brutal, surly, ungracious person … sordid, niggardly, grudging … a person disposed to … find fault … to deny human sincerity and the goodness of human actions and motives …' The same dictionary makes things clearer when it quotes the Victorian statesman Disraeli: 'The cynical smile … the signal of a contempt which [he] was too haughty to express'. We all know that.

What follows is not cynical at all (even if it was at the early draft stage when David read it), but it is sceptical. And that is a different matter. A sceptic 'doubts the validity of what claims to be knowledge in some particular department of enquiry' (*SOED* again). I certainly have doubts about certain claims to knowledge here. But I will finish my book with a few words as far removed from scepticism (or, come to that, cynicism) as they could possibly be. But first some scepticism is in order.

Words are central to all human life. Imagine a football crowd, a medical consultation, an over-the-fence relationship with a neighbour, the most banal of television programmes, a report on some new atrocity, a conversation in a pub garden with the one person whom we feel can make us laugh out loud after a terrible time. Now imagine any of these without words. It is impossible, of course.

So, because words are central to life, they are central to education as well. In teaching, the main thing is to use the right words, both spoken and written, with children. And, even more, it means paying the attention that love requires to their words. A six-year-old girl wrote, 'I used to hate myself but now I like me'. But we'll come to children (or a particular child) later.

We must also listen hard to the words that teachers, inspectors, government officials and advisers say and write, partly because they have more experience than we do and partly because they are sometimes cleverer than we are. 'Listen to everyone' says Grey (2003) in his advice to teachers just arrived in a new school. Our elders and betters might encourage us and they might discourage us, but we need to listen to them. We have to be alert to the ways things are moving in the educational world and their words will help us to do that. They will also help us to avoid falling into those traps that surround our energy, enthusiasm and creativity when we are tempted to take risks with words.

We are all betrayed at times by the words we speak and the way we speak them. But words can betray government officials and advisers too. Those people say something, but often mean something else. Sometimes, for the inspectors', government officials' and advisers' own reasons, they mean nothing. There are words and words and phrases that, once you begin to teach, will, on courses and in staff meetings, appear time and time again. They are, as far as I can see, unique to this profession. Here are some, chosen at random after two minutes' thought: 'broad and balanced'; 'learning curve'; 'the kids round here'; 'best practice'; 'aims and objectives' (this is exceptional, being US military in origin); 'what works'; 'special needs'; 'senior management team'; 'mission statement' (these two also have origins from outside education); 'basic skills'; 'phonics'; 'behaviour modification'.

If I were a cynic, I would sneer haughtily and long at these phrases, but instead I pay them sceptical attention. 'The kids round here …': in my experience, this is often followed by judgements like '… they aren't creative', or '… they don't have any language in the home', or '… they have *all* the material benefits, but nothing cultural goes on'. Does the speaker really mean *all* the children? Every single one? *All* the homes? They don't have *any* language? They have *all* the material benefits? They have *no* experience of anything cultural?

And just because the speaker sees them like that, does it mean that everyone does, or that it's a fair judgement? Lumping them together as one failing, philistine, unspeakable and unspeaking lumpen mass is not only insulting to the children and their homes. It is also insulting to the listeners. It implies that while the listeners may have energy, enthusiasm and creativity, and may think of themselves as good teachers, and while they may be ready to work their socks off, they are going to fail here because of 'the kids round here'. It makes a judgement about all the people living in the catchment area and, to say the least, that judgement is unfair, because it would be impossible to assess whether it was false or true. These words comprise an insult. They are cynical: 'brutal, surly, and ungracious'.

Many of these phrases pretend to be objective and because we've heard or read them so often, we all too often accept them as such. But are they? Do they not express someone else's view, someone quite likely in power and with a vested interest? Are they not, at least in part, the products of the baggage that the speaker brings to the situation?

What about 'best practice', for example? It begs the question, an obvious one when you reflect on it for a moment, whose best practice are we talking about? Is it merely what those in charge think we should be doing, or rather what we as intelligent professionals think we should be doing? Has someone tested what 'best practice' is? And how could you do that testing anyway? 'Broad and balanced' always implies a question that is never answered. To pursue the implied metaphor, where is the fulcrum of the balance?

'What works' presents a similar problem: what works for whom? Industry? Government? The parents? The teachers? The children? From my knowledge of governors of industry, I have no confidence that what works for them will work for the children. And as for 'basic skills', conventional wisdom has it that these skills are adding, subtracting, multiplying and dividing, and reading and writing correctly. They sound like what Victorian businessmen required from the young people they were to employ in their offices. Indeed, Scrooge would have demanded that Bob Cratchit in Charles Dickens' *A Christmas Carol* should have them, and he wouldn't have been interested in anything else, though now he would have had a few words to say about ICT skills. What about understanding and loving your neighbour, resolving disagreements, becoming a citizen, making a sad friend laugh in a pub garden, providing for your disabled son on Christmas Day? To me, these are basic skills.

As for 'behaviour modification', it reminds me of George Orwell's *Nineteen Eighty-Four*. Through torture with rats, Winston's views are modified so that he can learn to love Big Brother, the dictator who is the inspiration for the hidden camera in the reality television show. Do you (do I?) want to have my behaviour modified?

Watch the words, and you will be on the road to finding the truth. And, as Algernon says in Oscar Wilde's *The Importance of Being Earnest*, it will rarely be pure and never simple.

The truth

On the afternoon of the Dunblane massacre, when a class of children and their teacher were wiped out by a deranged gunman, I left a London primary at the end of the school day to find a pizza restaurant. I had been teaching and had foregone, on advice, a school lunch. Later I was booked in to lead an evening meeting during which some of the children were going to read to their parents the writing they had done with me.

I ate my Fiorentina, drank my glass of house white and my espresso. Making my way back to school, I stopped at a news stand. The posters said something like: CHILDREN MASSACRED IN PRIMARY SCHOOL. I remember thinking, to my shame, oh dear, more horror from far away ... Then, walking slowly along the pavement, I read the earliest reports in the London *Evening Standard* about those few minutes of hell in a school gym in Scotland.

Back at school, children and parents were gathering on the pavement inside that barrier that is there to stop excited children running out of school and into the traffic. Others waited in the playground and in the entrance hall. I wondered if they had heard the news. Some were probably spreading it around: some will have known it, some were about to be horrified. I pushed through them and found the headteacher. I showed her the paper. I asked 'Do you know about this? What are you going to say about it?' She had heard about it. 'Nothing', she replied. 'I'm not going to say anything'. I remember protesting. But we ran the meeting as though we lived in an innocent world, as though most of us weren't thinking, 'Are my children safe here?'

In assembly the following day, with two hundred children thirsting for reassurance and comfort, the headteacher told them a Bible story, led in the singing of a hymn, said a formulaic prayer, gave the children a mild rollocking about something or other … and we walked off to our classrooms.

Then a six-year-old, eyes glassy with tears, said to me in the corridor: 'Fred, a fox came into my garden last night and killed my chicks. He didn't eat them, he just wanted to kill them'. I said, lamely, 'I'm so sorry, Jenny' (or whatever her name was). I hope at the very least I touched her shoulders, but these days you never know how physical attempts at sympathy will be construed.

That girl was on to something. Here was 'the holiness of the heart's affections and the truth of the imagination' (John Keats). A light was dimly glimmering. A fox, her chicks, those class photographs of children, most of them now dead, seen on television with their teacher, also dead … all coming together, merging in her subconsciousness on one day. She wanted to understand the truth. She was searching for the truth through her distress: 'He didn't eat them, he just wanted to kill them'.

I have been thinking about this story on and off ever since, and one day, probably not this side of the grave, I will understand it. It is the most striking example I have, among hundreds if not thousands, of the truth of the Talmudic saying, 'Much have I learned from my teachers, more from my colleagues, but most from my students'.

May we as teachers always be, not like the headteacher, who hid from the truth behind that story, that hymn, that meaningless and invalid prayer, that rollocking, but like that child, who with her night-thoughts and her words to a stranger had begun to face up to it.

References

Bagnall, Nicholas (ed.) (1973) *New Movements in the Study and Teaching of English*. London: Temple Smith.

Beckett, Francis (2007a) 'Sell 'em cheap', *Guardian*, 3 April.

Beckett, Francis (2007b) *The Great City Academy Fraud*. London: Blackwell.

Bennett, Alan (2004) *The History Boys*. London: Faber and Faber.

Blishen, Edward (1980) *A Nest of Teachers*. London: Hamish Hamilton.

Boswell, James (1791) *The Life of Samuel Johnson LLD*.

Burgess, Tyrrel (2002) *The Devil's Dictionary of Education*. London: Continuum.

Carr, J.L. (1972) *The Harpole Report*. London: Secker and Warburg.

Clarke, Cas (1999) *More Grub on Less Grant*. London: Headline.

Curtis, Tony (1997) 'As the Poet Said ...' Edited from Dennis O'Driscoll's 'Pickings and Choosings' column, *Poetry Ireland Review/Eigse Eireann*.

Dixon, Peter (undated) *Display in the Primary School*. Peter Dixon, Cheriton Rd, Winchester.

Drummond, Mary Jane (1994) *Assessing Children's Learning*. London: David Fulton.

Fox, Seamus (2007) private correspondence.

Grey, Duncan (2003) *101 Essential Lists for Teachers*. London: Continuum.

James, Clive (2006) *North Face of Soho: Unreliable Memoirs, vol. IV*. London: Picador.

Larkin, Philip (1988) 'Coming' in *Collected Poems*. London: Faber.

MacNeice, Louis (2007) 'Snow' in *Collected Poems*. London: Faber.

Panichas, George (ed.) (1977) *The Simone Weil Reader*. New York: McKay.

Parker, E.W. (1940) *A Pageant of Modern Verse*. London: Longman, Green.

Paton, Graeme (2007) 'Children "damaged by exam factories"', *Daily Telegraph*, 1 May.

Plowden Report (1967) HMSO.

Roeves, Emily (1987) private correspondence.

Sedgwick, Fred (1991) *Lies*. Liverpool: Headland.

Sedgwick, Fred (2001) *Teaching Literacy: A Creative Approach*. London, Continuum.

Sedgwick, Fred (2006) *101 Essential Lists for Primary School Teachers*. London: Continuum.

Stenhouse, Lawrence (1967) *Culture and Education*. London: Nelson.

Stenhouse, Lawrence (1975) *An Introduction to Curriculum Research and Development*. London: Heinemann.

Willans, Geoffrey and Searle, Ronald (1999) *Molesworth*. London: Penguin.

Index

1-75

The Protestant Duke

VIOLET WYNDHAM

The Protestant Duke

A LIFE OF MONMOUTH

WEIDENFELD AND NICOLSON
LONDON

ISBN 0 297 77099 3

Printed in Great Britain by
Cox & Wyman Ltd
London, Fakenham and Reading

Contents

Illustrations

Dedicated
to
Rachel Wyndham
with love

March 1975

For these peasant followers of Monmouth, the dark Puritan faith glowed in all the colours of personal romance; they loved the young man more than they loved their lives. As of Napoleon, tales were told at nightfall beneath the thatch – and his return was still expected long after he was dead.

G. M. TREVELYAN *England Under the Stuarts* (1965)

Preface

THE story of the courageous rebellion of James, Duke of Monmouth, is the story of an expression of popularity for the House of Stuart just before its power came to an end. By estranging himself from the people of Britain in cleaving to the Catholic faith, James II thereby increased the popularity of his nephew, who was able to lead a rebellion that nearly succeeded and that, by its terrible aftermath, made possible the bloodless and easy revolution of William of Orange; it was an aftermath so terrible that the people of Britain, estranged now from the House of Stuart and from the very idea of rebellion alike, welcomed this representative of the Protestant House of Orange with friendship and peace. It is partly thanks to the Duke of Monmouth that England was eventually granted a Protestant monarchy without the pains and struggles of a second civil war.

I should like to offer my most profound thanks to Mr Claude Scott for having given me access to Lord George Scott's unpublished biography. I am also extremely grateful to Mr Timothy Purpus for his invaluable help with the research and for his inspiring enthusiasm which helped me to write this book.

I

Lucy Walter

On 9 April in the year 1649 a baby boy was born in Rotterdam – a child who was to develop great beauty and the power to inspire love, yet was to be the victim of the ambition of others and to go to his death branded, falsely as a traitor to England. His beauty came from his mother, a Welsh girl called Lucy Walter, who was aged about eighteen at the time of his birth. His father, aged nineteen, was the exiled Charles II of England, who had succeeded to the throne only ten weeks earlier, when his own father, Charles I, had been beheaded by the Parliamentarians against whom he had waged civil war for so many years.

Two months after his birth the baby, who had been named James, was taken from Amsterdam to Paris to see his widowed grandmother, Queen Henrietta Maria, who lavished affection upon him. Did she believe that his parents were married? Most probably her heart was too softened by their joy to wonder or to doubt, and by the gentle atmosphere of the convent in which she had taken shelter since her husband's execution. But many people believed at this time that Charles and Lucy were married (including one of the girl's relatives, George Gosfright, who was living in Rotterdam at the time of the child's birth), because of the King's 'inordinate love', of which 'all who were abroad with his Majesty at that time knew'.[1]

It is now necessary to go back four years, to the time when Charles I of England resolved to separate his eldest son from himself, to spare him the dangers of the civil war. The New Model

Army had just been formed by Cromwell and had changed the fortunes of the Roundheads for the better. Charles planned that Sir Edward Hyde, who had recently left the Opposition to serve the King, should accompany the Prince into that exile that the younger Charles would refer to in future – with typical irony – as 'my travels'.

At the outbreak of the civil war Queen Henrietta Maria had raised a large sum of money in Holland for the Royalist cause. In 1643 she returned to England to see her husband for what proved to be the last time; the result of this meeting was the birth of their daughter Henrietta the following June. The child had to be left in Exeter, where she had been born, under the care of Lady Moreton. In 1646 this ingenious lady, disguised as a French peasant woman, escaped with her charge to Calais. The Queen had already fled to France, her native country and, as the daughter of the late Henry IV and Marie de Médici, she was warmly welcomed. It meant much to her to be among Catholics again, after years in hostile, Protestant England.

In the turbulence of the year 1646 her greatest wish was, naturally, to have her eldest son with her in France, but there were mixed views on whether the Prince should join his mother or not. She was insistent that he should; Sir Edward Hyde was against it. In April 1645 Prince Charles had been welcomed in Jersey. But as he could not act against his mother's wishes for long, in July of the following year he embarked for France, with a small retinue of servants. Hyde remained in Jersey for another two years, where he devoted himself to his studies and enjoyed, as he was later wont to say, 'the greatest tranquillity imaginable'.[2]

Prince Charles lodged with his mother at Saint-Germain, where he found his brother Henry of Gloucester (whom Henrietta Maria ceaselessly tried to convert to Catholicism) and his little sister Henrietta. Charles truly loved his little sister and invented for her the pet-name of 'Minette' by which she later became generally known. The family lived at first in considerable splendour, until the Queen started to sell the more valuable objects that had been given to brighten her exile.

The refugee members of the English royal family were not permitted to attend the court at Fontainebleau; this was lucky for Charles, as he did not feel comfortable with the formal etiquette that surrounded his cousin Louis XIV, then only eight years old, but already *le Grand Monarque*. Charles's own pleasures in Paris were severely curtailed because his dominating mother allowed him only a small amount of money. Her ambition was that he should marry her niece Anne-Marie-Louise, the daughter of Gaston, Duke of Orléans. She was the richest heiress in Europe and was known as *la Grande Mademoiselle*. But she did not respond to Charles's chivalrous, though lukewarm, courtship and found his brother, James, Duke of York, handsomer. (York was his mother's favourite son, but much to her annoyance, he left her to go to Brussels as soon as he could.)[3]

George, second Duke of Buckingham, son of the all-powerful favourite of James I, was also in Paris. Orphaned in childhood, he and his brother had been brought up with Charles I's family. In Henrietta Maria's mind he was suspect, a bad companion for her son. Her instinctive doubts were not unfounded, and most of the two years during which Charles was in Paris were spent with Buckingham in impoverished dissipation.

Charles found a more sumptuous court when, in 1648, he visited his sister, Princess Mary of Orange, in The Hague. Here he was able to spend a pleasanter time than he had under the scrutiny of his mother. The reason for his visit to Holland at this time was the recent revolt from the Parliamentarian cause of some English ships, which had sailed away to Helvoetsluys. He was accompanied by his cousin, Prince Rupert of the Rhine, known as the 'Mad Cavalier'. The principal Royalist general, he was much admired by Charles. Rupert had accepted command of that portion of the English fleet that joined the Royalists. In eight days the two princes sailed, with their recently acquired fleet, for the Downs, off the south coast of England.

Charles left behind him in the Netherlands Lucy Walter, soon to become the mother of his son.

The date of Lucy's birth is uncertain. It could have been any time between 1628 and 1631. Her first home was Roche Castle, her second in Haverfordwest in Wales. But when she was about eight her parents' matrimonial disagreements became so scandalous that the Walters had to leave the town and move to London, where they lived in a house behind King Street, Covent Garden, then a most fashionable neighbourhood, where they had a number of interesting friends. By 1640 William Walter had left his wife and returned to Wales. Lucy remained in London with her mother.

Details of her pedigree on her father's side have been recorded in much detail in a book written by one of her descendants, Lord George Scott, in 1947. In the years when it seemed that her son might aspire to the throne of England there were attempts (encouraged by James, Duke of York, himself heir presumptive to the throne) to defame her family as well as herself. The following digression must be forgiven, since it is important to point out how false were the contemporary contemptuous remarks: the families of Lucy's parents were far from being the 'mean creatures' described by the diarist Evelyn.

A particularly interesting antecedent of Lucy's was her maternal grandfather, John Protheroe, an eminent astronomer. In 1609 he, with Thomas Harriot and Sir William Lower, the Welsh astronomer who was knighted for his work in that field, were privileged to be the first Englishmen to examine the heavens through a telescope. The telescope had been invented in 1608 by Hans Lippershey, a Dutch spectacle-maker. It is assumed that he never thought of using his invention for astronomy, and that it required Galileo, in the following year, to do this. Yet Thomas Harriot, known as a distinguished explorer and writer (his *Brief and True Account of the New Found Land of Virginia* is among the earliest known documents of English colonial exploration, and one of the best), mathematician and scientist, had earlier obtained some of these 'cylinders' from Lippershey and in July and August 1609 was observing and mapping the moon with their means. In this he was independent of Galileo, for the publication of the latter's *Sidereus Nuncius* did not come until March 1610 – so that Harriot was equal in priority, or possibly preceded him in some of his observations and telescopic drawings. These included the discovery of sun-spots in December 1609 and, later, the examination of the moons of Jupiter and the phases of Venus. The latter, as described by Galileo, were to deal a decisive blow to Ptolemaic astronomy and to point to the truth of Copernican theory by showing that the brightest of our planets moves round the sun.

John Protheroe, Lucy's grandfather, described as 'a bosom friend of Harriot,[4] assisted him in these epoch-making activities. He appears in an amusing letter of 6 February 1610 from William Lower, to whom Harriot had sent some telescopes for report. Lower is describing the moon: 'I must confess I can see none of this without my Cylinder. Yet an ingeniouse younge man that accompanies me here often and loves you and these studies much, sees manie of these things without the helpe of the instrument, but with it sees them most plainlie; I mean the younge Mr Protheroe.'[5]

Lucy's son, when older, was criticized for being unusually pre-occupied with magic, charms, soothsayers and fortune-tellers. He may have derived his taste for astrology from his great-grand-father's interest in astronomy. The Church viewed both activities with disfavour: the Catholic Church was particularly hostile to a sun-centred philosophy, while the Episcopalians disliked any hint of atheism, and the Puritans any hint of witchcraft. Though Puritanism gave much greater freedom of individual worship than either of the other creeds, and though probably many people under Cromwell's rule found in the sky hopeful lessons to be learned, or saw their destiny written in the stars, nevertheless, since astronomy and astrology were not sharply differentiated in the popular mind, either activity might provoke the hostility engendered by the other.

Through his friendship with Thomas Harriot, John Protheroe became a member of a wide circle of friends of the ninth Earl of Northumberland, whose dabbling in science and the occult earned him both the *sobriquet* of the 'Wizard Earl' and frequent terms of imprisonment in the Tower. (Protheroe considered himself to be the Wizard's nephew-in-law, as Sir Thomas Perrott, his wife's step-uncle, had married Lady Dorothy Devereux, who later married the Earl.) Harriot, who had formerly been tutor to Sir Walter Raleigh (now imprisoned in the Tower), was engaged to instruct the Earl's son and heir, Algernon Percy, who succeeded to the title in 1632. Through the Percy connection Lucy Walter could count among her distant cousins Algernon, Robert and Henry Sidney, sons of the first Earl of Leicester and nephews of the 'Wizard Earl'. Many years after her death a libellous rumour circulated that she had been the mistress of Colonel Robert Sidney and that his brother Algernon had boasted that he had paid 'fifty broad pieces' for her, before she fell into the arms of his brother. This unproved story was one of the many investigated by the enemies of Lucy's son.

Protheroe died in 1624 (at about the same time as Harriot), but his widow Elenour (*née* Vaughan) lived on in London and was frequently visited by her grand-daughter after the Walters' arrival in the city. When William Walter returned to Wales, Elizabeth Walter and Lucy moved into Elenour's home. Lucy's grandmother had by then remarried; as Mrs Gwinn she was the owner of a house in St Giles, a country village just outside London, and, like Covent Garden, an elegant district at that time.

Elenour was the sister of the first Earl of Carbery of Golden Grove, Carmarthenshire, who had been comptroller of the Household to King Charles I when he was Prince of Wales. There were times during the civil war when Lucy Walter's relatives crossed the path of the future Charles II. In 1645, for instance, he spent a full month at Exeter, the West Country being comparatively loyal to the Royalists, and it is probable that he lodged with Lucy's step-grandfather, Nicholas Chappell, at Brockhill. Lucy and her mother were guests there several times during that year, so it may well be that Lucy and her future lover first met there.

By 1648, however, Lucy was in The Hague, living in the household of her aunt, Margaret Gosfright. It was at this time that she became known as the mistress of Prince Charles. It was not long before news of his liaison with Lucy, 'perhaps the most beautiful of all the women who at one time or other enslaved [his fancy],'[6] had spread to England, and soon rumours of the romance were circulating round the Continent.

In 1648 the Prince was close to desperation in his efforts to keep himself and his small court comfortably alive in exile, to temper his mother's mania for interfering and for attempting to convert him to Catholicism, and to save his father's life. Lucy, and the son she gave him, brought him comfort at a crucial and painful time. In a story signed anonymously 'ST', in which the principal character was taken from Lucy and called 'Lucilious', she is described thus: 'A graceful bashfulness . . . embellished and gave an admirable lustre to her beauty, and every part of her was decked with some peculiar ornament; her mind was richly fraught with the rarest qualities; and she had a good wit and a quick apprehension.'[7]

The rumours of Lucy's importance to Charles were further increased when news came of their arrival together in Paris in July, to see the exiled Queen at Saint-Germain. Although it could have been an embarrassing meeting, Lucy had a proud bearing. The fact that the Queen had agreed to receive her would have seemed to her evidence that Her Majesty took rumours of their marriage seriously – a contract, perhaps, to be ratified later. Charles would not have risked a clash painful to his mother, particularly at this, the saddest time of her life.

The diarist Evelyn, who saw Lucy in Paris (and described her as 'a browne, beautiful, bold but insipid creature')[8] regarded her as simply Charles's mistress. But among those who believed that the pair had entered into a contract of marriage, much was made of the fact that Charles's sister, Princess Mary of Orange, time and again refers to Lucy in her letters to Charles as 'your wife'.[9] It was not in character for the Princess, who was extremely conscious of her own royal status, to refer to her brother's mistresses as her in-laws. And indeed Henrietta Maria herself, a strict upholder of court etiquette, received Lucy with marked informality – a courtesy never extended to her son's future mistresses.[10] Lucy was even allowed to be present at her sickbed, a very great honour indeed.

It is certain that at one time Lucy Walter had in her possession some document concerning Charles, and that it was of such consequence that the King and his advisers deemed it to be of the first importance that it should be taken from her. What was this document? Was it a certificate of marriage? Lucy's uncle George Gosfright blamed his sister-in-law, Elizabeth Walter, for leaving her daughter abroad in unfortunate circumstances. Mrs Walter retorted that he was mistaken, for Lucy was married to the King. Margaret Gosfright averred that she had seen under the King's own hand, a declaration of the marriage, which was taken from her niece in 'Oliver's time' – that is, during the rule of Oliver Cromwell in England, before the restoration of the monarchy.

On her return from Paris Lucy was lodged in affluence in Antwerp, while the young James was placed under the care of a nurse at Schiedam, near Rotterdam. Many of the arrangements for his well-being were made by Henrietta Maria. But Charles's advisers soon realized that the boy and his mother could be as much a liability as an asset in respect of the restoration of the monarchy. Any document relating to a marriage between Charles and Lucy had to be acquired as soon as possible – documents could be dangerous if they were in the wrong hands.

This must have seemed inexplicable to Lucy. Although she understood that he had to be kept in the background, Charles was so fond of his son that he could not bear to be parted from him. To avoid scandal it was arranged that the boy should be kidnapped from Schiedam. This caused Lucy so much grief that the mayor himself intervened, harbouring her in his own house and supervising an extensive search for the boy. At length, after about a fortnight, he was found.

The King's ministers viewed with alarm the public display of Lucy's plight. They were anxious to enhance the King's moral image in England, where Cromwellian propaganda perpetuated rumours of Charles's whoring, drunkenness, theft and debauchery. Lucy, already a sensation, proved even more annoying to the Royal Council by loudly bemoaning her wrongs to the mayor in public.

Lieutenant-Colonel Daniel O'Neale, a groom of the bed-chamber, wrote at length to the King, warning him of Lucy's loud protests: the inference was that the child's kidnappers had been actually directed by Queen Henrietta Maria, who may have been advised, now that a restoration of the monarchy was probable, that Lucy would be unacceptable as queen. Charles was living apart from her by now, but supported her financially and maintained a secret interest in her behaviour. 'Every idle action of hers brings your Majestie uppon the stage,' writes O'Neale, 'and I am noe less ashamed to have soe importuned your Majestie to have beelieved hir worthy of your care.'[11]

As we have seen, Charles's sister, the Princess of Orange, considered Lucy to be his wife. She wrote to Charles from The Hague on 9 November 1654: 'Your Mother says that the greatest thankfulness she can show for the honour of your kind remembrance is to have a special care of your wife for feare her husband there may make her forget them that are absent. Your wife thanks you in her own hand and still [sic] though she begs me very hard to help her!' This letter also reveals that in Lucy's situation as an extremely attractive, temporarily deserted wife she was inclined to encourage admirers. It was situations such as the one to which Princess Mary refers that were later used to vilify Lucy's character.

Among the shrewd gestures made by Charles in his first years of kingship was an overture to his German relations. In the candid

memoirs of his attractive first cousin, the Electress Sophia of
Hanover, we read of their meeting in 1649, she a young princess
and he a poor exiled bachelor king: 'He and I had always been on
the best of terms, as cousins and friends, and he had shown a great
liking for me with which I was much gratified. One day, however, his friends Lord Gerit and Somerset Fox, being in want of
money, persuaded him to pay me compliments . . . among other
things he told me that I was handsomer than Mrs Berlo and that he
hoped to see me in England.' Although the young Princess was
much offended when she learned the financial reasons for that
flirtation, she none the less speaks with greater warmth of Charles
than of his mother – 'I was surprised to find the queen (so beautiful in her picture) a little woman with long lean arms, crooked
shoulders, and teeth protruding from her mouth like guns from a
fort.' Henrietta Maria's kindness to her, especially when the
Queen compared her to Charles's adored sister, made her change
her mind and 'from that time forward I considered her quite
handsome'.[12] Sophia's engaging disposition did not win her the
crown of England, although, as the Princess was the first to admit,
'the English desired for their prince a wife of their own religion,
and at that time there were no Protestant princesses of birth
superior to mine for him to choose amongst'. The irony is that
while Sophia did not gain the penniless hand of Charles, she none
the less managed to come within reach of the English throne –
missing it by a matter of weeks when the crown passed to George
I, her eldest son by the Elector Augustus of Hanover.

Lucy had meanwhile given birth to a daughter. The date of this
event is not known. Neither is it known if Charles was the father.
Although he saw little of Lucy, he gave financial help to the
child, which suggests that he believed that she was his. She was
called Mary, which suggests that she may have been born during
Henrietta Maria's guardianship.

The kidnappers had failed and, although she was viewed with
ever-increasing disfavour among those who hoped to see the
monarchy restored, Lucy was granted an annuity of £400 and

sent back to England, with her children, in June 1656. It was
hoped that this move would put a stop to the scandals that seemed
to attend her. Her most loyal maid, Anne Hill, was to precede her
mistress by three weeks, on the understanding that they would be
united in London. Anne declared later that the king had not lost
interest in Lucy, as they had spent 'a night and a day together'
before Lucy's departure,[13] and he had left behind a pearl necklace
worth £1500 as a gift for her.

Thomas Howard, brother of the third Earl of Suffolk, accompanied Lucy to England. It is now known through official state
papers that he was a spy in the pay of Cromwell. Could Howard
have been the 'husband' referred to in the Princess of Orange's
letter to Charles quoted above? Allan Fea, in his *King Monmouth*,
asserts that he was Lucy's lover, while Lord George Scott was
convinced that Lucy's brother was included in the party to protect her from Howard's advances.

Once in London, 'Mrs Barlow', as Lucy was generally called
after a family with whom the Walters had intermarried, lodged in
an apartment above a barber's shop close to Somerset House (on
which Henrietta Maria was later to spend so much money). She
entertained those active in the Royalist cause and was treated with
such respect that the fact of her marriage to Charles seemed
obvious to those who paid homage to her. While in London she
also stayed with a relation of William Harvey, the celebrated dis-
coverer of the circulation of the blood. He was a contemporary of
her grandfather Protheroe and is mentioned by Aubrey: 'Warner
did tell . . . that when Dr Harvey came out with his Circulation of
the Blood, he did wonder whence Harvey had it; but coming one
day to the Earl of Leicester, he found Dr Harvey in the hall, talking very familiarly with Mr Protheroe to whom Mr Warner had
discoursed concerning the exercitation of his *De Circulatione
Sanguines*, and made no question but Mr Harvey had his hint
from Protheroe.'[14]

William Harvey was physician to James 1 and Charles 1 and had
witnessed the Battle of Edgehill in October 1642, in the company

of the young Prince of Wales. Another Harvey, presumably William's nephew, was to serve as Royal Treasurer to Queen Catherine of Braganza after the Restoration. As he was a relation of Lucy's friends, he may have introduced the rumour in the King's most intimate household that Charles really had married Lucy Walter.

It was not long before Lucy and her seven-year-old son were arrested, and a 'paper containing something relating either to a Marriage or Pension of Maintenance from his Majestie' was confiscated by Cromwell. For two weeks mother and son were held in the Tower, where Lucy cautiously withstood an extensive interrogation and denied that she had received any attention from the King for the past two years. She also claimed that his son had died and that young James was fathered by a Dutch captain, who had also died.

The Protector did not believe Lucy, but felt her to be harmless enough not to merit prolonged captivity. On 15 July 1656 he ordered the Lieutenant of the Tower to release 'one that goes by the name of Lucy Barlow, who for some time hath been a prisoner in the Tower of London. She passeth under the character of Charles Stuart's Wife or Mistress, and hath a young son whom she openly declareth to be his; and it is generally believed, that the boy being very like him, and both the mother and child provided for by him. ...'[15] Perhaps the lovely miniature painted in this same year by Samuel Cooper had been seen by Cromwell – hence his comment on the likeness to Charles. Thus Lucy was expelled from England and, to her displeasure, sailed for Flanders.

Within the month she was involved in more scandal, when an envoy of Charles's was stabbed in the street by her order, for his attempt to steal her private papers. Her servant wounded the young man dangerously and a lawsuit was to follow. The documents had become a matter of the utmost importance to Lucy, and equally – it appeared – to Charles. The King then prepared yet again to abduct the child (and the papers) as quickly and as quietly as possible. The first attempt failed, and Lucy fled with her son to

Brussels. There, yet another envoy tried to have her imprisoned. The arrest was made in the street; she resisted with loud cries, embracing her son. Her weeping and wailing created local sympathy for her and at length the Governor of the Spanish Netherlands, Don Alonso de Cardenas, brought the brawl to a halt by ordering both Lucy and the boy under his own care, where they were to await the King's pleasure. Nevertheless, Charles subsequently had his son abducted and put into the care of William Crofts.

Eight months later, in late 1658, Lucy died in Paris, where she had gone to be near her beloved child who, now known as James Crofts, was living at Colombes. Her age at death could have been twenty-eight, twenty-nine or thirty. Lord George Scott writes that she was buried by the late 'master of the Charter House', William Erskine. He was uncle to Lady Anna Scott, who would one day marry Lucy's son and become Duchess of Monmouth and Buccleuch. John Evelyn falsely asserts that Lucy died miserably, with no one to bury her.

It is difficult to understand why this beautiful young woman refused the status that King Charles II's later mistresses were happy to accept. Possibly she believed that she was married to him, and that one day they would go through a second marriage ceremony; or maybe she felt too acutely the insult of being forcibly separated from her son.

Charles had appointed for his son an English Protestant tutor called Thomas Ross. In April 1658 the tutor had written to the king giving his opinion of the nine-year-old boy: 'It is a pity so pretty a child should be in such hands hitherto to have neglected to teach him to read or tell twenty though he hath a great deal of wit and great desire to learn.'[16]

For the next two years James went to two schools connected with the famous religious house of Port-Royal, first at Le Chesnay and afterwards at the academy of Jouilly. Ross was proved right, in that James had indeed a great desire to learn. He

13

picked up what was required from pupils at Port-Royal remarkably well. One of these was 'good manners', or 'gentlemanliness', that virtue that has been so well defined as 'sympathy with self respect for others'.[17] Some of the other tenets of Port-Royal were enthusiastically adopted by James: hunting helps a man to bear the fatigues of war; dancing helps to give gracefulness; 'don't boast, don't flatter, don't interrupt' – these came under 'good manners'. When he was not at school young James, or Jemmy, as his doting father liked to call him, spent his time with his grandmother Henrietta Maria, at her court, which was then at the Louvre.

2

The Restoration Court

THE restoration of the monarchy, which placed the crown of England on the head of Charles II in 1660, was achieved through the influence of that great soldier General Monck, who had been sent by Cromwell to restore order in Scotland in 1654. Monck had personal magnetism and became a universal favourite there. Those who were jealous of his success whispered to Cromwell that he was too popular, whereupon the Protector wrote a quaint letter to Monck: 'There be those that tell me there is a certain cunning fellow in Scotland called George Monck who is said to be in wait there to introduce Charles Stuart: I pray you use your vigilance to apprehend him.'[1]

When Cromwell died in 1658 his son Richard had been proclaimed Protector in Scotland. But Monck was soon distressed by the anarchy resulting from the new militant Commonwealth. At first resisting Royalist pressures, he was later converted by his own chaplain and agreed to help to bring the dictatorship to an end. On 8 December 1659 he had assembled his army at Coldstream and personally led their famous march to London: 'The frost was great and the snow greater, and I do not remember that we ever trod upon plain earth from Edinburgh to London,' wrote the chaplain. All Yorkshire came in arms to aid Monck, and as he marched resistance crumbled away.[2] On 3 February 1660, they arrived in the capital where, it is said, the general declined the role of dictator.

It was on 25 May in the year 1660 that a crowd stood on the beach at Dover to greet their 'king from over the water'. A tall dark man got out of a boat. When the mayor of the little seaside town placed the English Bible in his hands, the king displayed his usual exquisite tact in his first words, to the effect that it was the one thing he loved above all things in the world. Nothing could have given greater confidence to his new subjects.[3]

A few days later, on his birthday, the King entered his capital. He was dismayed by the list of Presbyterians presented to him by Monck for the Privy Council, but the General showed no displeasure when Charles selected only Ashley Cooper and a few more Roundhead nominees. The real power would be in the hands of Charles's advisers in exile – Ormonde, Secretary Nicholas and Chancellor Hyde, the latter being President of the Council. (These three men had not only dealt with political problems when in exile with the King but were also his private advisers on the question of Lucy Walter and her son.) Monck, created Duke of Albemarle, became a great lord, retaining the respect of the people, but he was less and less in the inner circle of the king.

Queen Henrietta Maria's first visit to England after her long exile in France took place in December 1660. She must surely have gone with some trepidation, for before the civil war, she had been the most hated woman in England, due to her jealous Catholic convictions and her mania for conversion. At the time of her wedding, as a girl of fifteen in 1625, she had brought with her from France some four hundred Catholic attendants, in addition to priests and a bishop – they were soon packed off home. It would have been hard then to foresee that she was bringing into England hideous feuds between parties yet unformed, feuds that would still be resounding by the end of the century. In spite of the Protestant nation's memories of Popish subversion, however, the Queen Mother's visit in 1660 was unmarked by any public protest. The impact upon her former subjects may have been tempered by the natural grief caused at Christmas by the death from smallpox of her daughter Mary, Princess of Orange, who had accompanied her. Nevertheless, Charles had his mother removed from the deathbed at once, for fear of any last-minute attempted conversion, and she was sent back to France within the month. The king loved her, but he resented her attempts to dominate him.

Queen Henrietta Maria naturally wished to see her son united to a wife of her own religion, and it is supposed that negotiations for a Portuguese bride opened towards the close of the Queen's visit to England. The idea was put into words by the Portuguese ambassador, godfather of his king's sister, Catherine of Braganza, whom he proposed as Charles's future wife. In reply to the ambassador's first hints, Charles's chamberlain replied merely that the king would think about the matter. The next morning, the ambassador was more explicit and informed Charles that Catherine's dowry was £500,000 sterling, the annexation to England of Tangier and free trade for the English nation with Brazil and the East Indies, plus 'the Island of Bombay, with its spacious towns and castles'.

Clarendon's comments after hearing of Charles's choice was: 'Had His Majesty given up all thoughts of a Protestant wife?' Charles replied that he could not find one except among his own subjects.

Charles now wrote to the Queen Regent of Portugal and to the King, her brother. He had listened to the offer of £½ million with ill-suppressed delight and told Clarendon that the proposal pleased him and that he considered that the alliance might prove to be of notable advantage to the kingdom. He assigned two ships to the convoy of the ambassador, who immediately set sail for Lisbon. The court there was filled with great joy, and the ambassador was rewarded for his diplomatic skill with the title of count.

The ambassador was soon dispatched back to England with full powers to conclude the marriage. But on his arrival in London he found that the King had changed his mind, for the jealous Spanish ambassador had told him that 'Catherine was deformed, had bad health, and it was known she would never have children'.[4] Spain was against the marriage, presumably because it would strengthen Portugal, while France was in favour for the same reason. Charles, meantime, had made inquiries that gave Spain the lie and resulted in his determination to announce that he would not receive orders as to how to dispose of his own person in marriage. But a communication from Louis XIV offering 300,000 *pistoles* if Charles would ally himself to Portugal by marriage settled the matter, and the King agreed with his French counterpart that he could not do better than bestow himself on the Infanta.[5] He knew that she was a Catholic who would never give up her faith, but it was said, rightly, that she had been brought up by a wise mother never to interfere in state affairs.

No sooner was the king married than he summoned his mother to return to England. His most ardent wish was that she should bring with her his beloved son. Thus in the year 1662 young 'James Crofts' arrived in England in the retinue of his grandmother, who had become Queen Dowager on Charles's marriage.

Typical of Charles's half-serious, half-teasing manner was his warning to those who went to meet the Queen Mother at sea: he maintained that they were in grave danger of losing their lives, for Henrietta Maria seemed to attract bad weather. 'Mam's ill-luck at sea,' he called it.[6] (Charles himself gloried in waves, the bigger the better, and seasickness was unknown to him.) The English party did indeed meet the travellers from France in a raging storm. But they landed safely, and the Queen Mother and her grandson made their way to Hampton Court.

'The King's bastard' proved a most exciting surprise to the English court. The thirteen-year-old son of Charles and Lucy Walter was outstandingly handsome and had charming manners. Though Charles had not legally or formally acknowledged the boy as his own son, he treated him as such – not realizing at the time how fierce were to be the future controversies regarding the boy's possible right to inherit the throne. 'Jemmy' was so beautiful and appealing that he immediately won the hearts of the English, both rich and poor. Even Queen Catherine did not resent having a child who was not hers living at court and succumbed to his sweetness. This is much to her credit, as it has been said that she believed in his legitimacy.

It was not long before Pepys, the diarist, was able to record:

> In the Queen Mother's presence-chamber with our own Queen sitting on her left hand (whom I did never see before) . . . . Here I also saw Lady Castlemaine, and, which pleased me most, Mr Crofts, the King's bastard, a most pretty spark of about fifteen years old [James was in fact thirteen and a half], who I perceive do hang much upon my Lady Castlemaine and is always with her; and hear the Queens, both of them, are mightly kind to him. By and by in comes the King, and anon the Duke and Duchess of York; so that, they all being together, was such a sight as I never could almost have happened to see with so much ease and pleasure. They stayed till it was dark, and then went away. The King and his Queen, and my Lady Castlemaine and young Crofts in one coach and the rest in other coaches.[7]

What is auspicious in Pepys's observations is the presence of Lady Castlemaine, the King's current mistress, so confidently at the side of 'Jemmy'. She was a most powerful woman – more powerful than Queen Catherine – and by her mere presence at the court début of 'the King's bastard', she was countenancing his introduction into the court's inner circle. (Lady Castlemaine, later to be made Duchess of Cleveland, herself bore Charles three sons, later to be created Dukes of Southampton, Grafton and Northumberland.) She proved to be a suitable friend to the boy, in spite of the Duke of Sutherland's description of her as an 'enormously vicious and ravenous woman'.[8] (She was inclined to look upon one-time friends, such as the Duke of Buckingham, who had helped her into nightly contact with his old friend, the King, with furious demoniac hatred.) But Jemmy would have been an ornament and an added pleasure to his father at her convivial gatherings and at the little suppers where Charles sought to drown, in wine and ribaldry, criticisms and dull advice from Clarendon, his chancellor.

There is no doubt that, of all his sons, this eldest inspired in Charles a tender, almost passionate love. One can even say that, in his joy at having such a beguiling first-born, he appears to have lost his head. One might think that to have twenty-five honours bestowed on one at such an early age would be an embarrassment; but this bejewelled ewe-lamb, certainly raised no objection to receiving them. This should not be taken as criticism of his character since his extreme youth absolves him from the accusation of an overt desire for display. But the King, for his part, was showing appalling irresponsibility in his conduct. It was obvious that he could not bear to part with Jemmy: at the theatre, at Newmarket, at court balls, during audiences of foreign ambassadors, hunting, sailing on the Thames, making a royal progress – always by the side of the tall King was his dazzling son. It is strange that Charles did not foresee the tragic events that might result from his own indulgence.

When Jemmy first came to England he was befriended by his uncle the Duke of York, who would take him out hunting. The boy's love of sport soon inspired accusations of intellectual laziness and reluctance to learn. He was too physically active to make a serious scholar. Pepys suggested this in his description of the boy as 'the most skittish, leaping gallant that ever I saw; always in action, vaulting or leaping or clambering.'[9] Later Jemmy complained that his education had been neglected. Sir John Reresby wrote: 'Though he was quite finished as to his exterior, his inside was by no means apiece therewith.'[10] Jemmy's pocketbook reveals his interest in charms, in magic and in fortunetellers, and his fondness for keeping lists of recipes and medicines and of other facts that interested him. As we have seen, his interest in the occult may have derived from his great-grandfather's interest in astronomy. It would be interesting to know what he thought of one of his father's first actions when he became king: Charles granted a royal charter to a group of scientists, who now called themselves the Royal Society. Did he realize that, with a great-grandfather such as his, it should concern him?

Jemmy had inherited his father's sweetness of character and

charm and was much in demand among the court ladies. He had, despite his youth, a short period of dalliance, then married, though it cannot be denied that marriage did not put an end to his love life. The match had been arranged even before he left France, and the bride his father chose for him was Lady Anna Scott, daughter of the Countess of Wemyss and the late Francis, second Earl of Buccleuch. Anna, then eleven years old, was heiress to the richest family in Scotland.

Only two years earlier Lady Wemyss's dominance and ingenuity had been brought to the King's attention. Her behaviour at this time was shocking. After feuding with her own brother, Lord Rothes, she had aligned herself with the Earl of Highchester, and had made arrangements for the Earl's son to marry her eldest daughter, Mary of Buccleuch, and thus receive the considerable fortune of the eleven-year-old heiress. Mary was a countess in her own right, and by consent of the Countess Dowager (now Lady Wemyss), the title and revenues of the Buccleuch earldom would pass to Mary's husband immediately upon the King's ratification. Highchester, seizing upon the anger Lady Wemyss felt towards her meddlesome brother, consented to whatever terms she suggested, and when Lady Wemyss took her daughter to London with her to pay her respects to the King, it seemed certain that the Earl's fifteen-year-old son would also soon become an earl.

Once in London, however, Lady Wemyss quickly patched up the feud with her brother and plans were drawn up secretly for the young son of Lord Highchester to become Earl of Tarras, as opposed to Buccleuch, and to secure property of less considerable value. Mary was at this time very ill, and Lady Wemyss frantically swept her daughter into the King's presence, hoping that his royal touch would cure her. The girl's illness continued, however, and there were fears that she might die and leave Highchester's son with no claims whatsoever to the Buccleuch fortune. The Earl of Highchester adhered to the new marriage contract and married his young son to the eleven-year-old Countess, but the fatigue of her journey had made her illness worse and by 1661 she was dying.

The battle over her deathbed between Lady Wemyss, Lord Rothes and her new in-laws led to four different wills being drawn up and signed by the dying child, each with a more shaky and disjointed signature. The final will excluded her husband and her adored sister Anna from a good deal of her fortune. Anna received the title of Countess of Buccleuch, Tarras a small yearly annuity and the wilful Lady Wemyss the bulk of her daughter's fortune, to be divided between herself and her brother. To make matters worse, the patent on the will was received at court even before Lady Wemyss entered mourning, and the claims for the Buccleuch fortune were settled upon Lady Wemyss's brother with the power of executor. With some immediacy Lady Wemyss shrewdly manoeuvred Scottish law in such a way as to decree the marriage void, on the grounds that her daughter was still a child at the time of her wedding. Highchester's son was allowed to keep his title as Earl of Tarras, but it brought no revenue and little rank, and was granted for his lifetime only. The entire fortune was thus secured for the Countess Dowager and her brother.

With the prospect of his son's marriage, the King decided to consult Clarendon about giving him a title, since at the moment he was nameless. Clarendon's reply reveals how much he must have bored the King by his prudent ideas:

He need not give him any other title or honour than he would enjoy by his marriage by which he would by the law of Scotland be called Earl of Buccleuch, which would be title enough; and he desired his Majesty to pardon him if he found fault with . . . the title they had given him who prepared that draft; wherein they presumed to style him the King's natural son, which was never, at least in many ages, used in England, and would have an ill sound in England with all his people, who thought that those unlawful acts ought to be concealed, and not published and justified. . . .

Though the King did not appear to be at all offended, he asked Clarendon whether he had 'conferred with the Queen his mother upon that subject'. Clarendon replied that he had not, nor with any other person. The King then said he had reason to ask the question, because many of those things which he had said had been spoken to him by his mother, who was entirely of his (Clarendon's) opinion, which she used not to be; and concluded 'that he would confer with them together'.[11] Naturally, given Charles's character, he would certainly not have spoken again to either of them on the subject, but instead signed the draft as it was already written. He thus created James Duke of Monmouth.

On 14 February 1663 the King knighted his son under the name of Sir James Scott, Baron Scott of Tindall, Earl of Doncaster and Duke of Monmouth. Then on 28 March he was elected a knight of the Order of the Garter, and on 20 April 1663, the day of his wedding, he was created Duke of Buccleuch as well. In the following year, on 13 October 1664, the right of the ducal honours was extended to the Duchess. Previously she had enjoyed only her right of Countess of Buccleuch and, on her marriage, the courtesy title of duchess.

Charles wrote to his sister Minette describing James's wedding, telling her how he had supped and danced with the young couple (James aged fourteen, Anna only twelve) and seen them to bed. But,' he added, 'the ceremony should stop there'[12] – meaning, no doubt, that they were too young to consummate the marriage. Pepys records: 'This day the little Duke of Monmouth was married at White Hall, in the King's chamber; and tonight is a great supper and dancing at his lodgings near Charing-Cross.'[13] Another entry from Pepys's diary reads: 'A week after his marriage, when at Windsor, he was dancing with the Queen with his hat in his hand; the King came and kissed him, and made him put on his hat, which everybody took notice of.[14]

There is no doubt that Pepys found Monmouth of interest, because before the wedding he appears several times in the diaries. On 8 April 1663, for instance, we read: 'Up betimes and to my office, and by and by, about 8 o'clock, to the Temple. Thence by water to White Hall to Chappell. . . . Here also I saw the Duke of Monmouth, with his Order of the Garter. I am told that the University of Cambridge did treat him a little while since with all the honour possible, with a comedy at Trinity College, and banquet and made him Master of Arts there. All which they say, the King took very well.'[15]

The Countess of Wemyss had hoped that her son-in-law would live abroad until his wife had reached maturity. The King agreed to this plan at first, but later changed his mind and co-operated with Lady Wemyss only in her wish that Anna should remain in Scotland. So there she was, poor girl, depending on her mother for companionship, and with only her half-brother, Lord Elcho, as her playfellow. A letter she wrote to her stepfather, Lord Wemyss, on 4 June 1663 is typical of her narrow outlook at this period:

I have obeyed your Lordship's commandment in keeping my Lady [her mother] merry. She is in very good health, and so is all friends hir. The Duke [Monmouth] is your servant, and I hope your Lordship will be pleased to present my servis to my dear sister Lady Margaret, and to all the rest of your good companie. I hope you will be pleased to pardon this troball from, my Lord, your Lordship's most affectionate daughter, and homb servant.

Anna Buccleuch and Monmouth[16]

For the time being at least, Anna's grandiose title was the only gain she had derived from her new status.

Monmouth was not so restricted, for he was already a permanent member of the court. Since the Restoration, Charles had become a disgracefully lavish spender and kept a brilliant court. It seems that even his yearly grant of £1,200,000 a year, accorded in the first flush of his love affair with Parliament, was not enough for his needs. Either his many mistresses were rapacious or he was too generous, and although his many illegitimate children were very expensive, this did not stop him begetting more. When he sought to remedy his financial straits in 1663, he ordered an economy drive consisting of sending away many of those who lived free of charge at court. He also issued an edict that only he and the Queen and the Duke and Duchess of York should have ten courses at dinner.

The morals of Charles's court were already a source of scandal. His *penchant* for variety in his love-making originated from his days in exile, when he found that this kind of diversion helped him to bear the humiliation, the poverty and the constraint that were inevitable in his position. Mistress after mistress appeared. The little Queen made a brave stand against her husband's wish that she should have his mistress Lady Castlemaine among the ladies of her bedchamber, but finding that her numerous objections were always ignored, at length she gave way and tried to make of her rival a special friend.

When the King offered Jemmy the pick of his own mistresses, the offer proved to be redundant, for the Duke of Monmouth was already the terror of husbands and lovers. This success was, indeed, the cause of the first rupture between him and his uncle, the Duke of York. Both were numbered among the suitors of a court belle named Moll Kirke, but they had a serious rival in one Lord Mulgrave. Revealing a mischievous and revengeful side of his nature, Monmouth watched Mulgrave depart from a stolen visit to the siren and had him arrested by guards, who kept him in custody all night. The Duke of York, sharing his nephew's resentment, prevented Mulgrave from taking command of the 1st Regiment of Foot Guards, but the noble lord, in his turn, retaliated by opening the Duke of York's eyes to the fact that he had a rival for Moll's affections in his own nephew. York had hitherto believed that she loved him alone, and the knowledge that her favours were shared by Jemmy did not endear the radiant nephew to his uncle.[17]

Pepys reveals in his diaries a surprised disapproval of the way in which Monmouth was being lionized and of his behaviour. Of the great supper and ball given at the duke's lodgings on his wedding day, the diarist wrote: 'I observed his coat [of arms] at the tail of his coach: he gives the arms of England, Scotland and France, quartered upon some other fields, but what it is that speaks his being a bastard I know not.'[18] The arms in question had been granted so that the Duke's banner might be placed at St

George's Chapel at Windsor, preparatory to his installation as a Knight of the Garter. Pepys, and Monmouth himself, little knew that, in about twenty years, Monmouth's banner would be kicked into a ditch on the orders of James II. Pepys was even more affronted that Monmouth wore all day and all night the robes he had been granted for the ceremony of the Garter: 'Nay and he tells me he did see Lord Oxford and the Duke of Monmouth in a hackney coach with two footmen in the Parke with their robes on; which is a most scandalous thing.'[19]

3

'Wenching and Rogueing'

IN 1665 Monmouth, the Duke of York and Prince Rupert of the Rhine rallied in a naval battle against the Dutch at Southwold Bay. Monmouth served at the side of his uncle, while Prince Rupert led the fleet. The battle was gruesome, lasting long into the night, and many of Monmouth's shipmates were either killed or maimed. A young seaman is said to have been decapitated by the chain-shot – his head actually knocking down the Duke of York.

Upon their return, after victory at sea, the hot summer was setting in and bringing with it the dreaded plague, which lasted from June to December 1665. A hundred deaths were recorded in the first week, and seven times that number in the following week. The panic that caused the rich to leave London also stirred the higher clergy and nearly all the much-needed physicians. Bodies of plague victims were stacked in the streets and the churchyards. 'Lord have mercy on us' was written on nearly every door. But young Monmouth, with his father's courage, appeared to be personally undisturbed by the pestilence.

Royal father and son remained in London for a full two months as the plague reached its peak. They were noted surveying the fleet together at Greenwich, where Pepys referred to Monmouth's 'skittishness'. Even when they made their way to the country (to Oxford, for instance, to visit Lady Castlemaine, or to the West Country villages), they made certain to return soon to the capital, in order, by their mere presence, to soothe the terror of the citizens running rampant in London.

Charles was as fearless in the Great Fire that followed as he had been in the Great Plague. He went directly into the most dangerous sections, riding up and down the streets with a bag of guineas at his side, commanding, threatening, imploring, personally taking charge of his people and even dismounting to stand ankle-deep in water, handing buckets for hours and working the fire-engines. The Duke of York led a similar campaign, often risking his life by standing within feet of buildings being pulled to the ground or blown up. Their valour was heroic: 'All that is left of city and suburbs is acknowledged to be wholly due to the King and the Duke of York.'[1]

At this time Monmouth moved from Whitehall to a house in a street near Charing Cross, called Hedge Lane – indeed it was lined with hedges. The young man had it paved for his own carriages. This investment, along with many others, brought him deeply into debt, in spite of the many residuals that his father secured for him. The King had never intended his son to rely solely upon Anna's fortune and therefore instructed Thomas Ross to make an inventory of his accounts and debts. His clothes and jewels were lavish, and his wife's tastes in both were even more so, once she was established at court. Monmouth was soon to be subpoenaed by the Westminster court for debts incurred on the Hedge Lane property, relating to items such as pavements and gutters. The King established a commission to oversee expenditure in both the Monmouth and Wemyss households, and also to manage their joint incomes – including the occasional gift by the Privy Seal of £13,000.[2] Eventually their official London residence would be in the King's Mews, situated on the site of the Trafalgar Square of today.

With his usual high spirits and confidence, the reckless Monmouth would boast privately at this time that the King had married his mother. Pepys was told by the brewer for the King's household that the young Duke had stated that his mother was 'an honest woman with Charles', a remark that especially annoyed the brewer, who referred to her, says Pepys, as 'a common whore before the King lay with her'.[3] When Monmouth's remarks were brought to the notice of the Duke of York, the latter was naturally alarmed, for he had seen his own future on the throne secure as long as the King lacked legitimate children.

The court under Charles II was liberal in its etiquette and lax in its morals. Charles himself was known not only as a great lover of beautiful women but as a tolerant and easy-going host. When many of the courtiers, including Monmouth, were being hounded by intrigues and by various plots against their lives, Charles surveyed their plight with curiosity and would intercede only at the last moment, when he felt that the games had become too rough. When the murder of the Duke of Ormonde (who feared an assassin under every tree) had only just been avoided, he staunchly protested to the King that more severe treatment of ill-wishing courtiers, and better treatment for himself, would be in order. Protests of this kind, by the old Duke were common, and repeatedly embarrassed the King. So obvious was his irritation with Ormonde that the Duke of Buckingham inquired of him: 'I wish your Majesty would resolve me one question, whether it be the Duke of Ormonde that is out of favour with Your Majesty, or Your Majesty that is out of favour with the Duke of Ormonde? For of the two you really look the more out of countenance.'[4] Buckingham was especially appealing in such a mood. The King could not resist it, and even young Monmouth was kept fascinated by such wry observations.[5] That the accuracy of the remarks was masked behind the witty dialogue only encouraged the liberties he took.

The touchiest subject of all for the King was the Duke of York's blatant Catholicism. As heir presumptive, York's religious indiscretion was considered to be suitable for private rather than political discussion at court. Charles could laughingly insist that York's confessor imposed mistresses for penance upon his brother, since they were of at least comparable ugliness to his sins; but it was Buckingham who acidly declared that Charles could see things if he would, whereas York would see things if he *could*.[6] These remarks were delivered with such sportive humour that the joke outweighed the impertinence.

Buckingham was an outrageous rake, and Monmouth found him likeable. His notoriety was widespread, his zest for wanton behaviour hardly diminished at all by impending bankruptcy. Regardless of plague-infested London, he led the highly born (and mostly middle-aged) band of hell-raisers into drunkenness, rabble-rousing and destructive disturbances among the populace. He was a loose and extravagant libertine at a time when the average citizen had all but adjusted himself to plague and the squalor of London at its worst. Although nine years younger than the most junior of Buckingham's friends, Monmouth trailed after them in their habits of debauchery with the determination that might be expected of a sixteen-year-old boy first thrilling to the sense of sin. His taste for women and excitement had developed since his wedding two years earlier, when the King had already felt sufficiently apprehensive to stop the ceremony just short of the bridal bed. Thomas Ross, the well-intentioned tutor, lamented over Monmouth's 'wenching and rogueing', and insisted that he should concentrate on studying history.[7] It seems incredible that such a gentle father as Charles should be so infatuated as to think it necessary to issue so astounding a public proclamation as the following, drawn up for royal signature and seal, by which Charles grants his 'gracious pardon unto our dear Sonne James, of all Murders, Homicides, and Felonies, whatsoever at any time before ye twenty eighth day of Febry past, committed either by himselfe alone or together with any other person or person'.[8]

The following lines from John Dryden's *Absalom and Achitophel* (1681) apply very well:

> How easy it is for parents to forgive:
> With how few fears a parent might be won.
> Nature pleading for a darling son.

Charles and Monmouth were in fact the inspiration of the whole poem and among the principal characters in it.

The radiant youth became a more poetic inspiration when, along with the Duke of Albemarle (the son of General Monck), the Duke of Somerset and another friend, he went wenching about the alleyways north of Lincoln's Inn Fields. The beadle, Peter Virnell, not knowing the identity of the gentlemen, approached them to inquire about their raucous behaviour. They fell upon him at once with their daggers, and it was rumoured that it was the Duke of Monmouth's hand that drove the fatal knife into the innocent man. The incident was noteworthy enough to merit a Dryden elegy to the Beadle, and Monmouth's popularity was lessened, though not severely, by the incident. A gorgeous saddle and horse-trappings were given by Charles to his son upon the occasion and are still preserved at Bowhill. (They were used at the coronation of Queen Victoria by the then Duke of Buccleuch.) It was also in the year 1668 that Charles bestowed upon his son the appointment of Great Chamberlain of Scotland, and, on the death of the Duke of Albemarle in 1670, there was talk of his being made Captain General of all the King's forces. The latter honour disturbed the Duke of York, and for good reason. Had not General Monck been granted the same appointment, and although the army was loyal to Charles, was there not much criticism of its being granted to a mere subject? The appointment was abolished, for the time being.

Still in 1668, the King sent Monmouth to visit Henrietta, Duchess of Orléans, in Paris. Charles warmly thanked his sister for her and her husband's care and kindness to his son and wrote that, since they had taken the trouble of lodging him at the Palais-Royal, he was sure that James could not do better. 'I am very glad,' he wrote, 'that you have put the thought of going in the army out of his head, for it were not proper that he should appear in any army, now that I have become a mediatuer, by the Treaty have lately made with Holland, and I am not dispatching an envoye to the King of France . . . againe thanke you for your kindnesse to James, and beg you to be assured that my kindnesse and tendernesse to you is more than I can expresse.'[9] (Monmouth's outstanding gift of generalship and his talent in all matters concerning the army had not yet revealed themselves.) Charles wrote later to his sister: 'I cannot say much to you yett, in answer to the letters you have writt to me, concerning the good correspondance you desire there should be between the King of France and me.'[10]

The following letter is mysterious: 'I did order James to speak with you about one part of the commands you payd upon Trevor, which, if we can bringe to passe, will be the greatest happiness to me imaginable.'[11] Sir John Trevor, whose coarseness in manner was at first sharply criticized by the Duchess of Orléans, was the official political envoy to her court. The letter suggests that Monmouth had a role to play, however innocent, in the sinister secret Treaty of Dover, to be signed in 1670 by Charles and Louis xiv of France, without the knowledge of the English people. Was Charles persuaded by his adored sister that the end (the conversion of England to Catholicism) justified the means, or was he interested only in receiving enough money from Louis to establish his independence of Parliament? It is most likely that he had acted from religious considerations, as he had already, in 1662, made an offer to the Pope to reconcile England to Rome. That he did not carry out the religious part of the Treaty of Dover, 'because he found it too dangerous, and Parliament too Protestant',[12] does not prove that he never meant it.

Monmouth was called back to England by the news that his wife had fractured her thigh and was in great pain. She recovered, but it was thought that she might always be a little lame. Pepys reported the accident, adding pessimistically that the leg was likely to grow shorter and shorter.

In July Monmouth was able to return to Paris in time to be present at the festivities held at Versailles that summer. The greatest of these, allegedly held to celebrate the conclusion of the

Treaty of Aix-la-Chapelle, was in reality in honour of Madame
Montespan, Louis XIV's new mistress. Orangeries, grottoes, whole
fields of flowers and countless statues were scattered upon the
lawns of Versailles. At the feast itself three hundred ladies sat at
the King's table, which made it more like a sheikh's harem than a
Christian banquet. Descriptions of the event flooded Europe in
countless letters from those at court. It need hardly be said that
Monmouth's all-conquering charm was as devastatingly potent in
France as in England, and the Duke of Orléans even became
dangerously jealous of his wife's affection for her nephew.

The scientific and astronomical tastes of 'the young Protheroe'
revealed themselves in a slightly distorted manner in his great-
grandson when Monmouth, in an ecstasy of excitement, met the
Italian monk Abbé Pregnani in Paris; he was the rage of the
moment, and had so impressed the Electress of Bavaria that
she had recommended him to Louis XIV. The Abbé cast
Monmouth's horoscope, telling him things that enchanted him
about his past and giving him great hopes for the future. It was
probably Pregnani who prophesied that if Monmouth survived
St Swithin's Day, all would go well for him. He was to remember
this prophecy at the all too appropriate time. They became great
friends, and later Monmouth presented him to Charles, to the
delight of Louis, who saw in Pregnani another possible influence
at the English court. Charles was interested to know the Abbé
because he was not only a fortune-teller but an alchemist, and
anything relating to science fascinated the King. But his failure to
predict the winning horses at Newmarket lost him Charles's
favour.

Much has been written about Monmouth's extraordinary gift
for dancing, of his natural grace, good manners and irresistible
charm. All these attributes appealed to the courts of England and
France, and particularly to the English populace. Indeed he had
been their idol from the day he landed in England. It is parad-
oxical that his power to inspire love led to his undoing.

But there was more to him than this. Historical records of the

British army describe his gallant conduct in 1673 during the Dutch campaign. 'The heroic Monmouth and Churchill [later first Duke of Marlborough] – with the Life Guards, who cast aside their carbines and drew their swords, now led the troops they had rallied to the charge, and with such invincible courage that they drove back the Dutch and regained the outward half-moon (His Grace being the first who entered it), to the admiration of all who beheld their gallant conduct.'[13] Admittedly this battle took place five years after the *fête* at Versailles in honour of Madame de Montespan, but the records reveal that the courage Monmouth had displayed at Southwold Bay, at the age of sixteen, had in no way declined.

The adulation he received had not caused him to become effete. It may be true that he had a weak character and was born to be the tool of others; that he had taken part in drunken revels in which innocent people had been killed and wounded; yet he was known by poets and others as 'gentle Monmouth'. When his father remarked, after the battle that Monmouth had won so dramatically, that if he, Charles, had commanded the troops, there would have been no prisoners, Monmouth replied, 'I cannot kill men in cold blood; that work is only for Butchers.'[14] He was praised for his clemency, which is an admirable quality in so spirited a young man.

Among his biographers, George Roberts was nearest in time to Monmouth. Though his *Life* appeared as late as 1844, the opinions of people at that time were likely to be more exact than those of, say, a hundred years later. Roberts writes: 'The éclat of the Duke's first appearance at Court, the beauty of his person, the natural endowments with most engaging manner for exciting popular favour which he possessed . . . the absence of a regular education (which he deplored). . . . How many would have been spoilt by the adulation of a court to which they appeared as idols? Few would have been proof against the flattery to which such a position exposed them. He also had the art of inspiring the love of those who followed him.'[15]

4

The Protestant Hope

MEANWHILE Clarendon had been becoming increasingly unpopular. His love of luxury and display had never pleased the
Cavaliers, who were a good deal poorer than he was, and had
always irritated the Puritans. The suspicion that he had advocated
Charles's marriage to Catherine, as well as his organization of the
sale of Dunkirk, had heightened his unpopularity. The war was
over, and he had become the country's scapegoat; Charles had
tried to induce him to resign, but Parliament had been resolved on
impeachment. From this distance in time it seems as though he
was treated unjustly: the King had banished him from England in
1667, after thirty years of single-minded devotion to the Stuarts.
The Duchess of York, who loved her father, was passionately
distressed about this, but to no avail. For Clarendon himself, the
sentence was not as painful as it might have been; he now had
time for writing, his favourite occupation, and the result was his
classic *History of the Rebellion of England*. It is ironic that he was
never to know that his grand-daughters Mary (who would marry
William of Orange, Stadtholder of Holland) and Anne were to be
successive Queens of England and the last of the Stuart monarchs.

Clarendon died in Rouen in 1674 at the age of sixty-six, after
pleading unsuccessfully to be allowed to die in his own country.
Had his later years been spent in England he might have overcome his innate prudence and divulged what he thought to be his
knowledge that Monmouth was the King's lawful son. This
seemingly rash statement can, to a certain extent, be corroborated
by reference to the 1933 volume of the *State Papers* (*Domestic*).

Here we find 'A Letter to a Person of Honour concerning the King's Disavowing the having been married to the D. of M's Mother'. It is dated 10 June 1680. The anonymous author may have been one Robert Ferguson, known to his contemporaries as 'Ferguson the Plotter', though this theory has not been proved. Part of the letter runs as follows: '. . . and yet that very Lord [Chancellor Hyde], being in danger of an impeachment in Parliament for advising and persuading the King to a Marriage with Queen Katherine, excused himself from all sinister ends in that affair by affirming that his Majesty had a lawful son of his own by a former marriage (specifying by name the D. of M.) to succeed to his Crown and Dignity.'[1]

Monmouth was so loved by his father that affection alone held him secure from the political storms outside the royal household. He had been among the first peers after the Restoration, with Lords Rochester and Mulgrave, to sit in the House of Lords before reaching adulthood. This created a scandal at the time and was much resented in both Houses, but the King and the three peers weathered it well. Once he was in the Privy Council, it was not long before he was well in the political arena, with one foot firmly in his father's household. But it was long before his real gifts as an army commander, and his love of all things military, were to come well to the fore.

He became a member of the Privy Council three weeks after his twenty-first birthday. His political significance was obvious: he was amazingly good-looking, surpassing in beauty every other courtier – a sure way to the hearts of 'the people'; he had been proved to be brave; and he was, significantly, a Protestant, at a time when the heir to the throne appeared to be suspiciously Catholic.

It was not long before those in the highest state offices were paying homage to Monmouth and his intelligent young wife. There was Lord Clifford, amiable and sentimentally pro-Catholic; and Lord Arlington, also inclined to Catholicism; on the other hand there was also Buckingham, whose hedonism was shared both by the King and by Monmouth, who was a friend of the Independents. Most important, however, the politician who took the deepest interest in Monmouth was Anthony Ashley Cooper, later Lord Shaftesbury (the shrewd but bigoted man who was mockingly called by the King 'Little Sincerity'). He was fierce in his Protestant principles and keenly ambitious. Finally there was the powerful Duke of Lauderdale, who was a Covenanter at heart, and a persecutor. There was not one real Anglican among them. These five men are bound together in history by the word 'Cabal', formed by their initials – yet they were of widely diverse character. Together they had prime power in the King's government: a government already so riddled with intrigue and deceit that only the King's use of secrecy (with all or some of its members) could maintain the illusion of unity. When Monmouth became a member of the council, which was a generation older than himself, he dismissed their capacities as those of mere secretaries to his father. Yet these men and the implications of their actions would soon elevate Charles's favourite son to the status of national hero and the 'Protestant Hope'.

Monmouth was frequently flattered for his adherence to Protestantism. It was a time when Catholicism represented to the people the cause of disorder: the civil war, foreign intrigues, burnings. The people were violently anti-Catholic, especially in London, where the Catholic churches and ceremony seemed to represent wealth ill spent. As the Pope had for centuries been as political an influence as he was spiritual, belief in his word over that of the King represented treason to the English.

In 1669 the Queen Dowager, Henrietta Maria, died at Colombes in France, where she had often entertained Jemmy during his childhood. She had been warned by a fortune-teller that she must never take a narcotic, but she was in such pain in her last illness that her fear was overruled. She accepted some opium. It soothed her to sleep, but she never woke again.

Eight months later Charles's sister, the Duchess of Orléans, arrived in England. She came on behalf of Louis XIV, who wanted to induce Charles to withdraw from the Triple Alliance of Britain, Sweden and the United States of the Netherlands. Charles was in a predicament – he was tempted by Louis's offer of 2 million *livres tournois* and military assistance (in case of rebellion among his subjects) to the tune of sixty thousand infantrymen. In return, however, he was to commit England, as an ally of France, to war with Holland, to undertake to make public, at an unspecified time, his reconciliation with the Church of Rome and to reinstate Catholicism as the national faith of his country.

Anthony Ashley Cooper, who would have revolted against such terms, did not realize what was going on, and did not know that the prime diplomat for Louis's secret treaty was Charles's sister. Charles thought it very funny that he had fooled Ashley; to make it (for himself) funnier still, he created him Earl of Shaftesbury the following year. Charles signed the Secret Treaty, as did Clifford and Arlington, the only members of the Cabal with whom he could trust his secret. A different document was shown publicly – one that would be acceptable to his Protestant subjects. This 'Sham Treaty' was almost the same as the Secret Treaty, with only one important difference – Catholicism was not mentioned.

In fact Charles never fully lived up to his side of the bargain: he never revealed his pledge to change his faith and that of his nation. Louis did not criticize him for this. He seems to have been more concerned with the war against Holland. This was just as well. Had the English people known of the King's concessions in the Secret Treaty, they would certainly have opposed him with all possible force. Ashley would risk death to condemn so many concessions to the Catholics.

It was only by direct order of Louis XIV that the Duchess of Orléans's jealous husband had allowed her to go to England to secure the signing of the alliance. He had been enraged when he had read her intimate letters from both Charles and Monmouth.

But it was the last time that Charles and Minette were to meet: she was dead sixteen days after she had left Dover for France. Deeply grieved, Monmouth wore purple, the colour of royal mourning. Needless to say, this did not escape without a comment from Pepys, who felt that he had no right to wear this strictly royal sign of bereavement.

A further link with France had been forged by Minette's visit. She had brought with her to England one Louise de Keroualle, her childish-looking lady-in-waiting, who soon knew better than anyone how to usurp Charles II's affections and stimulate his passions. She returned to England after the Duchess's death and became the King's mistress. Her power over Charles became ascendant: there was nothing he enjoyed more than visiting her apartments at Whitehall. It was not long before she was created Duchess of Portsmouth, and her son by the King (Charles Lennox) was later created Duke of Richmond. Everywhere it is whispered that she was a French spy.

Monmouth's political involvement, as a member of the King's Privy Council, did not run into any opposition from his wife. She had considered herself to be 'a man in my own family'[2] before marrying James and she was strong-willed, intellectual and far more intelligent than her husband. But she was never heard to address him disrespectfully in or out of his presence, and there is little doubt that she was completely faithful to him, even in her close friendship with the Duke of York.

It was about ten years before the Earl of Tarras had sufficiently recovered from the shock of being disinherited by Lady Wemyss to appear on the Monmouth doorstep with a casual request for £40,000. 'I dined with the Duke of Monmouth,' wrote Tarras to his father in 1671, 'and after dinner he carried me with him to the Duchess of Cleveland's house, where the King was, and there I presented him with my petition.'[3] The kindness shown to him by Monmouth was typically generous, particularly now that the Earl was no longer connected with his wife's family. When he realized the extent of Tarras's claim he was certainly startled, but he continued to be a kind and generous friend. He pressed Tarras to accept a pension from the King and be thankful for it. Tarras would not hear of this. He did not believe in pensions. Had he heeded Monmouth's advice he would certainly have emerged the better for it, but instead he pressed Monmouth to obtain for him something 'less ill-paid and uncertain'[4] – in short, hard cash. Monmouth must have realized that such a request was useless, but he promised Tarras that his wife would speak to the King and perhaps come to a settlement. Tarras must have felt the fortune almost within his grasp, for Charles was known throughout his kingdom, and indeed farther afield, as a generous monarch, as fond of civility as of ribaldry. He was the most dignified man to be seen at Newmarket, yet the same man who watched Lord Digby walk five miles within the hour through a heath, stark naked and barefoot – and the same man who kissed the Bible at Dover with an awe-inspiring reverence. But in the case of the Earl of Tarras's petition,[5] he simply could not be bothered with it.

The Duchess of Monmouth, much loved and admired by both the King and his brother, alternated between the roles of daughter-in-law and diplomat. But the Monmouth home no longer saw as much of the King as formerly. Charles now rested elsewhere. In Rochester's words:

> Restless he rolls about from whore to whore,
> A merry monarch, scandalous and poor.[6]

In Tarras's case, as in the case of the country, the word 'poor' was a telling one. Whatever the influence the Duchess of Monmouth might have had over her father-in-law was also determined by the amount in the Treasury and the extent to which she was in league with the King's greedy but influential mistresses. Such diplomacy took time. Lord Tarras's pestering, for instance, quite exasperated the Duchess, and in the end his petition was forwarded to Lauderdale, who declined it. 'My Lord Lauderdale will do me all the ill offices he can,' wrote Tarras, 'because I make all my address wholly to the Duke of Monmc , and that galls him. . . .'[7] One might guess that it also ga ed the Duke of Monmouth, though there is no record of his complaint.

Towards the end of 1673 Charles II addressed himself to the problem of finding a second wife for his brother, the Duke of York, who was now without a male heir, six of his children, four of whom were boys, having died young. Their mother, Anne Hyde, who had been converted to Catholicism and was largely responsible for York's own conversion, had died in 1672. The Earl of Peterborough, who had been employed on a similar mission two years earlier, without success, was dispatched incognito to the Continent to find a suitable match. After visiting the court of Neubourg and finding no one to his liking, he passed on to Modena, where he found the Princess Mary d'Este to be just right for the position. She was only fifteen years old and had never heard of the Duke of York, or indeed of such a country as England, her intentions being entirely centred on becoming a nun. But Lord Peterborough obtained the necessary approval of her mother, who was then regent, and the Pope obliged them by writing the girl a letter telling her that her duty was to marry the Duke of York. She was eventually persuaded to agree, at which Lord Peterborough himself married her by proxy on York's behalf.

As Monmouth's popularity increased, so did York's need for reassurances. The promise made by the King in writing that he would certainly inherit the throne upon his death seemed less and less valid as the populace and Parliament aligned themselves against Catholicism. Peterborough's choice of Mary d'Este as York's wife created rampant anti-Catholic sentiment. This politically unforgivable step caused an outbreak of bonfires and more pope-burnings. These pope-burnings became so commonplace that visitors to London from the country regarded such happenings as one of the better tourist attractions offered by the capital.

In October the House of Commons had voted an address that protested against the marriage. Although this had not succeeded in preventing it, most of the court was so 'frighted' by it that few people accompanied the Duke of York down to Dover for the wedding in November 1673. None of the bishops, except that of Oxford, offered to officiate. The Duke and Duchess of York, with the Duchess of Modena were together in the room where all the company was present. The bishop asked the Earl of Peterborough whether he had married the Duchess of York as proxy for the Duke. This was affirmed, and the bishop then declared it a lawful marriage.

Although the King had not publicly interfered with his brother's wish to make a second Catholic marriage, he was forced to make a declaration that York's new wife would be forbidden the royal chapel and that no known Catholic would be permitted in the King's presence, palace or park. So severe was this declaration that the Duke of York admitted privately to a French envoy that he was afraid of being excluded from the succession.

The King and his Parliament were uneasy enough with one another without having to worry about a Catholic heir presumptive. For instance three years earlier, in 1670, during a debate on a proposed Entertainment Tax, the King's ministers had voiced their opposition to the tax on the grounds that the players were servants of the crown and part of Charles's pleasure. With reckless wit, one minister rose and made a crude reference to Nell Gwyn and Moll Davies, both actresses who had borne the King a bastard: 'Does his Majesty's pleasure lie among the men or women players?' Shortly after this Parliament adjourned for the evening. The minister was to pay for his wit when guards under Monmouth's direct command cornered him outside his own home and slit his nose to the bone.

Although nose-slitting was commonplace in Restoration London, Parliament was outraged at such revenge being taken upon a minister exercising his right to free speech. An act was

42

passed immediately that made the cutting, maiming or disfiguring of any man a felony without benefit of clergy. The two guards themselves were not tried for their crime, but were banished. Monmouth, who had given the order, and had afterwards dressed the wound of one of the guards at his own home in Hedge Lane, escaped the wrath of Parliament, though not the pen of Andrew Marvell:

> To contrive an act so hateful, O Prince of Wales by Barlow?
> For since the kind world has dispens'd with his Mother
> Might he not well have spared the nose of John Brother. . . .

(Barlow had been the adopted surname of Lucy Walter.)

By March 1673 Parliament had vigorously resolved upon their first steps towards what would later be known as the Test Act. The King's year-old Declaration of Indulgence, giving liberty of conscience to Catholics and Nonconformists alike, had been retracted. A week later it had been resolved that all those holding public office, even members of the royal family, were to take the sacrament in accordance with the Anglican ritual. This was a direct offence to the Duke of York and to Lord Clifford, both of whom were greatly trusted by the King and were in regular attendance at the Privy Council. The decree implied that they would have to lay down their offices or revert to Anglicism, yet Charles had signed the bill almost at once, to the great surprise of everyone. The King and his Parliament had, it seemed, buried their old grudges; and throughout London there had been great patriotic bonfires and bells had been rung with enthusiasm such as had not been seen in the capital since the Restoration.

Lord Clifford had resigned his position. The Duke of York, though always submissive to his brother's wishes, had not been able to bring himself to take the sacrament and had therefore laid down his offices. Though with anguish, he had consented to his daughters being baptized into the Protestant faith and raised strictly in the Anglican teachings. Buckingham, who six years earlier had privately implored the King to declare Monmouth his son and rightful heir, had now pressed for the prospective marriage of York's elder daughter, Mary, to her cousin, William of Orange. This would unravel the succession crisis should York prove to be unsuitable to a hostile Parliament.

The presence of Catholicism at court had been rammed home by Dutch propaganda in that turbulent spring of 1673. One pamphlet in particular, *England's Appeal from the Private Cabal at Whitehall*, had illuminated the designs of Louis XIV against European Protestantism and stressed the religious articles in his declaration of war against the United States of the Netherlands. England's leading ministers had been implicated in their connection with France. Isolated clauses in the Dutch pamphlet had pointed with marked evidence to what appeared to be a secret Treaty of Dover. Lord Shaftesbury, suddenly enlightened and horrified by his own part in this mockery, resigned from the Privy Council in November 1673. 'It is only laying down my gown,' he is reported to have said, 'and putting on my sword.'[8]

Shaftesbury was now regarded by the majority of the public as the chief protector of Protestantism, and, more puritanical than ever, he had fought with much venom against the ever more suspicious intrigues of the court. Charles had even been pressed to divorce the Queen at once and to seek a Protestant bride. These suggestions had been countered by rumours that the Queen was considering retiring to a convent, where she might either gain a more fulfilling spiritual life or, as more painful rumours had it, pine in disgust at her husband's dissoluteness.[9] The rumours had been so outspoken and publicly known that the Pope himself was alarmed. He had attempted to intervene and to press Catherine not to retire to a convent, but his messengers had found the situation so turbulent in London that even the most private audience might cause hysteria and seriously threaten English Catholics.

Two weeks after the most violent anti-Catholic celebrations of Guy Fawkes Day, Mary d'Este of Modena – now rumoured among the townspeople to be the Pope's eldest daughter – was, as we have seen, married to the Duke of York. This action of York's had, not surprisingly, fanned the flames against the Catholic succession still further.

Performing almost the only act of sanity among such anarchy, the Duke of Monmouth arrived home in glory from France to take the sacrament at St Martin-in-the-Fields. No politician could have missed so golden a vision as the enthusiasm for Jemmy that swept through London. The clamouring was unparalleled. To the Earl of Shaftesbury the sight must have represented the greatest hope for Protestantism and therefore a greater power for himself. He was particularly eager to secure a Puritan base, on any terms, and no base seemed more secure than the King's beloved son. Shaftesbury was as vulnerable as Monmouth to the waves of popular Protestant support.

At this point the King's Catholic mistress, Louise de Keroualle, whom Nell Gwyn described as 'the Catholic whore', decided to test her power over Charles: 'Why not make Jemmy Lord Lieutenant of Ireland?' one can imagine her pleading in her irresistible French accent. At first the King agreed: how could he refuse anything to his two loved ones? But the Duke of York, understandably, held that the post should be given to his own candidate, the Duke of Ormonde. He won. This decision did, in fact, suit the King better, since he could at one and the same time please his brother and have Jemmy near him; and as far as he was concerned, Ormonde was expendable. He had distinguished himself in the rebellion of 1640, and at the Restoration had been awarded with a dukedom. But as in the case of Clarendon, the King, not unnaturally, found the younger, pleasure-loving members of the court more interesting.

Charles's kindness to his son was extended to Lucy Walter's daughter Mary, who was cared for and pensioned both by himself and (secretly) by his two successors. When her pension was in arrears, Mary wrote to the Secretary of State; 'I will content myself with that which will but just keep bread in my mouth, rather than be troublesome to His Majestie.'[10] The King saw to it at once that the promised annuity of £400 was paid. By the example set by his father, Monmouth also took care of the welfare of his sister. Writing to a friend in autumn 1671, he requested: '. . . not knowing whether I may bee so happy as to see you before I go, my request to your Lordship is, when you come to Ireland to govern there that you would would upon my account bee as kind to Mr William Sarsfield (who married my only sister) in his respective concerns. . . .'[11] (However, Mary was left a widow in Ireland four years later, and returned to London to marry again.)

In this letter Monmouth was alluding to his imminent departure for the Dutch War. It had opened in 1672 (to the disgust of both Parliament and people), and Charles now sent Monmouth to France with six thousand men to fight with Louis XIV against the Dutch. Monmouth commanded his troops with so much heroism, under the guidance of Louis XIV (who personally witnessed his leading of the Life Guards to victory), that the latter presented him with valuable gifts, including a diamond ring worth 17,500 *livres tournois* and a sword set with diamonds worth an additional 38,000 *livres*.

News soon spread back to England of Monmouth's sensational siege of Maastricht, of his personal courage and of his modest insistence that Captain Jack Churchill (the future Duke of Marlborough) was responsible for saving his life in the battle.

In August 1672 a son had been born to Anna at Monmouth's new country home at Moor Park in Hertfordshire. He had been named Charles and the King and his brother, with the Countess of Wemyss, were his godparents. Sadly, the child had died the following February. But the young Duke and Duchess, who had taken up permanent residence together only the previous year, were to have numerous other children. A second son, christened James (afterwards Earl of Dalkeith), was born in May 1674; then came a daughter, named Catherine Laura, to whom the future

Queens Mary and Anne and their father, the Duke of York, stood as godparents; Henry, afterwards Earl of Deloraine, was born in 1677 and survived until 1730; another daughter, Anne, died in the Tower shortly after her father's execution.

Meanwhile Monmouth was by no means a faithful husband. 'The Duke of Albemarle,' wrote the King's Secretary of State, 'hath carried his Duchess into ye country in some discontent. Fancying the Duke of Monmouth cast his eye that way.'[12] Monmouth was always casting his eyes in the way of pretty ladies, but it was not until he was twenty-five that he had his first serious love affair. Eleanor Needham was his choice, and she remained his mistress for several years, bearing him four children – who were given their father's original surname, Crofts. It seems from their portraits that they inherited Monmouth's good looks, and the youngest daughter, Henrietta, who became Marchioness of Winchester, also had her father's talent for sport.

Neither Eleanor Needham nor Anna Monmouth had a part in a masque written in 1674 by the Poet Laureate, John Dryden, at the command of the King. There were to be only seven characters in it, all acted by ladies of the court. It was a story taken from Ovid and was performed at Whitehall on 15 December 1674 under the title *Calisto: Or the Chaste Nymph*. The parts were taken by the two English Princesses, Mary and Anne; Lady Sussex, a daughter of the King and Lady Castlemaine; Lady Mary Mordaunt; Margaret Blagg, a friend of John Evelyn; Sarah Jennings, who was to marry Monmouth's friend Jack Churchill; and Lady Henrietta Wentworth. Only two of these young ladies were allowed to dress in men's clothes, and none of them was older than fourteen.

Henrietta Wentworth acted the part of Jupiter. Monmouth could not have guessed what this child was soon to mean to him, that she would one day be the greatest love of his life. Nor could Sarah Jennings have foreseen her own strange future: her future husband would be created Duke of Marlborough, and would be given Blenheim Palace, built by Vanbrugh, by a nation grateful for his victories in war; she herself was to be a powerful and dominating influence in the life of one of the other little girls performing in the masque, who in later years was to become Queen Anne of England. Margaret Blagg played Diana. She wore jewels worth £20,000, and mislaid one worth £80 lent to her by Lady Suffolk – a loss the Duke of York made good. In addition Moll Davies, who was the mother of one of Charles II's bastards, impersonated the River Thames and sang as Sylvia in the choruses between the acts.[13] The Duke of Monmouth, who was renowned for his dancing, 'danced a totally irrelevant minuet in the prologue and apparently appeared as the hero attended by warriors dressed as Roman combatants.'[14]

More serious matters, however, were demanding Monmouth's talents at this time. In late December 1674 Louise de Keroualle, now Duchess of Portsmouth, wagered that he would be Master of the Horse within two weeks. She lost her bet. It took Charles eleven weeks to suspend the unstable Duke of Buckingham from the post and pass it on to Monmouth. He had also recently been appointed Commissioner of the Admiralty when York was forced to relinquish the post.

The Duke of York continued in his regard for both the King and his beloved son, although both seemed politically distant from him. It was particularly distressing to York to have to be constantly separating in his mind the Protestant Monmouth from his nephew Jemmy. Yet the unhappy uncle and his gallant nephew continued to go to balls and to hunt together. While dining with Monmouth, it was 'observed by those that are nere his Royall Highness the Duke of York that he had a particular kindnesse and affection for his Grace of Monmouth, upon whom, indeed, all the world now looks as a riseing sun.'[15]

5

The King's Eldest Son

MONMOUTH had ascended with a speed not fully recognized as dangerous. In the eyes of Londoners he was the most arresting, even heroic, of the king's courtiers. Charles had used his son's Protestantism and thrust him into the political offices of state left vacant or in chaos by the rejected Catholics. Ardent Puritan ministers, such as Shaftesbury, rejoiced at the honours falling upon the shoulders of so sound a Protestant as Monmouth. The immediate passage of a title from a Catholic to a Protestant candidate brought temporary reassurance to Parliament; Monmouth became Chief Justice in Eyre, south of the Trent, Lord High Chamberlain of Scotland, Lord Lieutenant of the East Riding of Yorkshire and of Kingston-upon-Hull, Lord of the Admiralty (with Prince Rupert as Admiral of the Fleet) and Steward of Kingston-upon-Hull. All these honours brought him into greater prominence and, as he was conscientious in his duties, he was appreciated by the provincial soldiers, who would rally in support of him when necessary.

Shaftesbury, his most whole-hearted supporter, even went so far as to insist that he should be made Commissioner for Scotland. But the suggestion, with the historic undertones of that office's role in the start of the civil war, was rejected by Monmouth long before his father could hear of it. He must have been well aware of the implications of that appointment, for even Anna was informed of the suggestion, and she boasted of her husband's tactful decision long before it was known by Parliament.

Just as the debates in both Houses were reaching a peak of

opposition to the Dutch War, Charles gave the command that his son was to oversee all military documents before presenting them for the royal signature. This position of power was casually referred to by the King's secretary as 'initiating him into business, and he is not like to be denied anything he shall be found capable to manage'.[1] This further concession to the Protestants did not lessen the hostility they felt at England's battling with the Catholics against their Protestant neighbour. The war, the French and the Catholics were all unpopular.

The money secured from the secret Treaty of Dover, an annuity from Louis's own privy purse, was not enough to enable Charles to bribe ministers *and* keep expensive mistresses. The money went, of course, the way of the women. Lady Castlemaine, now Duchess of Cleveland, squandered the King's gifts of jewels, paintings and landed estates as quickly as he could give them to her. Phoenix Park in Dublin was her latest request, but the Lord Lieutenant of Ireland protested even before the King could consider it. Instead he made a gift of it to Monmouth, but the Duke declined it of his own accord. He had no wish to leave his father for Ireland.

In July 1674 Monmouth returned to Moor Park from the chaos of London, to be with his wife in the country. Charles had granted him an increase in his pension from £6000 to £8000 and had made securities for his wife and son should they outlive him. Having rejected the Irish estate Monmouth had asked to remain comparatively near his father in case of any last-minute escalation of the war. The King was pleased with his son's show of affection and sent him back happily to Anna.

The rains that July ruined the crops all over England, and the disillusionment among the people was severe, approaching hysteria in the capital. Seventeenth-century Englishmen saw such vagaries of nature as ominous marks of God's judgement. Eight years earlier, during the Great Plague, one friend had written to another: 'It seems to me that every day at London is now (as it were) a Day of Judgment and that all our thoughts are placed on death, on Hell, on Heaven, and upon eternity.' The divine mystery alone was frightening and God's apparent warnings were brutal: 'If you be taken away by this dreadful pestilence you have had a fair warning and a very long time to prepare yourselves for Heaven.'[2] Englishmen were quick to demand repentance from the King – the French alliance and Popery were blamed for the rains and the famine that would follow. This sign of God's displeasure was increased by the bankruptcy of the Exchequer and the ominous death of York's only surviving son by Anne Hyde.

The superstitions of the common people were unreliable and, the King felt, dangerous. The fear of witchcraft – a common fear throughout Europe – made the dissenters tolerated by Charles all the more vulnerable among their fellow-Englishmen. If a man were protected by his kind, yet killed by his neighbours, the royal prerogative was then looked upon with some spiritual dubiousness. Inadvertently, this problem was temporarily solved by the Royal Society. Already under royal patronage, the fellows familiarized the minds of their countrymen with the idea of law in the universe and of the scientific methods of inquiry designed to discover the truth. Isaac Newton lived, worked and died in the faith that the Society's methods would never lead to any conclusion inconsistent with biblical history and miraculous religion, though the spread of scientific belief (as well as his own calculus and laws of universal gravitation), thanks to the absence of theology in their methods, could not help but alter and distort the character of all western faith. Could John Protheroe have foreseen this?

Trevelyan, in his *Social History of England*, points out that Englishmen were receptive to these new ideas. The future Industrial Revolution would come to full flowering once science was applied to manufacture, and already under Charles II this new spirit of exploration was influential in agriculture, industry, navigation, medicine and engineering. Englishmen, with that comfortable first breath of science, could now laugh with good conscience at the theory of 'Popish miracles' – not only because they were Popish but because they were miracles. The Bishop of Rochester, hoping to curb common superstition still further, warned his flock 'not to be hasty in assigning the causes of plagues, or fires, or inundations' to the judgement of God for sins.[3]

Yet in spite of this new attitude, the rains of July 1674 and their effects swept the people back to their old superstitions in panic and disillusionment. They looked to the head of their Church for the answer. And to their King.

In the coffee-houses, when men were not moaning about the weather, they talked of their hatred of France and of Popery. Only the court remained cheerful. Balls were given every night. The Duchess of Portsmouth, for instance, gave one at Barnes Elms, intending to dance with her guests in the meadows, with torches lighting the trees,[4] but the wet weather drove them indoors.

As at the time of his economy drive nine years earlier, Charles was desperately in need of money. When Louise de Keroualle told him that a diamond necklace she longed to possess could be paid for only with ready money, he suggested that she should make friends with the new Treasurer, the Earl of Danby, who seemed to work wonders with the small amount of funds available. Yet this situation did not dampen the King's eagerness for entertainment. Monmouth and York greatly amused him by their representation of the siege of Maastricht on the terrace of Windsor Castle in August 1674. Many of the troops were involved in the spectacle, which was lit by burning torches and enhanced by the presence of both dukes in full military uniform. 'All the circumstances of a formal siege to appearance,' wrote John Evelyn, 'and, what is most strange, done without disorder or ill accident to the great satisfaction of a thousand spectators.'[5]

Monmouth's own efforts to create amusement were also successful: he hung ornate lanterns in his London garden, which lent a romantic atmosphere to a party held for the King. Henry Purcell's incidental tunes and operatic pieces were already familiar, and light little verse dramas were commonplace at court parties. Monmouth, seeing that his father was well into yet another political crisis, prepared these festivities in his honour. But the King insisted on dining indoors, because even for Monmouth the cold rain would not cease.

In January of 1674 Parliament had refused to continue the Dutch War. Although recognizing that Charles's aim was a mercantile one and that most or all the commercial City of London was originally in agreement, both Houses had yielded severely under the pressures of the populace. They did not see the war in the same light as the landlords in the House of Commons saw it, as a crushing defeat for Dutch trade and colonial expansion, but only as the Catholic heel of France stepping on the helpless Protestant nation. This they could not condone, and certainly did not wish to endorse with English troops.

Charles had concluded a peace with the Dutch in February. Louis XIV continued to pay him a pension which subsequently enabled him to prorogue Parliament for five months. With the King at last able to bide his time, without financial help from either House, he could sit back as peacemaker, indifferent to his Catholic-hating Parliament.

Monmouth was not so idle. He took a conscientious interest in those foreign regiments bearing his name, paying keen attention to their services, their actions and their families. His correspondence with the regimental heads and with the admirals was surprisingly active during this period, especially for a man who, unlike his father, was not prone to letter-writing. His humane interest was well publicized among the troops and seamen, who welcomed his reforms and unselfish patronage. His aim was to form an efficient, well-equipped, regularly paid army. In this he was well ahead of his time; the influence of his friend Jack Churchill can be inferred.

Monmouth was made Privy Councillor of Scotland in May 1674 (having, as we have seen, refused the title of 'Commissioner' lest he draw the envy of York), but as he was not fond of long journeys to Edinburgh, it is doubtful if the Royal Commissioner, Lauderdale, felt the influence of his counsel. In July Monmouth was appointed Chancellor of Cambridge University, where he exerted some influence regarding the manner of preaching. A sermon set to memory was, he said, preferable to the 'supine and slothful' way of preaching from a written text. Furthermore, 'having taken notice of yr liberty which several persons in Holy Orders have taken to wear their hair and peruke of an unusual and unbecoming length ... commands all such persons, who intend to study divinity, to wear their hair in a manner more suitable to the gravity and sobriety of their profession'.[6] These resolutions were adopted rather than risk the pain of the King's displeasure.

In the summer of 1675 the City of London was in chaos. Anti-French sentiments were encouraged by the weavers, who were stirred to a frenzy by a new loom that, it was rumoured, had been imported from Calais and allowed one man to do the work of twenty. The outbreaks were most serious in Westminster and Southwark. Charles immediately prevailed upon the Duke of Monmouth to ride into the trouble spots and quell the riots. The ease with which he took control and brought the panic to an end was much praised in both Houses of Parliament.

Parliament was not always so well attuned to royal policy, however. It was tending so strongly towards disaffection from the crown that it seemed to one man, Thomas Osborne, Earl of Danby, that he should intervene personally in the cause of the nation's unity. At the age of thirty, in the year 1661, Osborne had become Member of Parliament for York. Ten years later he had been created Treasurer of the Navy and, in 1674, Lord High Treasurer and Earl of Danby. In his now ridiculous role of treasurer of a penniless bank, he was, in 1675, quick to note the breakdown of trust between the King and his Parliament. One neglected Cavalier MP complained: 'The King's conscientious good friends are (as they have always been) little regarded, both in themselves and in the principle they own. .... Undoubtedly if such men and their principles were but as this day regarded, all would speedily do well.'[7] On just such sentiments Danby based his hopes of regaining the political ground that the court had lost. He immediately set out to recapture the support of the old Cavaliers and brought some cohesion to the unorganized supporters of the court in the Commons. He also disbursed bribes and overenthusiastically negotiated with Louis XIV for money for Charles. (This filled the English treasury, but was to cause Danby's impeachment a few years later.)

Danby also sought to enforce the laws against Roman Catholics. Moreover, in the cause of Protestantism he was strongly in favour of the marriage of the King's nephew, William of Orange, to Princess Mary, daughter of the Duke of York, when she came to a suitable age. (Much later, in 1688, Danby was to sign the invitation for Orange to claim the crown as William III).

Danby's strict and, at times, intolerant Anglicanism naturally upset the Duke of York, who now strove to offer Catholics and Protestant Nonconformists active protection against the new policies. However, the zeal with which he assumed this new role overshadowed his judgement; so many petitions had reached him for privileged exemptions that he soon felt that the greater part of the population of the realm were not only religious dissenters but in active opposition to the recent policies. It was even said that he had declared that most Englishmen were not Protestants at all.

News circulated quickly in England at this time. It was already a nation of diarists and letter-writers, and there was a regular circulation of newsletters written by hand in the capital and sent down to correspondents in distant towns and villages. The recipients would share these among neighbours or read them out loud. News of all sorts, including sports and politics, was reported. An army of scribes in London was employed to answer post and copy out the irregular newsletters. It was from these that country gentlemen would begin, for the first time, to align themselves with others of their political sentiments and thus bring the party system into Parliament. Village squires would read the poem written on the death of Thomas Ross in 1675, beginning with the line, 'Shame of my life, disturber of my tombe. . . .', and anonymously referring to a royal bastard.

In its January issue of 1675 Cologne's *Latin Gazette* had made mention of the crown of England's passing, upon the death of Charles II, not to York, but to William of Orange. Although Shaftesbury did not nurse the popular hatred of foreigners that inflamed a good many Englishmen at this time, he did feel that there were strong Protestant possibilities in his own realm. The most noticeable, of course, was the King's eldest son.

But it was not easy for Shaftesbury to approach Charles at this time without having to suffer some jibes. The King had greeted him once with: 'Here comes the greatest whore-master in England'; to which the Earl replied, 'Of a subject, sire.' It was a remark appropriate to the times for in 1676 London was welcoming a young woman of mixed Italian and French descent in the person of Hortense Mancini, niece of Cardinal Mazarin, the former ruler of France during the minority of Louis XIV. Charles had known and admired her when he was in France. She caused a sensation among the then 'beautiful people', and her pagan beauty broke many hearts. The aura surrounding her, when she received her illustrious friends, among whom Monmouth was of course more than acceptable, was made even more exotic by the appearance of the little Negro page who waited on her guests. Charles deserted Louise de Keroualle for her; and Nell Gwynn, the former orange-seller, went into mock mourning to celebrate the temporary eclipse of her rival.

Meanwhile Monmouth was conscientiously attending the meetings of the Privy Council, where he frequently spoke out in favour of better treatment for the military. His natural gifts had become obvious ever since the Dutch War: he possessed that care, which almost amounts to love, for his soldiers that marks a born military commander. Among the more liberal suggestions was one for freeing imprisoned deserters 'in compassion to their wives and children', and for better housing for English troops on the Continent.

With Parliament and the populace clamouring for some curbing of French power, provision was made for the raising of 27,000 foot, 4000 horse and 2000 dragoons. The Duke of York was to be Captain General in case of war; Monmouth would oversee as General of the Horse, and Prince Rupert would hold similar control at sea.

The King was not pleased with Louis xiv for breaking a promise to restore Flemish towns. He sent reinforcements into Flanders, and, in order to head off French advances elsewhere, also sent orders and battalions for the defence of Mons. A more conclusive treaty with Holland against the French was quickly drawn up.

On the other hand, Charles was pleased with Parliament's decision to come in on the side of Holland against France, as it caused the members to vote him revenues beyond his wildest dreams. This acceptance by the King of the prevalent anti-Catholic feeling drew away all the criticism he had received from Shaftesbury, who had declared that he smelled popery around the back stairs of St James's.

The military-minded Monmouth, being actually at the scene of war, was quick to sum up for his father the situation on the Continent. On his arrival in Holland, on 30 July 1677, he wrote: 'Your Majestie must be pleased to send mee mor men for Ostend, for I can not rely upon the many that belong to the garison; and besides I doe not thinke that two thousand men is enough to defend this place against so great a forse as the King of France had. Whatsoever you doe, bee pleased to doe it quike, for one day lost is a great matter here.'[8]

Was it diplomacy or cousinly love that inspired William of Orange to make arrangements for Monmouth to dine with him on the field of battle? As a military strategist William was a genius, and his actions were much admired by Monmouth. Whatever he thought of his cousin as a Protestant rival as future heir to the throne, Monmouth did not probe such thoughts and enjoyed his company as a fellow-military commander.

After a bitter struggle, William and Monmouth managed to secure control of Saint-Denis near Paris. Both commanders led their troops with great skill and seven thousand enemy soldiers were killed or wounded. France, so long as the powers of England and Holland seemed to be in league, was forced to yield to the Netherlands and a treaty between France and Holland was signed at Nijmegin in 1678. Monmouth had displayed tremendous courage, and he returned to England a triumphant hero.

Earlier, in February 1677, Shaftesbury had simply lost his head, and his viciousness was criticized by both sides of the House. He doubted the legality of their being a Parliament at all, since Charles had prorogued it for so long. He had not yet got over the shock he had received on learning of the Treaty of Dover, and he adhered to Buckingham's claim that the sitting of Parliament after such royal abuse should be declared *ipso facto* and an election called. It came as no surprise when he was sentenced to imprisonment in the Tower. Monmouth offered to stand bail for him, but his offer was refused. By the time he was released, in 1678, his followers were few and it seemed that this once influential figure would never again wield power.

Some of Shaftesbury's ideas and policies – notably on the question of the royal succession – were, however, gaining increasingly wide acceptance. Some people believed that Lady Wemyss had thought that Monmouth was legitimate and had therefore been more than willing to give her daughter in marriage to a man who had such a golden future. Duchess Anna was encouraging Monmouth in this belief. All this may account for the extraordinary way in which sumptuousness seemed to surround him in all circumstances. In the King's case it was plain to all that it was love that inspired him to shower his son with glory – and with presents, including the magnificent saddle still to be seen at Dalkeith Palace. The theory of legitimacy was quickly grasped by others, who made use of it for their own ends.

It was suggested years later by the Duke of York that it was Monmouth's tutor, Thomas Ross, who first impressed upon his pupil the political advantages that his legitimacy might bring. But this seems unlikely. Ross was a loyal servant of the King and when Monmouth came of age and was no longer in need of his services as a tutor, he was retained as his librarian. It is true that he was an adviser – but a conscientious one. By this time the brooding rivalry between uncle and nephew was well known at court.

Monmouth did not know that in 1667 Buckingham had suggested to the King that he should declare him as his heir – that was after Shaftesbury and Carlisle had failed to persuade him to divorce Catherine. Charles would not hear of doing so, and as for declaring Monmouth to be legitimate, he replied, 'I would rather see him hanged at Tyburn.' Now why did Charles express himself so strongly on this subject? Lord George Scott, a twentieth-century descendant of Monmouth, was convinced that Charles's relations with his brother were guided by fear. Could it be that this subtle monarch had hoodwinked people into thinking that his affectionate way with York was inspired by brotherly love, when in fact he was only too well aware that his brother was privy to the secret that the Protestant monarch had been a believing Catholic for several years before he was called back to England? If this were so, it would have been in York's power to send him on his 'travels' again. Whatever principles inspired Charles when he made so emphatic a remark, it is clear that, as regards Shaftesbury, the wish closest to *his* heart was that Monmouth should be king. Shaftesbury pictured him much beloved of Protestant subjects and well advised by counsellors over whom he, Shaftesbury, would have the chief power.

. . . . . .

Monmouth's captivating charm and beauty had, as we have seen, raised him to an enviable position at court. Even when he was in exile in later years he was treated as a notable figure. He retained his popularity in spite of ill-chosen friends, and in spite of the disgraceful acts he performed in the first recklessness of youth, though it should always be remembered that he was a privileged member of an extremely scandalous court. Nevertheless, in many ways he revealed a tender heart. His letters to his father are marked by consideration for his feelings and are written in a spirit of respect, showing the real kindness that lay beneath his occasional outbursts of violence.

The Duke of York was less spontaneously affectionate to the King, but treated him with dignified obedience. When banished from court, he held his distance; when asked to leave the country, he left willingly – returning only when the national fear of Charles's death brought him home, and then he came apologetically. Monmouth maintained his Protestantism with ease and grace, at the obvious expense of his Catholic uncle. He hinted with the same ease at the succession to a father sick of the dispute but determined that the law regarding the crown should not be altered. The most Charles would do was to consent to legislation designed to prevent a Catholic king from ever nominating officers of the Church or giving offices to co-religionists.

Monmouth's regard for the Country Party, later known as the Whigs, soon became the most forthright link to his political ambitions. The party had been founded in 1667 by Anthony Ashley Cooper, before he was granted the earldom of Shaftesbury, and all the members aligned themselves behind definite anti-Catholic sentiments, including a hatred of the Duke of York, though they were divided in their choice of a possible successor to the King. Historians have been quick to proclaim Monmouth as a leader behind whom this party rallied, but in fact this was not the case. Certainly he was more popular than York. But William of Orange was already held in high esteem by the Protestants for his efforts to restrain the Catholic armies from encroaching on his territories. The greatest diplomat of the party was Shaftesbury, who was hardly deserving of that cruel nickname 'Little Sincerity', for he was, if anything, a political giant, especially in his leadership of the dissident politicians who were unable to agree as to who should succeed the King. He managed to keep them in league and drove them with a political ferocity that seemed overwhelming even to the members themselves.

The stubborn pride with which York maintained his Romanism was as different to Monmouth's Protestantism as the imperialism of Domitian was to the policies of Alcibiades. Whether Monmouth's nature was capable of deep religious feelings is doubtful, but it is true that at all moments of crucial decision he would publicly acknowledge his Bible as his only authority and guide, and much of his life was spent in prayer. As we have seen, he also consulted astrologers.

Weary of his perpetual warring with France, in October 1677 the Prince of Orange journeyed to England to arrange an alliance, and at the same time to propose matrimony to his cousin, Princess Mary of York. On the question of the proposed marriage, the Duke of York told the Prince that he had all the esteem for him 'that he deserved or could desire', but until they had 'treated and brought to some rightness the public affairs of War and Peace' it was 'not proper' that the 'discourse of any other matter' should take place.[9]

That same evening York informed the King of what had passed between him and the Prince of Orange; Charles said that he had answered very well, yet 'the King did not seem best pleased'. York was somewhat surprised, and no doubt disappointed. He said that he could 'have wished his Majesty had been more pleased to have acquainted him before with his mind . . .'; at which the King cut him short, and said that he would speak to him of it another time.[10] Evidently the King did, however, 'acquaint his brother with his mind' to the effect that he had no objection to the proposed marriage.

Sad to say, Princess Mary was very unhappy about these plans for her marriage. The only man to whom she had shown any affection was the Duke of Monmouth, and she found the Prince of Orange slight, ugly and reticent, and suffering from uncertain health. But she had no choice and the wedding took place as planned, in England. William hurriedly swept his young bride off to the Continent. Later, the Duchesses of York and Monmouth went to The Hague to visit Princess Mary. 'Wee are to ley in a hous nigh the Princess verie preevitly,' wrote Anna to her mother, 'which they are used to in that countray.'[11] Holland appeared unusually tranquil to the young Duchess of Monmouth.

6

The Popish Plot

IN 1678 Monmouth again asked his father for the title and powers of Captain General of the army in England, though for eight years this appointment had been in abeyance. His wish was granted, both as a mark of the trust his father placed in him and in recognition of his fine military record while fighting for Louis XIV in Flanders. The patent that was drawn up described him as Charles's 'natural' son. Monmouth objected to this and ordered the offending word to be omitted before Charles signed the document. York objected loudly to this interference, protesting that someone, perhaps the secretary, ought to be punished. He himself took the commission to the King, who was taking his usual walk in the garden, and complained of the secretary's conduct. Charles took out his scissors and wearily cut the document in two, ordering that another should be prepared for him to sign, with the word 'natural' in it. York pressed him to have the secretary punished. It eventually came out that Monmouth had made his own secretary erase the word. Later York pointed out that this was a time when Monmouth's ambition, and the King's favour towards him, were both at their height. Monmouth asked for control of the Scottish army and was again granted his wish. This time it was Lauderdale who insisted that he should be named the 'natural' son of the King in the patent for the declaration in Edinburgh.

If power is the symbol of a successful life, Monmouth had reached the summit of his own. 'The King's bastard' was now in sole military control of the British Isles, with the exception of Ireland.

In the autumn of 1678 London was far from tranquil. Titus Oates, a penniless chaplain's son, had pretended to be reconciled to Rome the previous year, and having, as he said, been admitted to secret Catholic conclaves, now offered 'evidence' of a Popish plot. Jesuits, disguised as Presbyterians, were to be sent to stir the Scots to revolt and, according to Oates, French troops in the pay of the Jesuits were to overthrow Ireland. Once the soldiers were in Dublin, the Duke of Ormonde was to be assassinated.

The plan for England itself was directly linked to Monmouth, as it spoke of establishing false titles and improper claims to the throne. This, with the debasing of the currency, was to be followed by the King's death and a rising of twenty thousand Papists to murder a hundred thousand Protestants. The City was to be set on fire once more, and the Duke of York was to be crowned king, with special provision being made for direct papal supremacy. Oates referred to the Pope's claim that England and Ireland were to be liberated from their heretical prince, and that thirty thousand masses would be said for the man worthy enough to assassinate the King.

Oates's story was neither original nor convincing. The King was openly sceptical, especially when Oates swore that York was not a part of the plot but Queen Catherine was. Secretary Coventry thought it possible, but was reluctant to take the word of one man, especially when Oates's own religion was a matter of doubt. Yet the story seemed to be confirmed later when the magistrate who had taken Oates's first deposition was found murdered at Greenberry Hill (now Primrose Hill). Londoners gave way to panic. The citizens felt that their own safety lay in weapons, and many slept with a knife for protection. One alderman admitted that when he went to sleep 'he did not know but the next morning they might all rise with their throats cut'.[1]

The unpopular standing army was increased, much to the dismay of Parliament, and interrogations of leading Catholics became frequent. One Catholic member of the House of Lords, already cited by Oates, was to note that 'wicked principles are alleged to make a good plot, which, being denied, the Plot is introduced to make good the principles'.[2] Monmouth was asked to interrogate a silversmith, a known Roman Catholic, who had been arrested in connection with the magistrate's murder. Dubious evidence had been levied against him. He confessed that two men of the Queen's chapel had killed the magistrate. Later, after a full report from Monmouth, Charles himself interviewed the silversmith, who this time admitted to having accused the two men falsely. None the less, a Mr Green and a Mr Hill, both named by the silversmith, remained in custody. Later, and probably more because of the coincidence of names than because of actual guilt, a third alleged murderer of the magistrate was sentenced to death by hanging. Green, Berry and Hill were all executed at Tyburn.

Early that winter Titus Oates stood at the bar of the House of Lords and accused Queen Catherine of high treason for wishing to kill the King, either by poison or by shooting him with silver bullets during his walks in St James's Park. Monmouth, as Captain General, was recommended by the Lords to care for Mr Oates's safety, and apartments were secured for the latter and his bodyguards at Whitehall Palace, along with a pension of £1,200 per annum. Since he was the great attraction of the day, three men were to fight viciously for the right to hold Titus Oates's wash-basin, and the Archbishop of Canterbury was pleased to receive this arch-deceiver at Lambeth Palace. A secretary to the Privy Council was to remark acidly, following the great gratitude expressed to Oates by the House of Lords, that 'it was the preparation of some men's minds and not the witnesses that gave it entertainment'.[3]

Much weightier evidence was provided by the letters of the Duke of York's secretary soliciting funds from Louis xiv. As a counter-measure, Charles pressed for the Test Act of 1673 to be extended to restrict membership in Parliament to Anglicans. This act was to remain in force until the days of Wellington.

Many events occurred to intensify the excitement. Men did not distinguish between their fears of Popery and their dread of an arbitrary government (excited by York's private secretary and Danby's standing army); nor did they distinguish between Popish treason and the fear of massacre (outlined by Oates and confirmed by the magistrate's murder), coupled with the possibility of cruelty and persecution under a Catholic successor. All these fears were fused into a general fear of Popery. By November 1678 the Commons were trying to persuade the King to raise a militia, though whether this was to protect the nation against the Catholics or against the standing army was not made clear. By Christmas the fear had died down in the provinces, and the plot became primarily an urban phenomenon. Nevertheless, two thousand men in trained bands watched the streets of London every night, and daggers bearing the magistrate's name were sold to women for protection. All streets were chained at night.

In January 1679 the Duke of York rode out to help the men dealing with a fire at the Temple and was dismayed to find that the people openly displayed their hatred of him. He left early for fear of the crowds. Of the hundreds of Jesuits thought to be surrounding him, later investigations revealed only two, and they were so hidden at his court that their political significance was negligible.

Charles took the crisis seriously. First he enforced the penal laws and pushed Monmouth forward while he investigated the plot, in the hope of allaying popular fears. Secondly, rather than accept his brother's exclusion from the line of succession, he offered to limit the powers of a Catholic successor; these would obviously prove ineffectual upon his own death. Thirdly, he anticipated an Exclusion Bill and approached it with such diplomacy as had not been seen since the intriguing secret Treaty of Dover.

The Popish Plot must have been one of the most damaging practical jokes in the history of England. Its perpetrator, Titus Oates, was brought to trial in 1685 for perjury and sentenced to be flogged through the streets of London. He survived to enjoy a small pension from the Whigs.

The position of the Duke of York was so precarious that he was forced to confess to the Prince of Orange in May 1679: 'Unless something very vigorous is done within a very few days, the monarchy is gone.'[4] There is irony in this when one considers that less than ten years later York did in fact lose his throne, and that he lost it to the very man to whom he was then speaking – his own son-in-law. The Duke of York's autobiography shows much bitterness towards the parliamentary parties. Of the first Test Act he writes that it 'gave them but too fair an opportunity of venting with success their malice against [himself, York], which hitherto had proved ineffectual'.[5] He noted the position of his own nephew: 'They also encouraged underhand the Duke of Monmouth to be legitimate, and consequent right heir to the throne, who of himself was ambitious and weak enough to give in to the snare.'[6]

The second Test Act had been specifically aimed at York and it was carried on its second reading, with much rejoicing throughout London. But there was an article to appease the expected anger of the King, for though no 'Catholick' was allowed in the King's presence, the bill did have a proviso, passed by only two votes, excepting the Duke of York. It put the Earl of Shaftesbury out of humour to such an extent that when he heard of this exception he is reputed to have said that he didn't care what became of the bill (about which he had taken so much pains) if it had that proviso in it.[7]

Charles had gambled on the people's losing interest in such anti-Popery, and by the summer of 1679 his predictions had largely come true. Country people were more cautious that town-dwellers in what they declared and less prone to swing from one side of the political spectrum to the other. They were religious and conservative and sought political as well as social enlighten-ment in the tranquillity of local churches rather than in the frenetic tavern atmosphere of the city. It was in these country pulpits that Monmouth's strength lay. They were loyal to the King, and to the King's son, and were disinclined to uphold the virtues of his Catholic heir. Sermons not only romanticized the ideals of Charles II but also unfolded with grandeur the exploits in defence of England of his beautiful grandson, Monmouth. The loyalty of these country parsons to the Protestant Duke, and their adherence to those stipulations laid down by him at Cambridge concerning sermons and deportment, were to place Monmouth in a far higher position than that of his unpopular uncle. He was later to see the evidence of the esteem in which he was held by the tremendous welcome afforded him on his royal progress of 1680.

The City, however, needed more than rumours. To a Londoner, who lost interest as quickly as he gained it, new evidence of grandeur was constantly in demand, and anywhere round Monmouth such evidence was not difficult to find. Most of the emphasis on mob pressure was made by the members of the Green Ribbon Club. They were stalwart Protestants, but they were hardly all-powerful in manipulating the city riots. Meeting at the 'King's Head' tavern – so named for the bounty on Charles's head during his 'travels' – their direct function was to sway Parliament into taking a firmer religious stand. In this they were not so successful, and their importance in mob control extended only as far as financing the more spectacular pope-burnings of the day. Many Londoners began identifying with the display, as opposed to its significance, and both Evelyn and Pepys were to note that after the people had filled themselves with alcohol, and watched the celebration, 'every man and boy went to his own home and so that play ended'.[8] As such displays became better financed and more spectacular, the response to anti-Catholic tensions became instead a celebration of the Protestant past. Such evenings were great fun. Persons of quality not only paid for the alcohol but rejoiced with the poorer classes at what seemed a better evening than the Lord Mayor's Show.[9]

The Duke of Monmouth as a child.
Miniature by Samuel Cooper

His father, Charles II,
painted at approx-
imately the same age
by Dobson

Lucy Walter,
Monmouth's mother

Charles II

The Duke of Monmouth in
his teens

Letter in Monmouth's own hand,
date 11 July, 1663

My Lord

about ten dayes since, the King was pleased
to write, either to my Ld Comp^{ner}, or to my Lord Lauderdail,
to haue an Act to pass to conferme my Contract. I hope it will
not bee negelected, but least their much busines should put it
sometime out of their thought, I begge the fauour of y^r Lpp..
to minde the Ld Comp^{ner}, or whom else you please for mee, that
no time may bee Lose in it. m^r Ross will informe your Lpp of
what else Concernes mee, I shall therefore add no more but that
I am

My Lord

y^r Lpp's

Whitehall
July 11th 1663.

very humble seruant

Monmouth

Above The Battle of Bothwell Bridge
Below The Duke of Monmouth by Henri Gascar

As far as Monmouth personally was concerned, the Green Ribbon Club brought him dangerously into politics. His position here differed greatly from his position as a member of his father's Privy Council, where he represented the loyalty of the King to his people. As he aligned himself and his associates behind the leadership of Shaftesbury, so then did York move still further away from his nephew, relying for his link with the King upon his faithful friend, the gallant Cavalier Lord Peterborough. The only wisdom in this political tit-for-tat was that Peterborough, although he may not have amused Charles, was at least respected by him. Shaftesbury was not. At this time Monmouth was in no need of a link, however, as his presence, or at least his correspondence, was still a great delight to his father. He was also quick to charm his father's mistresses, who certainly had influence – though we must not assume that York was without such allies, for the long-suffering Queen Catherine was his friend and confidante.

In the early days of the Restoration the courtiers had regaled the King and themselves with the finest wit; Charles, who was happiest in this element, encouraged them, but in 1679 the fears instilled by Titus Oates had caused profanity and flippancy, to say nothing of horseplay, to go out of fashion. Titled drunkards who had once danced naked on the balconies of Covent Garden were now respectably employed in politics or held embassies abroad. Monmouth showed himself to be no less diligent than his contemporaries as regards affairs of state and he is no longer mentioned among the frivolous flock surrounding the Duke of Buckingham. In fact that flock had dispersed and grouped elsewhere, leaving only the second Earl of Rochester and a few obscure commoners as Buckingham's friends. Rochester could always inspire the King; it was he who suggested the following epitaph for His Majesty:

> Here lies our Sovereign Lord the King
> Whose word no man relies on:
> He never said a foolish thing
> And never did a wise one.

'This is very true,' the King replied, 'because my words are my own and my actions are my ministers'.

Lord Rochester also chose Monmouth as a poetic subject. He was being sarcastic when he named him 'Monmouth the Witty,' which suggests that the latter did not shine in the light-hearted talk between sophisticated gallants, though his letters show a certain wit. Lord Rochester ran the risk of the King's ever-increasing anger at his continual jibes. Yet it is certain that Charles took greater care of the treatment of those who amused him than he did of those who bored him. For instance although Buckingham did join Shaftesbury in the Tower he was the first to be freed. His speedy dismissal was such a surprise to the stern Parliament who had tried and sentenced him that even Monmouth protested that the proper authorities had been trampled upon. The fact was that the King found Buckingham's company entertaining, and the same applied to Rochester, though both fell out of favour periodically.

We have seen that John Dryden considered the Duke of Monmouth to be heroic in both love and war and mourned his deteriorating character. The poet was an accurate critic of the many misadventures at the court of Charles II, and of the King's behaviour in the company of his son, but he lacked the coarse bitterness often found in Lord Rochester's vicious word portraits. In his *Absalom and Achitophel* Dryden wrote of Charles and Monmouth:

> ... when nature prompted, and no law denied
> Promiscuous use of concubine and bride;
> Then Israel's monarch after Heaven's own heart
> His vigorous warmth did variously impart
> To wives and slaves; and made as his command
> Scatter'd his Maker's image through the land,
> Michel, of Royal blood, the crown did wear
> A soil ungrateful to the tiller's care:
> Not so the rest; for several mothers' bore
> To God-like David several sons before

But since like slaves his bed this did ascend,
No true succession could their seed attend
Of all this numerous progeny was none
So beautiful, so brave, as Absalom
Whether inspired by some diviner lust,
His father got him with a great gust,
Or that his conscious destiny made way
By manly beauty to imperial sway.

It was at about this time that Lady Wemyss, who loved her son-in-law Monmouth perhaps more than she did her own daughters, complained that the young man was neglecting her. He was quick to reassure her:

Madam,
You can not imagine how troubled I am that you should believe it is possible for mee to fergett you. I doe assur you that would bee one of the last things I should ever doe. But you have draune upon your selfe sutch a troubell that I can not imagine how you will ever gitt of it; for now their will not be a post goe for Scotland but will have onc of my letters with it, to show you how much I am, and ever will be, your most obedient and humble servant,

Monmouth.[10]

Her daughter, the Duchess of Monmouth, was an active conciliator in the breach between Monmouth and York. This was by no means a selfless act, for she was a loyal friend to the Catholic Duke, but she also had foresight enough to recognize approaching danger in the strained relations between her husband and his uncle and to try to prevent it. But naturally the gossips of the court were quick to attribute baser motives to the friendship: Buckingham, especially, made malicious innuendoes about her relations with the heir to the throne. Perhaps for this reason, perhaps because Monmouth dismissed his wife's advice and attempts at conciliation, he forbade her the company of York. Though we do not know her inner feelings, she adhered to this request and in every circumstance remained publicly loyal and devoted to him. She seemed to be a model wife and duchess, yet she was so fierce with her wit, so cool, reserved and intellectual – so unlike most of the women at court in fact – that, though she was everywhere respected, she was viewed with suspicion. That she had been York's confidante only added to the courtiers' wariness of her.

York himself was disconsolate at being deprived of her friendship, 'conceiving it a mark of his nephew's insolence'.[11] His distress did not go unmarked, though many of his closest friends and advisers were quick to point out the reason behind Monmouth's action. The young man was not, after all, merely insolent: his uncle might see him as a headstrong adolescent, but he was in fact nearing thirty and was deliberate in his behaviour and ambitions. In later years the Duke of York was to blame Anna for 'putting such high pretensions into her husband's head'.[12] It was a bitter *volte face*.

Monmouth's current convivial companion in 1679 was Ford, Lord Grey, the eldest son of Ralph, Baron of Werke. Grey was an exciting figure and (like Monmouth's former friend, Buckingham) reckless beyond belief.

The Duke of Monmouth has so little employment in state affairs [wrote the Dowager Countess of Sunderland to her brother Algernon Sidney, late in 1679 or in 1680] that he has sent two fine ladies out of town. My Lord Grey has carried his wife into Northumberland, and Lady Wentworth's ill eyes did find cause, as she thought, to carry her daughter into the country, in so much haste that it makes a great noise, and was done in some great passion. My Lord Grey was long in believing the Duke of Monmouth an unfaithful friend to him. He gave her but one night's time to take leave, pack up and begone.[13]

Lady Wentworth's daughter was the same Henrietta who had appeared in the masque *Calisto*, described by the diarist Evelyn as 'a comedie at night at court acted by ladies only'.[14] She was the only daughter of Lord Wentworth, son of the first Earl of Cleveland, who was captured after the battle of Worcester and released from prison at the Restoration. He died in 1664, whereupon Monmouth took command of his regiment of guards. As her father's heiress, the four-year-old Henrietta became Baroness Wentworth in her own right. She became a maid of honour to the Duchess of York on 11 August 1679, at the time of the Exclusion Bill. It was probably at about this time, when her mother swept her off to the country, that she began her love affair with Monmouth. The senior Lady Wentworth herself apparently soon fell under the spell of Monmouth's handsome face and charming manners and allowed him to visit her daughter at their manor of Toddington.

The apparently acquiescent manner with which the mother yielded to her daughter's lover is simply inexplicable, for this attractive girl, although she was by no means wealthy, could have married any of a number of desirable suitors, such as Lord Ailesbury, the Marquis de Blanquefort, the Earl of Shrewsbury or Nicholas Tufton, Earl of Thanet. Ailesbury wrote in his memoirs many years later: 'A noble Peer [Wentworth] ... very many years after ... agreed with me that had his cousin been bred up by a discreet good mother, that she would have made a perfect good wife.'[15] Apparently Ailesbury had no suspicion of Henrietta's infatuation with Monmouth at the time. Yet it is most unfair of the diarist John Evelyn to describe the unfortunate Henrietta as 'that debauched woman', for her only sin was that she was desperately in love with the husband of another woman. And Monmouth himself, married at the age of fourteen to a girl of twelve by an arrangement in which he had no choice, was later to profess that Henrietta was his wife before God.

In 1679 it had become apparent that Lauderdale's handling of Scottish affairs had deteriorated into a most violent and corrupt government. The Whigs of south-western Scotland now rose under the Covenant banner and initiated an attack. Lord Shaftesbury at once began supporting pro-Scottish agitation, which appealed strongly to English Protestants; there was soon a general outcry in opposition to Lauderdale's request for English troops.

(Any military movement of this kind was in fact illegal, as it implied invasion, and as such was specifically forbidden in the Pacification Treaty signed by Charles's grandfather, James I, though this clause seems to have been ignored.) Charles would not have braved the Opposition by sending soldiers to Scotland if he had not bribed Shaftesbury (that is, secured his favour) by appointing Monmouth, Shaftesbury's darling, as commander-in-chief.

But Monmouth's former intimate friend, Lord Grey of Warke, resigned his office as Commander of the Horse. Lady Sunderland declared that it was on account of a domestic dispute, implying that Lord Grey, Lady Grey and Monmouth formed an uneasy triangle, but in fact there were other reasons. Grey found it strange that so much trust should be placed in people thought to be deeply involved in intrigue with the rebels of both kingdoms. There was, as well, the matter of Grey's own massive estates in Northumberland, on the border, which were vulnerable to rebel reprisals. But Grey miscalculated the results of the military enterprise.

Monmouth and his troops conquered the rebels at the Battle of Bothwell Bridge on 22 June 1679. There was something Napoleonic about the Scottish campaign. So rapid a march, battle and victory had seldom been seen. It is surprising that such a fine exploit caused so little stir. On 6 July 1679 a letter from the Privy Council of Scotland was transmitted to the King of England: 'May it please your Majestie, the Duke of Buccleuch and Monmouth being pleased to acquaint us with his purpose to leave this Kingdome and to return to Court for attending your Majestie, wee find ourselves obliged in all humilitie and gratitude to acknowledge the great honour your Majestie has done this your ancient kingdome by this most signall testimony of your affection and care for it. . . .'[16] This, to the general populace of Scotland, was no understatement. Monmouth and his troops had won far more than a quick, if not glorious, battle: the mercy shown by him to his enemies on the field endeared him to his countrymen. He must have shown great strength in his clemency, for when many with high commissions in his force were eager for the massacre of *all* prisoners – an estimated twelve hundred – rather than troubling themselves with individual hearings, he refused to yield, and defended his clemency with marked sobriety.

In Edinburgh he was received with great enthusiasm and was given the freedom of the city and a golden casket. He returned to court the most loved commander in the two kingdoms. Yet even at Whitehall there was dissent over his kindness; much was made of his lodging all the prisoners at Greyfriars in Edinburgh, and sending his own surgeon to attend the wounded. There was more jealousy felt in Monmouth's renown than pleasure at the defeat of the Covenanters.

At this vitally important moment, in August 1679, the King fell ill. The Tories were without a figurehead – Charles had exiled York so that the popular hatred of him might diminish through his absence. Now he was summoned back from Brussels by Halifax, Essex and Sunderland, but instead of finding a country in deep mourning, as he had expected, he found a cheerful monarch, recently recovered. Arriving at Windsor in the early morning to visit his brother, he begged His Majesty's pardon for returning from Brussels without royal consent, offering the valid excuse that he had heard that he was dangerously ill.

The King's welcome was considerably warmer than that of Monmouth, who had done all in his power to prevent York's return. York and the Tories soon saw that they had only very narrowly avoided being vanquished and excluded by the returned conquering hero of Bothwell Bridge. The following letter to Colonel Legge from York seems surprisingly naïve: 'There is one thing troubles me very much and puts odd thoughts in my head, it is that all this while his Majesty has never said a word, nor gone about to make good understanding between me and the Duke of Monmouth, for though it is the thing I shall never seek, yet me thinks it is what his Majesty might presse.'[17] Perhaps Charles realized that he could never bring York and Monmouth together while Shaftesbury was doing his best to keep them apart.

In September 1679 the Duke of Monmouth suddenly fell from power and was sent into exile. The timing of the King's banishment of his son seems at first inexplicable, considering that he had only just put down the rebellion in Scotland and had won such popularity there by his clemency – but in these very triumphs lay his downfall, for he was gathering a potentially dangerous following. And it would be to belittle Charles's own acumen to believe that he was not aware of what the Tories, his own supporters, believed: that the ambition of his son appeared to have exceeded all limits. Added to this was York's grievance that his nephew was at liberty to pursue his designs against him in his absence. And to crown it all there was Charles's personal disapproval of Monmouth's amorous intrigue with the little Duchess of Southampton, wife of another of the King's illegitimate sons, Charles Fitzroy, one of the children of Lady Castlemaine. Charles therefore demanded that Monmouth should resign his commission as general and commanded him to leave England.

In the days that followed Monmouth arrived in London and began preparing for his departure, though with much uneasiness and discontent. He saw taken from him both his commission as general in Scotland and that as Captain General (a position that was not awarded to anyone else). And he saw his friend Sir Thomas Armstrong banished from court and the King's presence for ever – it was said that Armstrong knew of four witnesses to the fact that Charles had actually married Lucy Walter.[18]

A more personal hurt was the King's order to Cambridge University to 'chuse another Chancellor in the place of him', a royal command that could not be disobeyed.[19] This act pleased the Duke of York, himself lately returned from Scotland. The university's vice-chancellor made a short speech in Latin to the Duke of York when he was received at Cambridge, to which he replied, with characteristic hypocrisy, 'that he would use his endeavours and interest for the preservation of the King's person, and the government of the State and the Church of England as now established by law'.[20] Monmouth's portrait by Lely, paid for by himself as a present to the university, was taken down and burned.

The King was taking the air in Kensington Gardens, when the Duke of Monmouth came to bid him adieu. Softening somewhat, he promised his son that his sojourn abroad should not last long. Having said goodbye to his wife the Duke was taken by barge from Whitehall to Gravesend, where he boarded his yacht. He sailed the following morning for Holland. A contemporary anonymous publication describes his departure from England: 'What a general silence and consternation seized [sic] on the willing crowds that viewed his passage down the River [Thames], so eager and steadfast were their eyes fixed on him as if they would have gazed away their souls. . . . Braveness of spirit is the virtue which adorns a Prince . . . this doubtless made the Duke so much beloved and made the nation more concerned for him than he was for himself.'[21]

There was one mitigation of Monmouth's bitterness: Charles had ordered York and his wife to Scotland. The historian Trevelyan has pointed out that the presence of York at court 'kept the magistrates in perpetual fear of an uprising of the Protestants'; it was in his own best interest that he should be sent to Scotland.[22]

Thus the two claimants to the throne departed the same day, leaving their political supporters to fight it out in London.

7

The Black Box

MONMOUTH arrived in the country of his birth on 27 September 1679. A warm welcome was afforded him at The Hague by the Prince of Orange. The graciousness may have been superficial. The Prince was a shrewd politician, the ruler of a republic and ever conscious of the people's will. He had a keen eye on the throne of England and was therefore unlikely to have a great deal of sympathy for disgraced members of the English court. The melancholy Monmouth had a private audience with the Prince, which lasted an hour. His cousin Mary of York, though rumoured to have been passionately in love with him before her marriage to William, did not even interrupt her game of cards as he kissed her hand. The icy indifference thawed only when Monmouth announced that he would be leaving The Hague shortly, whereupon William invited him to dine with him that night.

Henry Sidney, brother of Lady Sunderland, who recounted in his diary the political intrigues between the royal parties, also attended the dinner, after which Monmouth whispered to William that he would like a private audience.[1] It was rumoured that William told Monmouth in confidence that if he made any claim to the English throne, he would have nothing to do with him whatsoever. Since he subsequently announced publicly that he regarded Monmouth as a man of honour, we can perhaps assume that Monmouth gave an assurance that he had no intention of laying claim to the throne.

William was the nephew of Charles II and of the Duke of York, and his position as regards the succession to the throne of England was very much brought home to him by York's arrival, shortly after Monmouth had departed for Utrecht (where Prince Rupert had lent him a house). Though York received warmer hospitality at the Dutch court than Monmouth, the tedium William felt in his uncle's company was apparent to all who were near them. It was not long before the Duke and Duchess of York and their entourage set sail for Scotland once again, to fulfil Charles's orders.

It is not surprising that the Dutch people warmly welcomed Monmouth at Utrecht. He had been a hero to their cause (more recently than he had been to the French) and news of his kindly disposition towards the soldiers under his command had given him a most sympathetic introduction to the people. But he showed little sensitivity to Charles II's feelings when he lodged with an Amsterdam barber named May, a known enemy of the English crown.

Meanwhile, London was still split between the Catholic and Protestant causes, between the supporters of York and Monmouth. Monmouth had lost one powerful friend at court: Louise de Keroualle, now Duchess of Portsmouth and the King's chief mistress. Formerly sympathetic to Protestantism, she quickly reversed her loyalty when Monmouth had crossed the Channel. No support could be relied on from this woman, who was both the English King's mistress and the French King's servant.

Shaftesbury was still at work, however. Although he had been dismissed from the council when the King regained his health, he was still vociferous that Charles should divorce his Queen, remarry and beget an heir to the throne, to prevent York's succession.[2] In this he was unsuccessful, and he therefore decided that it was time for Monmouth to return to England. Since by now York had returned from Scotland, why shouldn't Monmouth also come back to his own country?

Once this point had been made to Monmouth by the Green Ribbon Club, it was certain that he would respond with haste. The Club immediately planned the most sensational reception for the 'Protestant Duke'. Almost before he had set foot in England, on the night of 27 November 1679, they began their spontaneous welcome. Bells peeled and fires blazed. The next day Monmouth's friends announced that he had returned on the advice of the Prince of Orange. Shaftesbury offered him hospitality before he went to his lodgings at the Cockpit.

The King, however, refused to see his son. Indeed he commanded him to leave the country (though at least it was courteous to have such painful news delivered by such a close family friend as Lord Macclesfield). Though Anna implored her husband to obey the King, Monmouth refused and went to Hedge Lane. Here he was greeted with the tragic news of the fatal illness of his son Francis, who was only a year old and was the second of his four sons to die in infancy. Charles's kind heart was touched, and he permitted Monmouth to remain in England to be with his wife, though when Nell Gwyn 'begged of his Majestie to see him, telling him that he Monmouth was grown pale, wan, lean and long-visaged because he was in disfavour. . . . the King bid her be quiet for he would not see him.'[3]

In that winter of 1679 Monmouth, though divested of his honours, was still at the zenith of his popularity with the people of England, and receiving support from the City of London as well as from the countryside.

In the turbulence of that decisive autumn the numerous trials and debates over the issue of Popery in high places were becoming wearying even to the most ardent Protestants. His Majesty's chief justices began to turn on the informers and found that most of their testimony was manifestly and criminally perjured. If Titus Oates were no longer to be believed in all he said, declared one Parliamentarian, 'and the Queen be not a traitor, our business is at an end'.[4] This meant that when the dazzling Duke of Monmouth strode through the capital, he found a populace sharply divided between those who saw that they had been deceived by Titus Oates and those who blindly persisted in believing him. The latter could continue howling terribly, but times had changed.

Monmouth was not the only person to grasp the implications

of the situation. As far away as Scotland, York had news of his nephew's flaunting behaviour. But he also saw that he was making no headway with the King. The Earl of Mulgrave obtained the governorship of Hull and others of Monmouth's honours, while command of the army was awarded to the second Duke of Albemarle, heir to the late General Monck – even here the rightful hereditary succession seemed to be uppermost in the King's mind. If all these indignities were not enough to bring the headstrong Monmouth to his senses, then it is possible that Shaftesbury himself had pressed him to make apologies and excuses for his untimely arrival in England. For Shaftesbury had clearly miscalculated when he suggested that Monmouth should return.

Throughout these events Anna persisted in acting with prudence and sagacity. She continually opposed the advice of Monmouth's more precipitate counsellors and tried to prevent his acquiescing to the desperate schemes devised by Shaftesbury. When Monmouth was forbidden the court, he retired to Moor Park, 'where a day's conversation with his lady made him repent of his conduct, and willing to sign any paper of the same nature with that which he had signed before, and had got back in the manner related'.[5] But the King had grown weary of his continual actions and reactions and, insisting that the time had come to deal with him in another manner, forced him to declare the whole truth before the Court of Judicature.

Courtiers were quick to snub Monmouth: it was one thing to side with either him or York, quite another to disobey a direct order from the King. Accordingly, Monmouth tried the loyalty of his friend Nell Gwyn. But the King's most celebrated mistress, whom Lord Rochester called 'the darling strumpet of the crowd',[6] was not to be led by the nose: recalling an earlier pretender to the throne, she christened Monmouth 'Prince Perkin'. Although Nell was undoubtedly fond of him and dined with him often, she was not above teasing him for his headstrong behaviour. When he was unable to conceal his annoyance he called her ill bred. The sharper-witted 'Protestant Whore' was quick to retort: 'Was Mrs Barlow better bred than I?'[7] and the Duke was silent.

Shaftesbury pressed Monmouth's cause with force and persuaded Charles to admit, through an intermediary, that he could not believe ill of his son. This admission marked a diplomatic truce, until it was suggested to the King that, in his new spirit of forgiveness, the pious Titus Oates should now be prayed for in Nonconformist congregations. Naturally Charles would not consent to such a mockery, and Monmouth sank with Oates in his disfavour. Nor would he consider Shaftesbury's suggestion that all matters concerning the Queen, York and the succession should be left to Parliament.

All the time that Shaftesbury was working in harmony with the King's son, the Duke of York did no more than watch over the arena with keen interest. Charles was old, perhaps dying. The greatest enemy of the anti-York politicians was the slow-moving wheels of government: should Charles die before his brother was excluded as heir to the throne, all would be lost.

The lobby assembling behind the mutual cause of the King and his Catholic brother was not doing so out of any great love for the Duke of York or the rightful succession. Lord Rochester saw that the Houses of Parliament had gone too far in their support of Titus Oates to survive under a Catholic king. He also saw that, whether the feared Exclusion Bill were upheld or not, civil war was imminent, unless York was executed for the questionable crime of Catholicism. But the minority opposed to the Protestant alternatives was now increasing. The views of this opposition were based upon the fear of a second civil war, should anyone be excluded from the rightful succession. No doubt the fact that York bore his grudges with a marked viciousness, a trait that would surface later in all its bloody horror, also represented a threat that was much in the minds of those who stood beside him rather than against him.

. . . . .

But a new crisis was about to disturb the English court. Sir Gilbert Gerard, apparently unable to restrain his curiosity, had broken the promise made to his father-in-law, John Cosin, of Durham, that the 'black box' left in his custody should not be opened until after the King's death. Gerard maintained that he had found in it a certificate of the marriage of Lucy Walter and Charles. He also stated that the Bishop had officiated at the ceremony. Naturally such news was widely discussed, and the Duke of York persuaded his brother that there should be a full investigation, for if the marriage had in fact taken place, then the Duke of Monmouth would be the rightful heir to the throne.[8]

Gerard was the first to be called to Whitehall to testify; but now he denied all knowledge of the black box, though he prayed to be excused rather than declare such ignorance under oath. The general fury aroused by Gerard's dubious confession was inflamed by Monmouth, who, in the presence of many foreign ambassadors, happily boasted that his mother was descended from Edward iv and that he had Plantagenet blood. At the same time the King's popular image was enhanced by the story of how, when a lonely exiled prince, he had fallen in love with a beautiful country girl and married her. Oliver Cromwell's carefully cultivated picture of him as a scandalous royal rake thus merged into a romantic one. But it was too dangerous to hope that the rumour would simply die away of its own accord. Thus Charles ii became the only king in English history to take the trouble to disown a wife by public proclamation:

There being a false and malicious report industriously spread abroad by some who are neither friends to me nor the Duke of Monmouth, as if I should have been either contracted or married to his mother; and though I am most confident that this idle story cannot have any effect in this age, yet I thought it my duty in relation to the succession of the Crown, and that future ages may not have any further pretence to give disturbance upon that score or any other of this nature, to declare, as I do declare, in the presence of Almighty God, that I never was married nor gave contract to any woman whatsoever, but to my wife Queen Catherine, to whom I am now married. In witness whereof I set my hand, at Whitehall, the sixth day of January 1678. Charles R.[9]

As the investigation continued, most of the controversy was concerned with the location of the marriage ceremony; did it take place in Liège or in Wales? Among those who had shared Charles's exile there were many who could have attended the marriage; but there was danger in testifying to this effect and only Cosin's steward actually admitted that he had been present. The King grew more and more weary as the testimony continued; none would openly declare where the marriage was held, or who officiated at the ceremony, or even if it had taken place at all. The Earl of Macclesfield, who had served the King with marked loyalty and success while in exile, was questioned on the moral character of Lucy Walter. Charles himself posed the question earnestly. He examined Macclesfield 'upon his knowledge of the Duke of Monmouth's mother being a whore to other people, which that Earl did not remember, though the King gave him a token to call him to mind about it'.[10] Macclesfield was more suitable to give evidence than any living man in England, as he had been continually in the company of Charles, his courtiers and Lucy Walter throughout the latter's association with Charles.

Time and again the issue arose as to which document was the one confiscated from Lucy on Cromwell's orders while she was under arrest. The evidence, though almost all hearsay, was to the effect that it was a certificate of marriage. Many of Lucy's relations and servants were said to have talked of the marriage, and it is interesting to note that all records of births and weddings filed in Pembrokeshire, Lucy's home county, in the year of Monmouth's birth, were mysteriously destroyed at the Restoration.

Throughout the year there were few political debates other than that concerning the alleged marriage. The Dowager Countess of Sunderland wrote to her brother that there had been uproar in the playhouses: '. . . calling all the women whores and the men

rogues ... throwing candles and links ... calling my Lord
Sunderland traitor, but in good company; the Duke [of York] a
rascall. The people ended ... "God bless his Highness, the Duke
of Monmouth". Wee will be for him against all the world.'[11]

So many anti-Papist demonstrations took place and so many
pamphlets were issued that even the politically inoffensive Prince
Rupert of the Rhine headed a deputation of peers who appealed
to Parliament to meet on the topic. The King, however, simply
prorogued Parliament. The role of York in the proceedings
became more and more odious as the investigations continued.
Monmouth, the darling of the public, was viewed with increasing
seriousness as a contender for the throne. He was no longer simply
the jewel of the highest court circles – he was suitable for kingship.

In May 1680 *A Letter to a Person of Honour Concerning the
Black Box* was published anonymously. The author was probably
Robert Ferguson, known as 'the plotter'. The pamphlet concerned
the two most popular hatreds of the day: Catholicism and the
Duke of York. So bold was this treatise that it is remarkable that
no statement contained in it was ever contradicted. In the early
1680s the political pamphlets of Robert Ferguson became the
most sought-after documents in the City of London. Ferguson
was a skilled journalist and managed his Scottish wit with some
force, both while delivering his sermons at Moorfields and while
writing about political conspiracies at court. His document on the
black box was found under the King's own pillow at Windsor
Castle. A far wittier publication was *A Letter to a Person of
Honour Concerning the King's Disavowing His Having Been
Married to the Duke of M's Mother*', which appeared in the wake
of the whole black box argument.

The impact of Ferguson's pamphlets was twofold. On the one
hand those in favour of a Protestant successor now stridently
took note of Monmouth as opposed to his cousin William of
Orange, for Monmouth's image was noticeably improved and
taken more seriously by the pamphleteer. On the other hand

many of the more sober-thinking Londoners mellowed in their appreciation of the Duke of York once the hysteria of the opposition became apparent. He appeared at least sane, if not loyal to both the King and, nominally, his Parliament.

When the Duke and Duchess of York returned to Whitehall from their temporary exile they were greeted with a surprisingly cordial welcome from the City of London. Urban hysteria had cooled. The thinking man had had time to weigh the evidence while both dukes were in exile, and many men, Lord Shaftesbury in particular, were to note how public sentiments had mellowed in their absence. This was a gambit well played by Charles, who had anticipated just such a calm once his headstrong son and stubborn brother were out of the public eye.

While the ferment over Ferguson's declarations was still raging, in July 1680, Monmouth set out on his famous 'progress to the West Country'. The contemporary and anonymous *Heroick Life* of Monmouth, presumably written by Robert Ferguson, records how he 'went into the country to divert himself, visiting several gentlemen in the West of England, by whom he was received and entertained with a gallantry suitable to the greatness of his birth and the relation he stood unto his Majesty; incredible numbers of people flocking from all adjacent parts to see this great Champion of the English Nation who had been so successful against the Dutch, French and Scots'.[12] His Majesty seems to have been strong in his disapproval of this blatant exhibitionism. On 12 August Secretary Jenkins wrote to the Bishop of Bath and Wells: the King, he said, 'utterly dislikes the proceedings of the Duke of Monmouth. . . . He desires his friends not to show him any respect nor to have any commerce with him in this ramble; that the course he is now in . . . is very much against common prudence and the duty he owes to his Majesty.'[13]

But the successful progress of the wilful Protestant Duke continued unabated. He was acclaimed in Bristol and Bath and visited Longleat, where his friend Tom Thynne lived. He then turned south to Maiden Bradley, Bruton, Sparkford and Ilchester, and was greeted by thousands shouting: 'God's blessing to the Protestant Duke.' A dinner was given in his honour at White Lackington, and he was magnificently entertained by Sir John Sydenham at Brympton D'Evercy, near Yeovil. Sir John also received him at Hinton Park, about three miles away, and it was here that Monmouth received proof of the faith of the people in his royal quality. One Elizabeth Parcet, 'who had heard of the festive party, made a rush at the Duke of Monmouth and touched his hand. She was a martyr to the king's evil ... After touching the Duke, all her wounds were healed in two days. A hand-bill was circulated in folio setting forth this marvellous cure.'[14]

On 1 September he entered the city of Exeter. According to an eye-witness: '... the citizens, together with the people of all adjacent parts ... came all forth to meet the Duke with their souls and mouths filled with love and joy, trumpeting forth his welcome, and shouting out thus, God bless our Gracious Sovereign King Charles, God bless the Protestant Duke, God bless the Protestant Prince. . . . The great concourse of people, the amazing shouts, the universal joys were such, as are more easily related than can be credited.' This, writes the same eye-witness, was an example of the ovation 'that the Protestant people was willing to give to an illustrious Protestant prince'.[15]

The rejoicings continued for over a month, and Monmouth did not return to London until the end of September. His 'Western Progress' and the acclamations he received were remembered for many generations; but the heedless happiness that he was able to convey at this time contrasts only too vividly with the devilishness that was so soon to manifest itself in this same part of England.

Lord George Scott, in his unpublished 'Life of Monmouth', has suggested that 'the astonishing manner in which all classes of the community welcomed Monmouth during his Western Progress was due partly to the fact that he was 'the Protestant Duke' and partly to 'his abnormally good looks, perfect manners and charming disposition'. He also points out that in London Monmouth was welcomed by 'inordinate manifestations of affection', such as would not ordinarily have been accorded to him even had he been Prince of Wales.[16] It is not surprising, therefore, that many believed that he had been born in wedlock.

We should remember here that praise of Monmouth had, since his arrival in England, been preached from the very pulpits of the villages. The people were as united to him spiritually as they were to their king or their bishop, and by his presence he had at least become more accessible than either.

The 'Protestant Duke' had clearly become too popular to receive any backing from Catholic France. The French ambassador, Paul Barillon, writing to Louis XIV on 19 September 1680, told him that Monmouth had been received in many places with great demonstrations of welcome and that his party seemed to be growing stronger every day. Indeed at Oxford the rabble in the streets cried: 'A Monmouth, no York, no Bishop, no clergy, no University!'[17] These shouts went to the Duke's head: at dinner he shared a toast with the mayor of 'Confusion to the Vice-Chancellor and Bishop of Oxford'.[18] This was not good behaviour from one who, since 1674, had been chancellor of Cambridge University. In the same vein was the toast given at Penruddock Hall, the seat of Baron Lovelace of Hurley (a cousin of Henrietta Wentworth), where glasses were raised to the Duke of Monmouth and *Magna Carta*, the famed charter of English freedom.

While Monmouth was touring the west his name was kept on every man's lips in London by the seemingly miraculous powers of his 'sister', Mary Fanshawe. Monmouth always referred to her in his letters as if she and he shared the same father as well as mother, and as if both were born in wedlock, though the King never acknowledged that she was his child. The story of her particular spirituality originated in September 1680. When a

London boy named Jonathan Trott became ill with a very swollen throat, his mother was of sufficient means to consult specialists, all of whom advised her to seek the 'King's royal touch' as the only possible cure. But both Jonathan and his mother had identical dreams that night, directing them to seek not the King himself – Windsor was a fair distance to take a sick boy – but the Duke of Monmouth's sister, then living in St James's Street.

Mary was quite overcome with surprise at their arrival on her doorstep. She was in the company of Lord Macclesfield (who had befriended Lucy Walter in exile), when Jonathan fell to his knees before her. Lord Macclesfield was later to report to the King that Mary placed her hands over Jonathan's throat, and that the boy was healed within two days. A pamphlet was issued at once to commemorate the miracle of 'Princess Mary's royal touch'. There was also a vulgar elegy written that laughingly referred to the young girl 'gently stroking Mr Trot'.[19] The story indirectly elevated the dead Lucy Walter to royal stature, as the mother of such a miracle-worker, and this too became a great subject of coffee-house conversation after the 'Western Progress'.

On his return to London Monmouth was in disgrace: his own popularity and his sister's powers were too much for York to bear, and his complaints turned the King against his son. Yet he remained in England and continued to appear in public. (Indeed it was York who had to slink away to Scotland.) In November 1680 a contemporary wrote: 'The Duke of Monmouth was at St Martin's Church last Sunday . . . and all uncovered admiring him. He hath on his coach painted an heart wounded with two arrows, crossed, the plume of feathers, two angells bearing up a scarf on either side, which some say is Prince of Wales armes. He is mightily followed in the city.'[20]

8

Shaftesbury and the Exclusion Crisis

ON 4 November 1678 Parliament had witnessed a rousing debate between those who advocated reverence for royalty and those who denounced the dangers of Catholicism in the heir to the throne. Near the close of the argument a minister had risen to ask, 'whether the King and Parliament [might] dispose of the succession of the crown'.[1] With this single sentence Members of Parliament who ten minutes before had been shouting one another down in fury were silenced: who would have the courage to speak out against his King's own brother and heir?

Yet Shaftesbury continued to carry through a policy of exclusion against the Duke of York. An unexpected boost to his cause was a public admission by the Duke of York's private secretary, standing before a committee of the House of Commons, that his master had carried on a secret correspondence with the King of France concerning the restoration of England to the Catholic faith. Lord Shaftesbury was swift to propose that York should be withdrawn from the King's presence and councils.

A careful look into Shaftesbury's strategy is important if we are to understand how it was that the Duke of Monmouth was to fall under his influence.

Shaftesbury's use of anti-Popery was brutally simple: he delivered speeches harping on the dangers of Catholicism and of arbitrary government (indeed they became interchangeable terms), insisting that exclusion was the only possible solution to the problem and that anyone who disagreed was a Papist or had leanings towards

Popery. Almost all Englishmen shared a fear of Popery, and Shaftesbury stimulated that fear. Those who succumbed to his oratory and reasoning were fused into his new Whig party.

The issue of the succession was raised in coffee-houses and meeting-places throughout London. It was not always Monmouth who came under discussion, but it was certainly York who was constantly opposed – except by those who still entertained the likelihood of York renouncing his Catholicism and gratifying his people. But many favoured a plan for asking Prince William of Orange to come over and granting him an English dukedom. It seemed that he had proved a popular leader, a competent soldier, respectful to Parliament and (most important) consistently anti-Catholic, but unfortunately he also had a number of drawbacks on the personal level: He was ugly in face and figure; he was foreign; and there were some doubts as to his sexual preferences, for although he was married to the pretty Princess Mary of York, he showed some indication of homosexual tendencies. Favours shown to the male favourites of James I had seriously damaged the credibility of the crown and few would have welcomed a return to the days of the notorious first Duke of Buckingham.

Shaftesbury did not rely for popular support entirely on his greatest asset, the 'Protestant Duke'. He was cordially received in the City of London on his own account. As a gesture towards the powerful new middle class he had moved his residence from the fashionable Whitehall area to the merchant quarters of Aldersgate. His splendid coach, led by eight horses, was decked with green ribbons and became a vehicle of propaganda. He was neither youthful nor handsome, yet his impact on the City was not unlike that of Monmouth upon the countryfolk.

In the summer of 1680 he had added appreciably to his allies by means of a very shrewd manoeuvre. When he and his partisans Russell and Cavendish had presented the Duke of York to the Grand Jury of Parliament on 26 June, they had also made a move to indict Louise, Duchess of Portsmouth, as a common nuisance.

Beginning to fear the Whigs, the Duchess had entered into an agreement with the trio: in return for a sum of money she would seduce Charles into accepting the exclusion policy and a successor named by Shaftesbury. Louise was probably using her diplomatic cunning with the Whigs mainly to save her place at court, for there is no evidence of her needing additional subsidies from Shaftesbury. None the less, her desertion had carried with it Colonel Robert Sidney, by then Lord Sunderland, while the Earl of Essex, who was at heart a Whig, had also passed over to the Opposition.

Monmouth made an appearance at the House of Lords for the reading of the Exclusion Bill in November 1680. But there was a far more important personage than he at this reading, though merely as an observer – the King himself. Behind the scenes His Majesty had solicited votes in favour of his absent brother, and petitions were also sent round on his behalf. 'The fourteenth of November was one of the greatest days ever known in the House of Lords,' wrote Sir John Reresby. 'As the matter was extra-ordinary – i.e. the cutting of the lineal descent of the Crown – so also was the debate.'[2]

The French ambassador wrote of the proceedings to his master: 'Lord Halifax stood up [*tint tête*] to Lord Shaftesbury and answered him every time he spoke.' The debating powers of Halifax during this critical time were recorded in other places than correspondence to the French King, for he had secured his place in parliamentary history. Though unfortunately none of his actual speeches was recorded, historians would point to his performance before the House of Lords on this issue with a respect not rivalled until the days of Pitt. Yet Halifax was not consistent in the debates, and many of the court faction took note of his sudden switch from the defence of the 'Catholic Duke'. 'He [Halifax] is entirely in the interest of the Prince of Orange,' wrote Barillon to Louis XIV, 'and what he seems to be doing for the Duke of York is really in order to make an opening for a compromise by which the Prince of Orange may benefit.'[3]

The bill, instead of naming Princess Mary to replace her father, York, was purposely worded by Monmouth's supporters so as to make him a possible successor. It passed its third reading in the Commons but, thanks to Halifax, was thrown out in the House of Lords by a vote of sixty-three to thirty. Sir John Reresby wrote to Lady Sunderland on 14 November 1680 that it was Halifax alone who persuaded the House to reject the bill.

I am full of my Lord Halifax [Lady Sunderland wrote to her brother] and will tell you what perhaps nobody else will – that a day or two before the Duke's bill was carried to the Lords, one of the great actors came to him as a friend, I suppose, to tell him that if he did speak against it, he would be impeached by the House of Commons, or an address made to the King to remove him from his great place of Privy Councillor. He answered, neither threatenings nor promises should hinder him from speaking his mind. How he did it, you who know him, may judge.[4]

As so many correspondents of the day wrote, it was the most exciting debate since the days of the civil war. Among the more novel topics discussed in opposition to the Catholic Duke was the introduction of Duke of Monmouth's unacknowledged claim to the nation's crown. It was also made clear that there was no provision in the bill for the Duke of York's privileges, should he become Protestant. As we have seen, Monmouth and the King were both present. York was conspicuously absent, as his presence would probably have stirred the peers to dissension. Monmouth spoke boldly and uttered sentiments against his uncle for the first time on the floor of Parliament, 'because he knew of no other expedient to preserve the life of the King from the malice of the Duke of York';[5] and it was said that the King was heard to whisper loudly; 'The kiss of Judas.'[6]

The storm Lady Sunderland prophesied soon broke. Three days after the debate in the House, the King was petitioned by the Commons to remove Lord Halifax from the council, on the grounds that he was a promoter of Popery. Halifax had compromised in his debates and, while not standing against the Duke of York, had suggested that he should be banished for the King's lifetime and be allowed to return upon Charles's death with only limited privileges if he maintained his Catholic principles. Although York was pleased with Halifax's skill in winning over Parliament and defending the succession, he could not contain his anger at the thought of exile.

The House of Commons drew up a second petition for the reinstatement of Monmouth to his previous positions, as they had resolved that the stripping of his dignities was due to York's influence. This petition naturally alarmed Louis XIV, who was quick to dispatch a letter to his ambassador in London, telling him of his displeasure: 'I ask no other return from him [Charles] for the 500,000 francs offer to have paid each year than that he should strengthen himself in the rightful possession of royal authority by proroguing Parliament . . . and by then recalling the Duke of York to his presence, and I shall have to ask in my interests, but still more in his own and that of his crown, no longer to draw down the wrath of God by unjustly persecuting the Catholics.'[7]

The 'wrath of God' may have fallen upon Charles as a result of all his diplomatic struggles, but his calm mood was evident to all who met him. He excused himself from attending the Lord Mayor's banquet, pleading his wife's slight illness as his excuse, but Monmouth, along with Lord Grey and Tom Thynne, was there. Once again the crowds shouted 'Long live the Protestant Duke' and there were many who commented on the Prince of Wales's insignia on his coach, still with the bar sinister (denoting illegitimacy) conspicuously missing.

Parliament was prorogued for ten days and then dissolved for two months. The new Parliament was to meet in March 1681 in Oxford. This would keep the ministers out of the more violently anti-Papist capital and at the same time help them to resolve their grievances amid the tranquillity of a country town. This naturally displeased the Whigs. When the supporters of Shaftesbury arrived in Oxford they immediately set to the task of building up Monmouth's public personality. They had not expected the King to dissolve Parliament once again and then flee to Windsor, leaving behind the confused and angered ministers and even the royal mistresses.

The Prince of Orange now made plans to visit Charles in England – plans of such obvious political intent that both the King and his brother were averse to them. But the Prince arrived before any reply to his announcement could be made, and pressed the King to call Parliament to settle the succession issue without further delay. Himself the elected ruler of his country, William was firmly opposed to any principle of absolute monarchy (such as that which obtained in France at that time); he never lost sight of the fact that the Dutch people had made him their stadtholder and that they could dismiss him if necessary. He now carried the same principle into his dealings with the English succession. Charles was sympathetic to his nephew's request, but he would not yield.

Shortly after the break-up of the Oxford Parliament Shaftesbury was arrested (on undeclared grounds) at his London house in Aldersgate. His memoirs, his receipts and his notes for further debates were all seized with him. (Lord Ailesbury had the privilege of looking through many of these documents and discovered his own name at the head of a list of men deserving to be hanged.) After an examination before the court in the King's presence, Shaftesbury was conveyed by water to the Tower and was visited that night by Monmouth and Lord Grey.

Monmouth came forward as security for Shaftesbury's release – which greatly annoyed the King. The Green Ribbon Club issued a celebratory medal for their leader's release, but on the other hand only a few days later the poet Dryden published his *Absalom and Achitophel*, which rallied monarchist sympathies. He wrote of Shaftesbury:

> . . . the false Achitophel was first
> A name to all succeeding ages curs't,
> For close designs and crooked councils fit,
> Sagacious, bold and turbulent of wit
> Restless, unfixed in principles and place,
> In power unpleased, impatient of disgrace,
> In friendships false, implacable in hate,
> Resolved to ruin or to rule the State.

The poem had the desired effect of attracting great popular sympathy for the court party. The portrait of Shaftesbury is cruel and unjust, yet when seen against the background of those most violent years it seems an appropriate caricature.

After the Exclusion Bill had failed to pass, Shaftesbury and his followers were so disgruntled that they looked upon it as a test of loyalty to rejoice in or bewail the prospects of the Catholic successor; they preached with fury against Dissenters but thought it indecent to speak against the religion of the heir to the throne.[8] Shaftesbury and the Council of Six, consisting of Monmouth, Essex, Russell, Sidney, Hampden and Howard, discussed a general insurrection.[9] Monmouth and Russell were against any precipitate action, and it was decided that the true feelings of the people should be ascertained.

Lord George Scott believes that Shaftesbury was by this time nearly demented, not only because of the numerous political disappointments he had experienced but because of the effects of a serious injury incurred while riding in his carriage twenty years earlier. He was in fact dangerously ill and did not have long to live. On 30 September 1682, he left his house in Aldersgate and lay in hiding in the City, where Ferguson and his other accomplices daily visited him. If one can believe Lord Grey's statement, he had urged Monmouth, Russell and Sir Thomas Armstrong that it was absolutely essential to start a rising. But Monmouth and Russell, although recognizing Shaftesbury's ability, had no confidence in his military judgement.

Rumours of a potential rebellion were already spreading,

however. That summer the Earl of Argyll had been to London, having slipped away from Edinburgh, where the Duke of York had placed him in custody. He was as eager as Shaftesbury for a rebellion, and they discussed a plan whereby Argyll should raise Scotland, Lord Granard, Ireland and Monmouth, England. Though York was relentless in his enmity for Argyll and tried to persuade Charles to arrest him, the King said merely, 'Let the hunted partridge go.'[10]

In the autumn Monmouth set off for the north, to show himself to the people, as he had done during his Western Progress. The court was nervous of this journey. He was reported to be going to the races, but such gatherings had often been used before as a cover for political intrigues.

Coventry gave the 'Protestant Duke' a triumphant welcome. He had breakfast in the mayor's parlour, after which he left for Lichfield. There he was received coldly. Thirty country gentleman had come in for a horse race and were dining at the very post-house at which Monmouth dismounted, but not one of them so much as left the room to look at him. Monmouth was not used to such coldness. His reception was very different at Stone and Nantwich, however, and he rode into the towns to wild cheers. The inhabitants flung up their hats, and above the cheers only one word could be distinguished: 'Monmouth!' The Duke, with his customary charm, saluted them most courteously, his hat in his hand. In the courtyard of 'The Crown' in Stone women were waiting to flock about him as he mounted his horse to start for the next town.

He went out of his way to lay his hand on a child suffering from the 'king's evil'. His charm and captivating ways came from the genuine sweetness of his nature and were all the more potent for this. His enemies were wrong in attributing the warmth of his manners only to ambition, of which in fact he had very little. His apparently avid desire for popularity was in reality created by his supporters.

He crossed the water that night to Liverpool, and the next day found him with Lord Delamere at Dunham. He dined that night with open doors, that the countryfolk might come in and see him. Two of Monmouth's friends shared the local intoxication and went home shouting 'A Monmouth! A Monmouth!' After dancing and sports and hunting, and two attendances at church on the Sunday, he moved on on Monday to Newcastle-under-Lyme, then to Trentham, where the bells were ringing and bonfires flaming, and so to Stafford.

The mayor of that town, Sampson Birch, was reluctantly obliged to receive Monmouth publicly; on 25 September he wrote to the Secretary of State, Sir Leoline Jenkins . . . that he had been visiting and on his return:

. . . Sergeant Ramsey went to speak with me at a private gentleman's house when he took me aside and told me that his business was to arrest the Duke of Monmouth; he added that he would appear in the public room of the Duke . . . so I went with my staff and the mace to the door where the Duke, our High Steward was to come. . . . I did my obeisance to him and he put me to go before him where I spoke the words in the enclosed papers. When I spoke of abhorring the traitorous association, he said all good men should abhor it too. Then I drank to the King as the Duke desired me which he pledged and prayed God to bless His Majesty. Immediately after this, Sergeant Ramsay came in and produced his warrant, at sight whereof the noise abated.

The contents of the warrant explain the arrest: '. . . that James Duke of Monmouth hath lately appeared in several parts of this Kingdom with great numbers of people, in a riotous and unlawful manner . . . require you forthwith to repair to any place where you shall understand the said Duke of Monmouth to be, and him forthwith to apprehend and bring in safe custody before me or any of His Majesty's most honourable Privy Council . . .'[11]

The list of those guilty of the same riotous behaviour as Monmouth comprises virtually all the influential men in Cheshire and the neighbouring counties. This was a back-handed compliment to Monmouth, who could no longer be linked exclusively with the poorer and more ignorant countrymen. Shaftesbury and Essex presented themselves to Judge Dolbein to give bail, but found the magistrate in a quandary as to where Monmouth should be sent. The King vetoed the idea of committing him to the Tower, but he was taken to London.

Once in London he showed both determination and resourcefulness in the way he conducted himself as he faced the law officers of state. Secretary Jenkins, who had been granted a figurehead role as custodian to Monmouth, found that he had familiarized himself with the privileges of peers in his refusal to be subpoenaed by the Secretary's office 'unless for treason'. *State Papers (Domestic)* show that Jenkins could but adhere to this request, and that he later lured Monmouth to his office 'with a verbal message that His Majesty desired to speak with him, on which he immediately went, but found there Mr Secretary only'.[12] This was not so cruel a trick as it appears, for the King was in the next room deliberating in Council and ninety minutes later communicated through Jenkins a vague accusation of treason. Monmouth's fate thus hinged upon that cry of 'A Monmouth! A Monmouth! No York' yelled in Chester under the duress of 'seven hundred force'.

He was sufficiently military-minded to realize the implications of levying an armed *coup détat* in Chester. He replied that he had neither broken nor intended to break His Majesty's peace and knew of no crime he had committed. He was discharged, but he had not even reached Whitehall Gate before a messenger overtook him with a new warrant brought against him for causing a riot. He was again detained and this time bailed out by Lords Grey and Russell, among others. (This is typical of the spirit of those who sympathized with him. Some of Monmouth's closest friends, including Grey, Russell and Algernon Sidney, John Hampden and Henrietta Wentworth, were wholly sincere in their Protestant zeal.)

Two days later Monmouth was granted bail and went to Moor Park with his wife and children. Shaftesbury advised him to return to Cheshire at once and raise a rebellion, but Russell said that no plans for so grave an enterprise had been drawn up. It was decided that Grey should reveal the conclusion of the consultation to Monmouth, and Grey later asserted that Shaftesbury had privately urged him 'to cheat the Duke of Monmouth' and tell him that the advice of all his friends was to rise.[13]

Appearing before the King's Bench on 23 November 1682, Monmouth was discharged four days later. Shaftesbury suspected that there was a secret understanding between Monmouth and his father, and began almost to distrust the former. He was not alone in believing in the existence of such an understanding; some also believed that there was an understanding between the King and his nephew, Prince William of Orange. Lord Howard of Escrick now came to Moor Park and tried to persuade Monmouth and Russell to join Shaftesbury, declaring that Shaftesbury was complaining that Monmouth had failed to support him, to which Monmouth replied that he thought Shaftesbury was mad: 'I was so far from giving him encouragement that I did tell him from the beginning, and so did Lord Russell that there was nothing to be done at that time.'[14]

In December 1682 the Earl of Shaftesbury fled, undetected, disguised as a Presbyterian minister, to Holland. He died within six weeks, in January 1683.

9

The Rye House Plot

THE various intrigues that culminated in the unsuccessful 'Rye House plot' of 1683 are described in detail by Robert Ferguson (Advocate) in *Fergusson the Plotter*. Another contemporary described these events as in these words: '. . . indeed this plot as to the murdering part of it seems to have been contrived by the Duke of York for the staining of the Duke of Monmouth and Buccleuch, and getting him removed forever from the Court.'[1] Many involved, including Monmouth, were to suffer a more painful penance than mere banishment from the King's presence.

Once Monmouth had dismissed Shaftesbury's proposals for a general insurrection in London following his humiliating defeat at Oxford, there then developed a secondary plan of attack: if the Whigs would not seize the nation's capital, then why not take the nation's king? What was most appealing to the Whigs in this plan was the assassination of the Catholic heir (though this would have been repugnant to the tender-hearted Monmouth).

The King generally took the same road to Newmarket, passing close to Rye House in Hertfordshire, which belonged to one Colonel Rumbold. It was here that armed horsemen would wait to perform the royal massacre. Shaftesbury's role had been considerably weakened by his ill-health, and he had confessed to Robert Ferguson that 'he could not commit his life, his fortune or his party to the Duke';[2] he stayed at Ferguson's home, and convinced the pamphleteer that he had every intention of undermining Monmouth's reputation. His confession went further: he was stimulated by a 'disgust of monarchy'.

As to Monmouth himself, according to Ferguson his knowledge of the conspiracy was limited. In the whitewashed account given by Ford, Lord Grey some years later, Monmouth had walked in Soho Square all night and had expressed confidence that when they were in power both Parliament and the King would 'be accommodated' to a Protestant end. Such ingenuousness is unbecoming in a man such as Lord Grey, who asserted his own innocence at the same time as damning the unhappy Lord Macclesfield. Lord George Scott suggests that Macclesfield's years of devotion to Charles were not sufficient evidence to disprove Grey's charge that it was he who kept insisting on 'murdering his Majestie'.[3] Grey is consistent in defending his own boon companion: 'The Duke of Monmouth expressed himself with the greatest abhorrence that can be imagined of such an action, and said he could not consent to the murdering of the meanest creature (even the worst enemy he had in the world) for all the advantages under heaven; and should never have any esteem for Lord Macclesfield while he lived.'[4]

Shaftesbury continued his quarrel with Monmouth and assured him most indignantly that 'ten thousand brisk boys' would rise to a new Protestant monarch should an insurrection occur. Monmouth, no fool when it came to military fact, demanded to know their whereabouts. This time Shaftesbury promised *twenty* men in London who would rally recruits.[5] Although this figure was more reasonable than what Monmouth expected for his own active support, it was none the less disheartening. The plot was further confused by the faction who hoped that the bloody massacre would bring in a weak government led by Monmouth or an aristocratic republic. Those connected with this latter group were headed by a discharged Cromwellian officer, a sinister lawyer and a good many political fanatics: not the most wholesome of Monmouth's supporters. Both groups were initially encouraged by Shaftesbury, until he left England at the end of 1682. It is significant that Shaftesbury's will was found to contain a bequest of the then large sum of £40 'to my worthy friend Mr Robert

Ferguson',[6] one of the few personal legacies for which he provided.

Both Monmouth and Grey were far from preoccupied by the prospective ambush. Indeed their lives continued in the same sporting fashion as before. Monmouth journeyed to France to be present at Louis XIV's international race-meeting in February on the plain of Archères near Saint-Germain-en-Laye, and brought back to England the converted plate worth 1000 *pistoles*. His consistent showmanship did not go unnoticed: 'The honour of England was sustained by the Duke of Monmouth,' wrote a contemporary at the English court, 'who carried away the prize in the presence of Louis and the French Court.'[7] Lord Grey had proved valiant on another field by defending with his sword the seduction of his sister-in-law, Lady Henrietta Berkeley, the previous November. The resulting scuffle proved before the King's Bench that Lord Grey's resourcefulness was not reserved for the ladies only. The guilty parties were never called to judgement.

On 22 March 1683 the King went to Newmarket but, because of a fire in his stables, he returned home a week earlier than he had intended, thus frustrating the plotters. Narcissus Luttrell entered in his diary:

1683, June. About the 19th was discovered a dangerous and treasonable conspiracy againt the person of his Majesty and the Duke of York, by some of those called Whiggs. The 29th came out a proclamation by his majestie with the advice of his privy council, for the apprehending of James Duke of Monmouth, [Ford] Lord Grey, Sir Thomas Armstrong and Robert Ferguson, for conspiring the death of the king and the duke of York, to levy men and make an insurrection; promising the reward of £500 for taking any of them. His Majesty returned from Windsor about the 26th to Whitehall, where the councill sitts frequently concerning this plott, and the Duke of York sitts in council since this too; some persons are startled at it, the discoveries thereof being kept very private, and also the persons that have discovered it, however his majestie is so sensible thereof he hardly goes out but with a strong guard.[8]

Robert Ferguson knew more about the details of this Rye House affair than anybody; consequently his version is of great importance for valuing his character and attesting the opinion of others. It exposes the mistakes of Shaftesbury's last days and accentuates the capacity and perspicuity of Monmouth, although the latter was prone to be influenced by the company he was in. This may have been due to his Port-Royal training, since he had been taught 'never be afraid to reject an opinion if you are brought to see that it is wrong'.[9] The King pretended that he believed in the assassination part of the plot, but made it clear that he believed that his beloved son knew nothing about it.

Monmouth was sent for on 26 June but was 'said not to be at home'. On the next day Algernon Sidney was arrested in his house in Jermyn Street. With Russell and Grey, he was ordered to the Tower. Grey, by some extraordinary stroke of fortune, escaped. There was a price on the heads of James, Duke of Monmouth, Ford, Lord Grey of Werke, Sir Thomas Armstrong and Robert Ferguson.

Mrs Needham, still known as the Duke of Monmouth's mistress, in spite of his all-absorbing love for Henrietta Wentworth, was suspected of harbouring him, and it was thought that at 2 am he had embarked from St Saviour's Stairs. It seems likely that the rumour was true, and that Monmouth was hidden in the house of one of the doorkeepers of the House of Lords – probably William Snow, who lived in the Court of Requests. Hearing the guards coming for him as he lay in bed, Monmouth no doubt leaped out and escaped over the roof. He went to Toddington, Henrietta Wentworth's family seat, where he knew he would be received with open arms. One of the songs he wrote at this time reveals his mood:

> O how blest and how innocent and happy is a country life
> Free from tumult and discontent.
> Here is no flattery nor strife,
> For 'twas the first and happiest life
> When first man did enjoy himself.

This is a better fate than Kings.
Hence gentle peace and love doth flow.
For fancy is the rate of things,
I am pleased because I think it so.
For a heart that is nobly true
All the world's arts can ne'er subdue.[10]

He had managed to send word to Russell that if he thought he could do him any service, he would gladly do so. Russell answered that it would be of no advantage to have his friend die with him. As long as Charles lived, there was no hope for Monmouth.

The crown had its witnesses now: enough to send many deluded Whigs to their deaths.

In October 1683 there were hopes of a reconciliation between Monmouth and his father. Extracts from Monmouth's diary at this time are revealing.

October 13 [Halifax] came to me at eleven at night from [the King], told me [the King] could never be brought to believe I knew anything of that part of the plot that concern'd Rye-house; but as things went, he must behave himself as if he did believe it, for some reasons that might be to my advantage. [Halifax] desired me to write to [the King], which I refus'd; but afterwards he told me [the King] expected it: and I promis'd to write tomorrow, if he could call for the letter. . . . [Halifax] shew'd great concern for me, and I believe him sincere. . . .

In the original, the names were written in code.

The letters that Monmouth now wrote to the King were drawn up by Halifax. The first read as follows:

If I could have writ to your Majesty sooner with any safety to myself, I would have done it, to have told you that there is nothing has struck me so to the heart as to be put into a proclamation for an intention of murdering of you, Sir, and the Duke [of York]. I do call God Almighty to witness, and I wish I may die this moment I am writing if ever it entered into my head, or I ever said the least thing to anybody that could make them think I could wish such a thing. I am sure there cannot be such villans upon earth to say I ever did. But I am so innocent to this point that I will say no more of it; for I know God Almighty is just, and I do not doubt but he will put it into your heart, that I am clear of this most horrid and base accusation. But, Sir, the chief intent of this letter is to beg pardon, both of your, Sir, and the Duke, for the many things I have done that have made you both angry with me, but more especially of the Duke, though I might have some justification for myself, that many people made me believe he intended to destroy me: for to you I do protest, before God Almighty, and I wish I may never prosper more, that all I have done was only to *save you*, as I shall convince your Majesty, if ever I am so happy as to speak to you; and I hope you will let me do it before it be long; for I have that to say to you, Sir, that will for ever, I hope, settle you in quiet in your Kingdom, and the Duke after you, whom I intend to serve to the uttermost of my power. And, Sir, to convince him that I will do so, if your Majesty will give me your pardon, I will deliver myself up into his hands, that the Duke may bring me to you. Besides, Sir, I should be glad to have him by when I speak to you, but nobody else; and by this kindness of the Duke's if ever I should do anything afterwards against him, I must be thought the ungratefullest man living. What good can it do you, Sir, to take your own child's life away, that only erred, and *ventur'd his life to save yours*? And besides, Sir, I am sure I can be servicable to you; and if I may say so make the rest of your life happy, or, at least, contribute a great deal towards it. You may believe me, sir, for I do not tell you this out of fear, but because I do think myself sure of it. I do beg of you, sir, if you have any thoughts of mercy of me, that you will let me know it soon, for the sooner I speak to you the better. And now, Sir, I do swear to you that from this time I never will displeasure you in anything; but the whole study of my life shall be to show you how truly penitent I am for having done it. And for the Duke, that he may have a more firm confidence of the services I intend to do him, I do here declare to your Majesty, that I will never ask to see your face more, if ever I do anything against him, which is the greatest curse I can lay upon myself.

MONMOUTH

It is likely that Halifax, at Charles's instigation, had coached Monmouth on how to play his part. The entry in Monmouth's diary runs for 14 October 1683: '[Halifax] came as he promis'd.'

The next entry is dated 20 October (Saturday): '[Halifax] came to me at Stepney with a line or two from [the King], very kind assuring me he believ'd every word in my letter to be true, and advis'd me to keep hid, till he had an Opportunity to express his Belief of it some other way. [Halifax] told me he was to go out of Town next day; and that [the King] would send [an agent] to me in a Day or two, whom he assur'd me I might trust.'

The King came up from Newmarket that day, and the following Thursday the father and son met. The diary records on 25 October: '[Halifax] came to me . . . where [the King] was. . . . He received me pretty well and said 30 and 50 were the causes of my misfortune, and would ruin me. After some hot words against them, and against S, went away in humour.' Some think that '30' and '50' may refer to Sir Thomas Armstrong and Robert Ferguson, while 'S' may have been the late Lord Shaftesbury.

Monmouth's own submission to his father was bolstered by the usual sincere, tactful mediation of his wife. In this same month, October 1683, she wrote to the King:

Wednesday

Since I am so unhappy as to have no hopes of seeing your majesty to ask your leave to deliver this letter to you I had no other way of putting it into your hands, and finding by the Duke of Monmouth to me that it is necessary your majesty should have it as soon as I could give it you, which I was the more encouraged to do because he writes to me that except your majesty be resolved upon his utter ruin he is sure he can satisfy you that he will deserve your mercy and that he can at this time be servicable to you, so I do hope your majesty will not refuse to accept of the entire submission and great penitence from him which your goodness would not perhaps deny to another man, I beg your majesty will not be displeased with me since I doubt not but that his letter is of consequence because he pressed me to deliver it with all speed to your majesty.

I am your majesty's obedient dutifull servant

According to Lord Ailesbury, Monmouth 'negotiated his peace so well' that he was permitted to go 'in the dusk of the evening to Mrs Croft's [Anna's] lodgings in Whitehall, where the King used to go often, and after an intimate conversation Charles promised his beloved son that he should not be used as a witness, and after protesting his innocency as to any design against the life and person of the King, Monmouth referred to the evidence of Lord Howard of Escrick, Colonel Rumsey and Mr Sheppard.' 'After this secret conference', the King told his son where to appear at a stated time. 'Returning from Mrs Crofts wrapped up in a cloak', a court official, Colonel Griffin, saw Monmouth in a passage and ran in haste to the King to inform him, but 'the King answered, with a disdainful look, "You are a fool; James is in Brussels."' He had never liked Griffin, but 'after that officiousness, he could never hear the sight of him'.

Why was the King of England forced, for no ostensible reason, to resort to subterfuge, in order to interview the son whom he declared and genuinely believed to be innocent?

Monmouth was once more in a tight corner, for his diary entry for 26 October runs: '. . . was in danger of being discover'd by some of Oglethorpe's Men, that met me accidentally at the Back Door of the Garden.' The next entry comes a week later, on 2 November: 'A letter from [the King] to be tomorrow at seven at night at Stepney and nobody to know it.' Perhaps this refers to the Wentworth house at Stepney. The diary continues:

Nov. 3. He [the King] came not, there being an extraordinary Council. . . . Bid me come tomorrow at the same hour, and to say nothing of the letter, except [the King] spoke of it first.

Nov. 4. I came and found [the King] and [Halifax] there. He was very kind, and gave me directions how to manage my business, and what words I should say to [York].

Nov. 9. [Halifax] came from [the King] and told me my Business should be done to my mind next week; and that Q [the Queen?] was my friend, and had spoke to [York] and [the Duchess of York] in my behalf; which he said the King took very kindly and had express'd so to her. At parting he told me there should be nothing requir'd of me but what was both safe and honourable. But said there must be something done to blind [the Duke of York.] [Poor Charles was having to play a double game on behalf of the son he loved against the brother he feared.]

Nov. 15. [Halifax] came to me with a Copy of a letter I was to sign, to please [York]. I desired to know in whose hands it was to be deposited; for I would have it in no hands but [the King's]. He told me it should be so; but if [York] ask'd for a Copy, it could not well be refus'd. I refer myself entirely to [the King's] pleasure.

Nevertheless, Charles was so far gradually winning, especially if the contemporary diarist Woodrow was correct when he wrote that the Duke of York had engineered the Rye House Plot in order to have Monmouth banished for ever from court. Halifax says that York 'was perhaps more troubled at it [Monmouth's return] than at anything that ever happened to him in his life'. Could Halifax's reason for zealously supporting York in the Exclusion Bill have been that Charles had confided the reason for his fear of his brother and implored his help, lest the truth should come out? Bishop Burnet says that all the letters sent by Monmouth to the King at this time were drafted by Halifax.

His second letter, transcribed from a draft made by Halifax, was, according to the diary entry for 15 November, 'a letter I was to sign to please [York]', for unless assisted, the nephew was no match for the wiles of his subtle uncle:

You must allow me, Sir, still to importune you, not without hopes of prevailing at last upon your generosity, so as it may get the better of your anger to me. I am half distracted, Sir, with the thought of having offended you and the torment it gives me is perhaps greater than your forgiving nature would know how to inflict upon the most Criminal offenders. The character I lie under is too heavy for me to bear, – even death itself would be a relief to me could I have it without the aggravation of leaving the world under your displeasure. I must therefore throw myself upon your compassion, which being a virtue so agreeable to your nature, I hope your child, Sir, will not be an unfortunate instance of your denying it when tis implored. I confess, Sir, I have

been in fault, misled, insensibly engaged in things of which the consequence was not enough understood by me; yet I can say I never had a
criminal thought against your Majesty not pretending by that to insist
upon an absolute justification of myself. Your Majesty will consider
that whilst under *the apprehension of great anger and violence against me,*
it might easily corrupt my judgement, and by seeing things in a wrong
light betray me into very fatal mistakes. . . . I humbly beg, Sir, to be
admitted to your feet, and to be disposed of as you direct, not only
now but for the remainder of my life, and though my resignation is too
full to admit any reserve, your Majesty will permit me to offer to you.
Whether you will let pass anything as a penalty upon me which may
lay a stain upon my innocent children? Whether you will make me
undergo the ignominy of a trial before you give me your pardon? and
of what use or satisfaction it can be to you to forgive me and yet give
me the cruel punishment of hearing my self arraigned for treason
against such a King and such a father? And whether my being carried
to the Tower in case you be pleased to excuse my Trial can have any
effect but an unnecessary mortification of one who God knoweth is
already enough afflicted and some kind of blemish, too, to my family as
well as an useless limitation of your Majesty's mercy? Sir I lay these
things before you in the most submitting manner that is possible with
an entire resignation to what you shall determine. Neither do I imagine
to receive your pardon any otherwise than by the intercession of the
Duke, whom I acknowledge to have offended, and am prepared to
submit myself in the humblest manner; and therefore beg your Majesty
would direct how I am to apply myself to him, and I shall do it, not as
an outward form, but with all the sincerity of the world. If what I have
said can move you to forget my past faults it will be a grace I shall
endeavour to deserve by all the actions of my life, and I am so sensible
how ill a guide my own will hath been to me that I am resolved for the
future to put it entirely in your Majesty's hands that I may by that
means never commit a fault but for want of your directions or your
commands. Dear Sir, be pleased to receive by a kind answer the most
miserable, disconsolate creature now living,

MONMOUTH

Nine days later Halifax brought a note from Charles: 'If the
Duke of Monmouth desire to render himself capable of my mercy,

he must render himself in the custody of the Secretary, and resolve to disclose all he knows, relying entirely upon my mercy, resigning himself entirely to my pleasure.'

Narcissus Luttrell records in his diary: 'Nov. 24th. – the Duke of Monmouth surrendered himself to Secretary Jenkins, and the next day was before the Council, his coming in had surprised most people, some think he has not been out of Whitehall all this time.' And the entry in Monmouth's own diary reads: 'Nov. 24th. [Halifax] came to me from [the King], and order'd me to render myself tomorrow. Caution'd me to play my part, to avoid questions as much as possible, and to seem absolutely converted to [York's] interest. Bade me bear with some words that might seem harsh.'

In a letter dated 26 November Sir Leoline Jenkins wrote to Lord Dartmouth:

You will see by the Gazette of this day that the Duke of Monmouth is returning to Court again, and pardoned. All that passed after Council yesterday in the evening was . . . that the Duke of Monmouth came afterwards into my office, and that then the sergeant-at-arms, that had him before in custody, was discharged. Then I waited on him (as I had been ordered) to the Duke [of York]. His Royal Highness carried him straight to the King, the King carried him to the Queen, then the Duke brought him back to the Duchess [of York]. He was at Court all this morning; which is all the account I have yet to give. After a meeting of the Privy Council . . . the King brought Monmouth to kiss the Queen's hand: the Duke [of York] took him to kiss the Duchess's.

If we turn to Monmouth's diary we read: 'Nov. 25. I rend'd myself. At night [the King] could not dissemble his satisfaction; press'd my hand; which I remember not he did before, except when I returned from the French service, [the King] acted his part well, and I too: [York] and [the Duchess] seem'd not too ill pleased.'

That night the diarist Welwood recorded that the King was 'so little Master of himself that he could not dissemble a mighty Joy in his Coutenance and in everything he did or said: Insomuch that it was the publick Talk about Town, and strongly insinuated to the Duke of York, that all the King's former proceedings against the duke of *Monmouth* were but *Grimace,* and that his Royal Highness [York] being made an Instrument of the Reconciliation was all but a Trick put upon him.' The following day Monmouth 'was abroad with the King as usual'. This must have been a real joy to his devoted father.

Those of Monmouth's friends who had been implicated in the Rye House Plot were less fortunate than he, however. Essex, Sidney and Russell were arrested. Incidentally, it can only be to Monmouth's credit that these three, his closest friends, were greatly liked and admired, except by their political enemies. Rather than break with his brother, the King allowed the judicial execution of the excellent Russell in July. On 26 November Monmouth recorded in his diary: '[The King] took me aside, and falling upon the business of [Lord Russell] said he inclin'd to have sav'd him, but was forc'd to it, otherwise he must have broke with [York]. Bid me think no more on't. Coming home [Halifax] told me that he fear'd [York] began to smell out [the King's] Carriage. That all was done was but a Sham.' On 7 December 1683 Sidney, too, was due to be executed and the King sent Monmouth an order to leave Whitehall. Five days later he ordered that a copy of the letter he had signed for the Privy Council book should be prefaced with an account that, in view of the reports that had got about that Monmouth had confessed to no plot: 'His Majesty had thought it fit, for the vindication of the truth of what the said Duke had declared to himself (his Royal Highness being present), to require for him in writing, by way of letter under his own hand, to acknowledge the same. Which the said Duke, having refused to do in the terms that it was commanded to him, his Majesty was so much offended therewith, that he hath forbidden him his presence, and hath commanded him to depart the Court.' Another of Monmouth's friends to suffer under the law was

John Hampden, who appeared before Chief Justice Jeffreys on 6 February 1684. The contemporary historian Burnet writes: '. . . there was nothing but Howard of Escrick's evidence against him, without so much as any circumstance to support it. So, since two witnesses were necessary to treason, whereas one was enough for a misdemeanour, he was indicted for a misdemeanour, though the crime was either treason or nothing.' The examination of Howard ran as follows: 'My lord,' said the Lord Chief Justice, 'you seem to speak of a disappointment given to an undertaking by my Lord Shaftesbury. Pray make it as short as you can my Lord.' Howard made a long speech, in which he described how Shaftesbury had told him of his own disappointment, saying: 'There was such a preparation in the city, that if some lords did not unhandsomely desert them they should be in readiness for action quickly. I asked him who he meant? He told me, the duke of Monmouth and my lord Russell had very handsomely deserted him; for they had promised and undertaken to be in readiness with men of several countries [counties?] in which they had an interest.' Howard said that Shaftesbury 'proceeded to speak several sharp things of the duke of Monmouth, upon the account of his ambition, that he thought to have all under his command: which was a secret lurking ambition to him, that he said, he always suspected the duke to be guilty of. And now he found his suspicions true. That unless he might command all, he would do nothing.' Howard then described how he offered himself as mediator between Shaftesbury and Monmouth and went to Moor Park, where he saw Monmouth, who said of Shaftesbury: 'I think the man is mad, what does he mean? We did undertake to do this, it is true; but not by that time he speaks of, and things are not ready, I know what his own fears make him do, but he does act so preposterously that he will undo us all.' Howard suggested that Monmouth should meet Shaftesbury: 'With all my heart, says the duke, I would have nothing more, I desire to speak with him. This made me recoil back again to my Lord Shaftesbury, and told him all this.'

During the course of Hampden's trial Lord Chief Justice Jeffreys remarked: 'It seems my Lord Essex had such an opinion of my Lord Howard's evidence, that he thought fit to cut his own throat, rather than abide the trial.' Many people believed at the time, and many are convinced now, that Lord Essex was murdered in the Tower.

Monmouth failed to appear when called as a witness, and the Lord Chief Justice asked if he had been served with a subpoena. The Attorney General proved that he had instructed someone to serve it, but when his agent Atterbury was examined, he explained that although he went to Moor Park and to the Duke's house in the Cockpit . . . he could obtain nothing but evasive information of Monmouth's whereabouts. Three times an attempt was made to serve Monmouth with a subpoena, but in reply he simply 'nodded his head and smiled, and went away'.

The story of the Rye House episode and its aftermath is bewildering, and it still seems mysterious that even at the end of the seventeenth century a younger brother of the reigning King of England was able to manipulate a trial so effectively, and that his political opponents were judicially executed, owing to flagrant and bare-faced injustice on the part of the highest law officers, after an open trial. At the same time, even the King of England was unable to avert these murders, he himself being 'forced to it, otherwise he must have broke with [York]' – another indication of how real his fear of his brother was. Moreover, when the life of his beloved son, bereft of his murdered supporters, was in jeopardy, though longing to save him, the King was forced to suffer in preventing Monmouth's suffering the fate of his gallant, staunch and clever friends and supporters, Russell, Essex and Sidney (the latter was condemned by the new Lord Chief Justice, that sadistic fiend Judge Jeffreys). The only possible explanation seems to be that during the last few years of Charles II's reign, the Duke of York was the real ruler and even the judges had to conform to his behests.

The King's fear of his brother presumably rested upon his own Catholicism. He had placed his hands upon the Holy Bible and expressed his devotion to the principles of Anglicanism, accepting the crown of his nation and his nation's Church with such marked respect that his later dissension was a blow to all who had previously felt spiritually aligned to him. The Marquis of Halifax was to write years afterwards:

The company he kept, the men in his Pleasures, and the Arguments of State that he should not appear too much of a Protestant, while he expected assistance from a Popish Prince; all these, together with a habit encouraged by an application to his pleasures, did so losen and untie him from his first impressions, that I take it for Granted, after the first year or two, he was no more a Protestant. . . . I concluded that when he came into England he was certainly a Roman Catholick as that he was a man of Pleasure: both very consistent by visible Experience.[11]

Yet it is difficult to understand Charles's motives. Vatican transcripts dated as early as 1651 stress his desire to protect and favour Catholics in the three kingdoms. At that time the Pope declined to admit agents into the royal household until evidence of Charles's personal conversion had been produced. Two years later he again declined financial assistance on the grounds that Charles had not shown sufficient proof of his spiritual conversion. These overtures to Catholicism were not as private as Charles might have hoped, and by 1656 newspapers in The Hague were flaunting the news of the existence of a new Catholic monarch. In the Pope's eyes, Charles was more devoted to a financially stable monarchy than to the Roman faith, and indeed money perpetually dominated most of their correspondence. The added temptation of Louis xiv's model government – free from the parliamentary strings that hampered its English counterpart – may have appealed to Charles. But throughout all these negotiations for secret annuities, there remained in the background that conspicuously Catholic heir. Upon the issue of his brother, Charles would not yield or bend: the rightful heir would reign.

From a purely economic point of view, there was only one eligible prince in Europe whose wealth was comparable to that of the Sun King – Prince William of Orange. It is doubtful, however, whether the Stadtholder would have allowed his family fortune to go the way of Charles's – to his mistresses. Although the lively Restoration court was operating upon a far tighter budget that allowed far less waste than almost any other royal household in Europe at that time, the image Charles projected was to remain until his death that of a spendthrift and a shifty rake. Certainly history might have found him far more sympathetic as a monarch pensioned by a Protestant, rather than a Catholic prince – but what is the likelihood of William ever having considered such an arrangement?

The Prince of Orange did not rally his nation for religion's sake: his people feared political, rather than spiritual, domination. It is unlikely that he would have considered Protestantism essential to English sympathies, except in the advent of a military anti-Reformation. In this light, a pension would best be spent on the purchase of troops, rather than on deceptive English treaties.

That Charles could sidestep, ignore and even blatantly break the treaties he had previously laboured over with much enthusiasm did nothing to enhance his image as a diplomat. William had seen him move with such swiftness in and out of the Triple Alliance that he naturally felt that any treaty with him was not worth the paper it was written on, without tangible security. Louis might have foreseen this too, but then he had the security of Charles's heir and brother, the Duke of York. William's sole security was Monmouth – his only Protestant rival.

To be fair to Charles, it is doubtful whether his devotion to his brother's interests was based on money alone. In the early nineteenth century state papers concerning his friends and acquaintances while he was in exile were made public. Many of the Restoration documents, including the Duke of York's autobiography, were annotated and published during the reigns of George IV and William IV. Among them is an account of Charles's very early conversion, in Europe, before he was received at Dover: 'It was done in the absence of Lord Culpepper, who knowing of it at his return, fell into a great passion and told the King, that he must never expect to see England again, if it should be known there.'[12] This statement echoes Charles's own letter to his younger brother. Henry of Gloucester, who was rumoured at the time to be falling under his mother's Catholic influence. Culpepper's stern warning, written from Cologne, appears almost verbatim in the King's own (or Culpepper's) words.

Many historians, in particular Lord George Scott, stress the valid point that even if Charles did marry Lucy Walter, it would undoubtedly have been a Protestant wedding, and therefore, according to Charles's elastic conscience, not valid for an avowed Roman Catholic.

There is evidence in Clarendon's autobiography that both York and Charles adopted the Catholic faith, or at least entertained sympathy for it, long before the Restoration. York was of course more steadfast in his devotion, especially on the death of his first wife. Presumably, once the Secret Treaty had been signed he was in the position of a blackmailer. Lord George Scott believes this to be very much the case: York kept silent upon what he knew to be true, in return for which Charles secured the succession for him. However unlikely this may sound, the theory that York had a hold over his brother was discussed in the coffee-houses and mentioned in private correspondence. We shall also see that Charles 'became a Catholic' on his deathbed – at a time when York's hold was surely no longer valid. This deathbed conversion has baffled historians for three centuries: could the 'merry monarch', the Protestant monarch, have been a 'villainous' Catholic all along?

Exile

SEVERAL contemporary sources refer to Monmouth's visit to the Netherlands. According to Macpherson's *Original Papers*: 1684 Jan. Sometime after the Duke of Monmouth was forbid the court, he went privately beyond the sea; only one gentleman and a servant along with him. He embarked at Greenwich in a fisherboat, and landed at Tervere, thence he went to Bergen-op-Zoom, Antwerp and Brussels. . . . He said he would go to Holland; and he could say to the Prince of Orange, in a quarter of an hour, that which would satisfy him.'[1] In support of this Bishop Burnet writes:

The duke of Monmouth had lurked in England all this summer, and was then designing to go beyond sea, and to engage in the Spanish service. The King still loved him passionately. Lord Halifax, seeing matters run so much further than he apprehended, thought that nothing could stop that so effectually as the bringing the duke of Monmouth again into favour. That duke wrote to the King several letters, penned with an extraordinary force. Lord Halifax drew them all, as he himself told me and showed me his own draughts of them.[2]

And then we have the following diary entry from Narcissus Luttrell: '1683/4 March 13th. The Duke of Monmouth, since his being out of favour this last time, 'tis said has returned himself to Flanders and that he hath some command in the Spanish forces there.'[3] Meanwhile D'Avaux, the French ambassador in the Netherlands, tells us that Monmouth paid assiduous court to the Prince of Orange. He recounts how one day the Prince dropped his stick when out riding, whereupon Monmouth sprang from his horse, picked it up and handed it to him, 'who remained seated on his horse'. He emphasizes that William 'showed by his kind treatment of the Duke of Monmouth his lack of respect for the King of England and the Duke of York'.[4] In another letter D'Avaux wrote: '. . . that the Prince of Orange and the Duke of Monmouth were about to recover the good graces of the King of England; that his Britannic Majesty was very agreeable to it, provided that the Prince of Orange complied with his desires; that he had begun to conform to them, by no longer keeping Monsieur de Monmouth with him, and that he had detained him only to fulfil his duty.'[5]

What of York's views on the situation? In a letter to his daughter, the Princess of Orange, dated 10 June 1684, he wrote:

I see it troubles you to know that exceptions are found as to the Prince's behaviour to the D. of Mon. and Lord Brandon, and the excuse you make for him is not a good one, for, tho 'tis true that D. of Mon. had his pardon, yet all the world knows what an ill return he made the King for it, which obliged his Ma. to banish him his presence and tho, as the law is here in England, he could not be prosecuted for it, yet 'tis certain his behaviour has been so offensive to his Ma. that really 'twas in my mind as bad as what he was pardoned for; for can anything be more insolent and more offensive than the D. of Mon, refusing to own under his hand, when desired to do it by his Ma., what he declared to the King and myself was, to give both his Ma. and myself the lie, and to make the world believe that the King would have obliged the D. of Mon. to have put that under his hand he had never said? . . . .[6]

Two days later the indignant York fired off a letter to the Prince of Orange, from Windsor: '. . . and, though I believe what you say in that letter, that neither the D. of Mon, nor any of his faction can give you any ill impressions, yet the countenance you give them does encourage them and their party, does you no good, and has ill effect as to his Ma. service; and, let any of them say what they please, there is no trusting them.'[7] (Here the Duke of York, not surprisingly, reveals his intense irritation at the apparently cosy relationship between his daughter and his arch-enemy.)

Allan Fea quotes from 'a letter written by a gentleman' in Brussels to his friend in London, describing Monmouth's reception in the town. The writer welcomes the advent of 'many voluntary Gentlemen of most Nations, Christians, but especially English, in whose valour we have not a little confidence, but are more especially encouraged by having among us the Heroick Pattern of true Valour and Conduct, James Duke of Monmouth, whose brave Achievements at Mons are not, nor never will be erased out of our Memories, his Name being there such a terror to the French, that past doubt next Heaven, it mostly contributed to that Happy Victory.'[8] (This of course refers to Monmouth's part in the relief of Mons in 1678.) In a letter to the Countess of Rutland, Chaloner Chute gives a different view of Monmouth's reception:

1684, July
The Camp at Leffenes . . . The gratious Prince [Monmouth] is our neighbour here at Brussels, and as it is said here the Lady Harriet [Wentworth] with him. We were almost under the walls of the town the other day but yet we can give no other certaine account of him but only this, that he had an affront putt upon him the other day by the English officers in that service, all of them refusing to salute him at a review that there was there. It is said too that he had the same affront putt upon him in Holland.[9]

Concerning Lady Wentworth, Burnet claimed: 'Desperately in love with him, she followed the Duke to the Continent.'[10] Henrietta's mother was also there, and was largely responsible for her daughter's unconventional behaviour.

D'Avaux tells us that in July 1684 the Prince of Orange continued to show 'marks of friendship' for Monmouth and that 'the Prince of Orange ordered all the troops of the States to render Monsieur de Monmouth the same honours they gave the Count de Waldeck, their General'. Charles II had forbidden Englishmen to show Monmouth 'any mark of respect' – to placate York – but

William told the senior British officers in Holland that 'he would break the first who failed' to obey his own commands. D'Avaux continues: '. . . the Prince of Orange had not been content to entertain him [Monmouth] well but . . . he had had him received on his journey to Mineque with outstanding honour', and says that this was more marked, 'for in the towns of the Republic no honour is paid either to passing ambassadors or to other persons of distinguished character'.[11]

At this time William invited Monmouth, Lord Brandon and other Englishmen 'involved in the last plot'[12] to meet him at Diren. On 7 July he wrote to his friend Bentinck: 'I do not think I have given any occasion to his Majesty of being dissatisfied with me for seeing the Duke of Monmouth and Lord Brandon. The first is his son, whom he has pardoned for what he may have committed; and though he has removed him from his presence. I know that in the bottom of his heart he has always some friendship for him, and that the King cannot be angry that I have rendered him some civilities.'[13]

Again D'Avaux tells us that Sir Gabriel Silvius, the British ambassador, complained to the Prince of Orange 'that he was treating Monsieur de Monmouth so well', that he was told in reply that he was 'far from displeasing' the King of England who had said nothing 'except after he had engaged to receive Monsieur de Monmouth at Diren'; that Chudleigh, Charles's envoy, 'who was ordered to speak to him on this subject and who had a letter from the King of England, had kept it in his pocket and excused himself'; and that having received Monmouth, he could not 'drive him away'. D'Avaux proceeds to tell us that Silvius, 'on returning from England', had given a letter from the Duke of York to his daughter the Princess of Orange, 'in which the Duke of York reproached her for having recived the Duke of Monmouth', and that after reading it, she wept and said that 'since the Prince of Orange wishes it so, she must obey'. Silvius further relates: '. . . the Duke of York and the Prince of Orange, had for a month, written to each other twice a week.'[14]

In Leyden Sir Thomas Armstrong, having been detected by a spy, was seized as he was taking a boat to join his companions, and was brought in fetters to Newgate. Clearly William did not approve of this, for when the 'Bailly' of Leyden and his colleagues approached the Prince of Orange about choosing an alderman:

... the Prince of Orange came to them and without waiting for them to speak, addressed the Bailly of Leyden and told him he had been very impudent to dare come before him after the infamous act he had committed in handing over Armstrong to the King of England and asked him if he indeed knew that he was not safe at Diren and that the Duke of Monmouth was there; that he might avenge himself on him for the wicked action he had done; then he drove him in shame from the house and forbade him ever to appear before him.[15]

Armstrong was refused a trial, on the plea that he was an outlaw. The 'infamous Jeffreys' had Armstrong's money seized so that he could not pay any counsel on his own behalf, then told him that as he was an outlaw, he, Jeffreys, could not act 'but to award execution'. Armstrong died a traitor's death at Tyburn, having written: 'I take God to Witness I never was in any design to take away the King's life; neither had any man the impudence to propose so base and barbarous a thing to me. . . . I do verily hope I am going to partake of that fullness of joy which I believe is in his presence; and hopes whereof do infinitely please me.'[16] Lord Grey tells us: 'I received a letter from Monsieur Fuchs, wherein told me, that letters from the duke of Monmouth, directed to him, were taken in Sir Thomas Armstrong's pockets; that they had made a great noise in the court of England, and that not only Mr Godolphin had made a complaint against him to the elector's envoy, for assisting the King's enemies, but that the King had also complained, that the elector gave protection to some who had been in a conspiracy against his life.'[17] It is likely that these letters were entirely unconnected with any treasonable activity.

Armstrong had asked to be shot, having been a lieutenant in the 1st Troop of Guards and Gentleman of Horse to the King, but he was still hanged, drawn and quartered. His head was set above

Westminster Hall and one of his quarters on Wren's new Temple Bar; the other quarters were sent down to be displayed at Stafford, the town he had for many years represented in Parliament. Thus another of Monmouth's friends had been executed.

Meanwhile Monmouth was still in the Netherlands. 'The Duke of Monmouth is at Leyden and the Hague,' wrote Luttrell on 27 October 1684, 'and lives there in great splendour in one of the Prince of Orange's houses, attended by his guards and servants, serv'd from the Prince's own table, and is much respected there.'[18]

D'Avaux entirely misunderstood the situation between Charles and his son when he wrote, at this time, that the Prince of Orange 'was not content to show him [Monmouth] many marks of consideration and friendship on all occasions: he did a thing so offensive to the King of England and the Duke of York that everyone was surprised at it.'[19] Like many others at the time, D'Avaux little knew the extent of the King's duplicity over treatment of his son. But he did fully understand the current indentification of interests between William and Monmouth: 'The Duke of York writes twice a week to the Prince of Orange,' he wrote; and on receipt of these letters, 'The Prince of Orange shuts himself up for two hours with the Duke of Monmouth.'[20] It was an alarming situation for the French ambassador, whose monarch was so firmly in favour of the succession to the English throne of the Catholic Duke of York.

But by the autumn of 1684 Monmouth was already planning a return home – a secret visit in which he could meet his father and gauge how strongly their ties of affection were holding, and, as a contemporary wrote, 'being deeply depressed and troubled in his mind anent the d of York and his Jesuitical Cabal, then plotting how to take the King off the state, which made him resolutely and generously venture to come over to London incognito'.[21]

He arrived in England on 10 November, with no show and no official reception, though, as it turned out, his coming did not go entirely unremarked. Once in London he sent for

... the Lord Arlington, then Governor of the Tower, being his great friend and favourite, telling him that he must needs go to the King and acquaint him that he is in town, and has a business of great importance to impart to him, upon which his Maj sent him word with the bearer when and where to meet him. He was credibly informed that there was a design laying by the Duke of York and his cabal to cut him off, and he could not but venture all that was dearest to him to come and acquaint him therewith. At which the k was a little struck and amazed, not so much from his not being apprehensive of the thing as it should have come the length of his eare when abroad and that he should have shewed so much kindness as to make such a dangerous adventure to inform him; so that after they had discussed to the full ere they parted, the King gave him as many jewels out of his cabinet as were valued at 10,000 lib.sterg. and a secret order to his cashier to pay to the Lord Allington for the use of a friend of his 10,000 lib.sterg. as it is said; so he returned incognito again to Holland.[22]

D'Avaux had soon got wind of the visit, and put it down to the intrigues of Lord Halifax, 'who wished to reinstate the Prince of Orange and the Duke of Monmouth in the good graces of the King of England', his aim being 'to withdraw the Duke of York from affairs'.[23]

Monmouth had his secret interview with his father on 30 November 1684. On 1 December he went to Tilbury, crossed the sea and landed in Nieuport on 10 December, whence he went to Brussels.

By then the very person who Monmouth – and Charles – had least wished to know of the visit, the Duke of York, was fully informed of all that the gossips had to tell. He had written to William of Orange on 2 December: 'As for news, there is little returning amongst us, all things being very quiet here; what is most talked of is about the Duke of Monmouth to know where he is; 'tis believed he is here for several reasons, besides that he was neither in Holland nor Flanders when the last letter came from hence.'[24] A few days later he had written to the first Duke of Queensberry, the Lord Treasurer of Scotland:

I do not think it strange that where you are people have been alarmed at the Duke of Monmouth's being privately here in England, since many loyal people have been so here upon that account; but there is no real danger of it, his Majesty having no inclination to receive his deceiving submissions again. He had kept himself very close here, so that we could never know certainly where he was. I have been positively assured he came over in the same boat with Lady Henrietta Wentworth but whether he be yet here in England, I do not know. . . .[25]

Ten days later he wrote again to Queensberry, now glad to announce that Monmouth had certainly left the country and that so far there had been no dire event as a result of the visit: 'As for news, the Duke of Monmouth arrived at Bruxelles, I think the same day as Lady Henriette Wentworth did. They came over together, and I believe and am confident returned so too. What his business was here I do not know; 'tis said 'twas to get Lady Henriette Wentworth to settle her business upon him. I am sure he has had no other advantage by it, and all things go very well here.'[26]

Nevertheless, Monmouth had been cheered by his meeting with Charles. On 19 December he had had a letter from him, 'bidding me stay till I heard further from him',[27] but on 5 January he wrote in his diary: 'I received a letter from [Halifax] marked by [the King] in the Margin, to trust entirely in [William of Orange], and that in February I should certainly have leave to return, that matters were concerting towards it; and that [York] had no suspicion, notwithstanding my reception here.'[28]

Monmouth's return to Holland saw no lessening of his links with William of Orange. The Prince invited him to visit him at The Hague, and on his arrival 'received him with great demonstrations of joy'.[29] He wanted to bring his wife to see her cousin at once, but as it was late at night, 'she was already half-undressed, but the Prince of Orange made her dress and go to her audience chamber' to meet him.[30] He asked Monmouth to lodge in Prince Maurice's house (the usual lodging for royal guests), and offered him all his servants to attend him there'.[31]

D'Avaux was appalled at the trouble the Prince and his wife were taking to entertain the Duke and wrote on 18 January:

> The Prince of Orange could not flatter the Duke enough; very often there were new balls and parties between them; four or five days before, they had been in a sleigh on the ice with the Princess of Orange . . . and when there was dancing it was the Duke of Monmouth who led out the Princess of Orange. He went everyday to dine with this Princess, although she ate alone and in private; . . . It was even noticed that this Princess, who never walked on foot in public places, went nearly every day in the Mall [with Monmouth] . . . and it could not be understood how the Prince of Orange, born the most jealous of all men, suffered with all the airs of gallantry that everyone remarked between the Princess of Orange and Monsieur de Monmouth.[32]

Hitherto, he claimed, William had never allowed his wife to receive any man – or even woman – privately, but now he

> . . . himself urged Monsieur de Monmouth to go to the after-dinner [receptions] of the Princess of Orange to teach her the Country-Dances. They even made her play a part hardly suitable for a Princess, and which I [D'Avaux] should say would be ridiculous in an ordinary woman; for during the great frost there was this year the Prince of Orange . . . made her learn to skate on the ice, because Monsieur de Monmouth also wished to learn to do so. It was a very extraordinary thing to see the Princess of Orange with very short skirts, half tucked back and with iron skêtes on her feet, learning to slide, first on one foot, then on the other.[33]

Perhaps William was sure that the presence of Lady Wentworth in his city was a sure sign that Monmouth would not pay serious court to Princess Mary.

The generous entertainment that the Oranges afforded their cousin was enough to bring in a flock of flatterers from among the Dutch: 'Nobody considers they have conducted themselves well at Court with the Prince of Orange,' wrote D'Avaux bitterly, 'if they do not do the same to Monsieur de Monmouth, and all the persons of highest rank in Holland hastened in rivalry of each other to entertain him.'[34]

The reason for Prince William's kind treatment of Monmouth – who was, after all, the Oranges' main rival for the title of Protestant successor to the English throne – may just possibly have lain in his belief that Charles had married Monmouth's mother. He may have heard from his own mother that many years before she used to treat Monmouth's mother as a married woman. Tradition has it that Princess Mary had in her possession letters from her aunt/mother-in-law in which the elder Princess Mary referred to Lucy Walter as Charles's wife. Tradition also has it that after Monmouth's death Mary gave these letters into the safe keeping of his friend Archbishop Tenison, so that posterity might know the truth of his birth. But it is more likely that William and Mary had received secret instructions from Charles to treat Monmouth kindly. There was certainly a system of signs between uncle and nephew by which William could tell whether the contents of Charles's letters conveyed his own views or were written out of political expedience. The two of them had established a good relationship and some unity of purpose, as Bishop Burnet reveals.

The Prince [of Orange] had come for a few days to England after the Oxford Parliament, [ie after March 1681] and had much private discourse with the King at Windsor. The King assured him that he would keep things quiet, and not give way to the Duke [of York's] eagerness, as long as he lived; and added, he was confident whenever the Duke [of York] should come to reign, he would be so restless and violent, that he could not hold it four years to an end. This I had from the Prince's own mouth. Another passage was told to me by the Earl of Portland. The King showed the Prince one of his seals, and told him, that whatever he might write to him, if the letter was not sealed with that seal, he was to look on it as only drawn from him by importunity. The reason for which I mention that in this place is, because, though the King wrote some terrible letters to the Prince, against the countenance he gave to the Duke of Monmouth, yet they were not sealed with that seal; from which the Prince inferred, that the King had a mind that he should keep him about him, and use him well. And the King gave orders, that in all the entries that were made in the council books of this whole business, nothing should be left on record that could blemish him.[35]

William was convinced that Charles had not cast off his son, for 'though he removed him from his presence, I [William] know that in the bottom of his heart, he has always some friendship for him, and that the King cannot be angry with him'.[36]

Meanwhile Monmouth was convinced that his period of exile was nearly over. On 3 February he wrote in his diary: 'A letter from [Halifax] that my business was almost as well as done; but must be so sudden as not to leave room for [York's] party to counterplot.'[37] At last, he believed, the King would send York back to Scotland and bring him, Monmouth, home.

But even as he wrote, Charles II lay dying.

On the evening of Sunday, 1 February, the King had been enjoying his usual recreations. The diarist Evelyn was a witness:

> I can never forget the inexpressible luxury and profaneness, gaming and all dissoluteness as it were to total forgetfulness of God [it being Sunday evening] which . . . I was witness of the King sitting and toying with his concubines, Portsmouth (Louise de Keroualle], Cleveland [the former Lady Castlemaine] and Mazarin [Hortense Mancini]. A french boy singing love songs in that glorious galley, whilst about twenty of the great courtiers and other dissolute persons were at basset around a large table, a bank of at least two thousand in gold before them.[38]

This turned out to be a description of the eve of tragedy, for Charles's fatal illness struck him down the following morning, and he died on 6 February.

Monmouth felt it deeply that his father, who had demonstrated a deep love for him, failed to mention his name on his deathbed. When he heard the news of Charles's death, he gave way to great grief.

England now had, with the succession of the Duke of York as

King James II, a Catholic monarch. Monmouth could not bring himself to write to his uncle. Henceforth he could live only by his sword, on his wife's generosity or on Henrietta Wentworth's bounty. He knew that unless he went home as a conqueror, England was now closed to him.

Two Invasions

THE English exiles living in Holland in 1685 had mainly taken refuge there because they had been involved in plots againt the life of the King or of his brother, for the Protestant religion and Nonconformity, though in danger, were not being actively persecuted at that time. The Scottish exiles, on the other hand, were the victims of much more aggressive actions on the part of their Stuart persecutors. The English government was in fact plotting against the life of the Scottish Church. The Duke of York, who was a Royal Commissioner for Scotland, had ordered the confiscation of Church property, the imprisonment of ministers and wanton penalizing of innocent and sincere Presbyterians, who were denied their property and their freedom and sentenced to death at the slightest sign of trouble. For instance, Archibald Campbell, ninth Earl of Argyll, had been so sentenced for refusing to take the Test Act, but had escaped.

Consequently, the Scottish Earl of Argyll was more urgent in his purpose of rebellion than Monmouth and the other English malcontents. In the spring of 1684 he was preparing an invasion force with which he would return to his Highlands and fight the English, so as to preserve the liberties of the Scottish Kirk and the Scottish nation. He regarded himself as superior to Monmouth, whom he saw as nothing more than a military commander, and whom he did not want with him, on the grounds that his talents were inadequate for the partisan warfare among the Scottish clans that would result from the invasion.

Monmouth had refused to promise his services to the plotters of this rebellion while his father was alive, as his love for him was too great. But when his father died the die was cast. Argyll wished to invade without delay, but the English plotters deemed the adventure too hazardous for haste. Argyll, in his high-minded way, paid little attention to them, even to the point of refusing to acquaint them with the details of his plans and the adequacy of his resources. On 2 May he sailed with three ships, the *Anna*, the *Sophia* and the *David*, for the Orkneys, with a fair wind.

Arriving on the 6th, he found the Campbells of these islands apathetic to the call to arms, but, moving on to Campbeltown, on Kintyre, he successfully organized a gathering of the clans, round the isthmus of Tarbert. This new army was then divided into two halves: Argyll and Rumbold remained in the Highlands. while Sir Patrick Hume and Cochrane sailed east to land at Greenock. The attempt to rouse the Lowland people failed, and the whole army met again on the Isle of Bute. The news of the landing of Argyll's expedition did not reach James II until 22 May; he immediately informed Parliament, which had met on that very day for the first time since his coronation. It was thought unlikely that there would be a separate expedition on behalf of Monmouth, and the government expected him to join Argyll in Scotland, Though the West Country had long been viewed with suspicion as a possible place of rebellion, Monmouth's actual place of landing, Lyme Regis at the southernmost border of Devon and Dorset, was kept completely secret from James II's spies.

His force sailed on 24 May. There were eighty-three men in three ships: Monmouth with such men as Andrew Fletcher of Saltoun, Colonel Foulkes and Nathaniel Wade – all fine soldiers – and Robert Ferguson, who was appointed Chaplain-General to the rebel army. Though their destination was secret, the fact of their sailing was known through information sent from The Hague, and James II complained of Prince William's carelessness in allowing three ships to set sail. Their destination was unknown even to some members of their own party, including one Tillier, who was told by Colonel Foulkes that he was bound for service with the Elector of Brandenburg. When Tillier found out his true destination he was given the choice of being held a prisoner or accepting a commission in Monmouth's army. He chose the latter.

At daybreak of Tuesday, 11 June, after a long voyage with contrary winds, the three boats reached Lyme. The delay had been to their advantage, as the alarm caused by the news of their departure had by this time died down. They stood off the harbour all day while a customs official examined them. A certain degree of alarm spread among the local inhabitants, but the harbour defences could not shoot, as no gunpowder was available. Two of the arrivals disembarked and rode towards Taunton to seek out those Monmouth sympathizers who would be most helpful in the coming campaign.

All day long the town was in uncertainty, until at twilight the rest of the party disembarked. As the sun set Monmouth, dressed in a magnificent purple and red uniform, with a silver star on his breast, set his standard with the words 'For Religion and Liberty' on the Church Cliff. Monmouth now made his party kneel and offer up a prayer of thanksgiving for their safe arrival, then led them by a path over a cliff into the town, but with difficulty, as large crowds had gathered. At the market place he had the following declaration read aloud:

As Government was originally instituted by God, for the peace, happiness and security of the Governed, and not for the private interest or personal greatness of those that rule: so that Government has always been esteemed the best where the supreme magistrates have been vested with all the Power and Prerogatives that might capacitate, not only to preserve the people from Violence and Oppression, but to promote their Prosperity; and yet where nothing was to belong to them by the Rules of the Constitution that might enable them to injure and oppress them.

And it hath been the glory of England, above most other nations, that the Prince had all entrusted with him that was necessary either for the advancing the Welfare of the people, or for his own protection in the discharge of his office; and withal stood so limited and restrained by the Fundamental Terms of the constitution, that without violation of

The Duchess of
Monmouth with her
two children

Lady Henrietta Wentworth

The Earl of Shaftesbury

James, Duke of York

William and Mary

The Battle of Sedge-
moor

The death of the
Duke of Monmouth

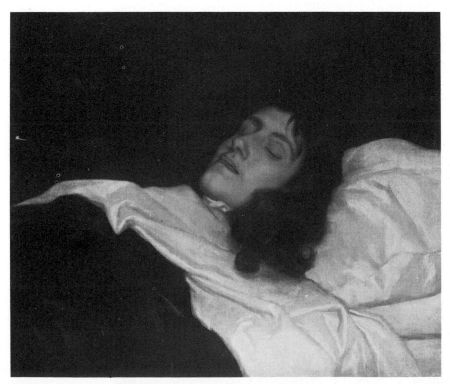

his own oath, as well as the rules and measures of the Government, he could do them no hurt, or exercise any act of authority, but through the administration of such hands as stood obnoxious to be punished in case they transgressed; so that, according to the primitive frame of Government; the Prerogatives of the Crown and the Privileges of the subject were so far from jostling one another, that the Rights reserved unto the people tended to render the King honourable and great; and the Prerogatives settled on the Prince were in order to the subjects' Protection and Safety.

But all humane things being libable to Perversion as well as decay, it hath been the fate of the English Government to be often changed, and wrested from what it was in the first settlement and institution. And we are particularly compelled to say, that all the boundaries of the Government have of late been broken, and nothing left unattempted for turning our Limited Monarchy into absolute Tyranny. For such has been the transaction of affairs within this nation for many years long past, that though the Protestant religion and Liberties of the people were fenced and hedged about by as many laws as the wisdom of man could devise for their Preservation against Popery and arbitary power, our religion has been all along undermined by Popish Councils, and our privileges ravished from us by Fraud and Violence. And more especially, the whole course and series of the life of the present usurper hath been but one continued conspiracy against the Reformed Religion, and Rights of the Nations.[1]

This declaration (the work of Ferguson) continued for many thousands of words and is too long to quote in full. It put forward the view that James II was a villain who should be brought to justice; a murderer who had caused the deaths of the Earl of Essex and Sir Edmund Berry Godfrey; a usurper who had poisoned his own brother; an incendiarist who had contrived the burning of London in 1666; and, above all, a traitor who had betrayed the English people by filling the legislature and executive with Papists and depriving Protestants of their freedom. It urged everyone to fight the King and his Parliament by bringing 'war and destruction' to the present seat of government, or else the whole nation would be forcibly converted to Popery.

Owing to the great length of this declaration, it is probable that Monmouth did not read it before attaching his signature. If he had, he would surely have objected to a sentence that ran: 'And forasmuch as the said James Duke of Monmouth, the now head and Captain General of the Protestant forces of this Kingdom, assembled in pursuance of the ends aforesaid, hath been, and still is believed, to have a legitimate and legal right to the crowns of England, Scotland, France and Ireland, with the Dominions thereunto belonging. . . .'[2]

The truth is that as an alternative to James II, Monmouth had a faith in Protestantism and a wish that it should prevail; a degree of toleration for dissent that also extended mercy to Catholics, provided they were not harming Protestants; and sufficient modesty even to refuse the crown, if the people of England did not want him. These virtues were obscured by the hot-headed proclamations that were delivered and widely published by his staff. It was perhaps his neglect to moderate their extreme ambition that caused the harsh treatment meted out to those of his followers who became prisoners of the King.

The problem of enrolling recruits was easily solved: 80 volunteers had joined Monmouth at the moment of landing, and by the end of the next day the total had grown to 1000 and 150 horses. The mayor of Lyme, Gregory Alford, was not one of the sympathizers. He sent horsemen to scour the country for the two men who had disembarked earlier, and that evening rode to Honiton; from there he continued to Exeter to warn the Duke of Albemarle, and to send word to Colonel Luttrel at Taunton. Both men were commanders of the local militia. Though the postal services at that time were not very reliable, a letter was also dispatched to London. Late that night two customs officers, Dassell and Thorold, who had been watching the events of the day carefully, decided to ride all the way to London, to give an account personally to James II. Calling at the mayor's house, they found him gone, but his daughter procured them a coach-horse, on which they galloped, the two of them on the one mount, sixteen miles to Crewkerne. Here lived Winston Churchill, the father of John Churchill, who became the great Duke of Marlborough. Calling at the Churchill home and mounting fresh horses, they rode all that night and all the next day. It was not until four o'clock in the morning on Saturday the thirteenth that they roused the King from his bed and were given each £20 each for their pains.

Parliament was called and a bill of attainder prepared, convicting Monmouth of high treason, with all the usual penalties of forfeiture and death. Dragoons and horse under John Churchill were sent from London, and Parliament voted a reward of £5000 for anyone delivering Monmouth, dead or alive.

Monmouth made the 'George Inn' his home during the four days he spent at Lyme. He had three thousand followers by the end of the fourth day. When a group of men volunteered to fight for him, Ferguson or another officer would take a note of their names, and they would be told to go with this list to the town hall, where they would be given arms. From there they would be sent to the various officers guarding the approaches to the town, where they would be put in order and exercised.

For the last day at Lyme Monmouth had planned an attack on the local militia at Bridport, ten miles away. He rightly thought that an early offensive was his best hope, since the odds would be greatly against him once the country's full military strength was mobilized. At dawn on Sunday morning, with the help of a thick mist, the rebel force, consisting of cavalry under Lord Grey and infantry under Major Wade took the Bridport militia by surprise. But at the first musket volley Grey's cavalry bolted and did not stop galloping the whole way back to Lyme. Monmouth then set out with a party of men to find out what had happened to the infantry, and happily found them marching home, in good order, with thirty additional horses and a dozen prisoners.

At 10 am on Monday Monmouth marched out of Lyme Regis with three thousand men. His first main objective was Taunton. On the way he passed through such small towns as Axminster,

Chard and Ilminster. Round Axminster his troops had a brush with the Devon and Somerset militia, but the militia fled, leaving arms, coats and more than half the Somerset men as deserters. If this was typical of their spirit, the future for the rebels was hopeful. On Tuesday the sixteenth they reached Chard, where they were joined by forty extra horsemen under John Speke of White Lackington. That night was spent at Ilminster.

By 4 am the next morning the streets of Taunton were already crowded, and when, twelve hours later, Colonel Hucker and a troop of horse entered the town, the excitement was redoubled. Monmouth camped in a field outside the town the following night, and did not enter with the main force until the morning of Thursday, 18 June.

The entry into Taunton was the most colourful highlight of the campaign. The roads were strewn with flowers and every inhabitant of the town was either out in the streets or gaping out of a window. At the market cross, once the declaration had been read out in the usual manner, a second announcement was made – the 'proclamation against pillage': 'Whereas, to the great scandal and reproach of the Cause we are engaged in, and contrary to our intentions and our express command, several lewd and dissolute persons [had robbed the people of everything they could find] to our unspeakable grief and trouble, our designs and intentions being only to relieve the distressed and oppressed and not to increase their grievances.'[3] The proclamation threatened with death anyone seizing anything without written authority. It also promised compensation for those who had been so deprived of their possessions.

During the three days he spent at Taunton, Monmouth lodged at Captain Tucker's house, near the 'Three Cups Inn'. On the second day twenty-seven young girls appeared outside his door, each with a Bible, and he honoured each of them with a kiss. This 'Presentation by the Maids of Taunton' became quite famous in illustrations and stories of the rebellion.

On his last day in Taunton Monmouth was proclaimed King.

In organizing this proclamation, he sought to protect his followers against the failure of his expedition by taking advantage of a statute dating from the reign of Henry VII that gave total immunity to all persons obeying a king, no matter how defective his title might later be considered to be. He himself had always said that if it were necessary to assume the crown for the purposes of establishing the revolution, he would later submit the question of his continuing as king to Parliament.

On the twenty-first he marched out of Taunton with seven thousand men. In the ten days since his landing the whole country had been alerted. Every moment of the day and night a watch had to be kept against attack from any quarter. Every day there came a scare that someone, such as Albemarle, the Lord Lieutenant of Devonshire, was attacking: guns would be dragged down streets, troops detailed to line hedgerows, or lie concealed with their muskets in neighbouring meadows, to creep furtively round the edge of the town to mask another approach road, or challenge a newcomer galloping down a country lane towards them with white-hot news. With a £5000 reward on his head, Monmouth was in perpetual danger from the crowds in the street where he was quartered. Nor could he count on the loyalty of his own volunteers: it is said that he was fired at on three different occasions by members of his own army.

Arriving at Bridgwater later on the twenty-first, he was greeted by the mayor and corporation, who willingly read out the proclamation at the market cross. He set up his headquarters in the ruined castle on the west side of the river, while his army camped in the castle field.

On the twenty-second he moved out of Bridgewater, choosing a road leading slightly south of east, through Weston Zoyland three miles away and across the level peat soil of King's Sedgemoor to Glastonbury, a distance of nearly fifteen miles. The drought that had gripped the land for the last two years suddenly ended, and rain poured down on the army, coinciding with the first change in direction of the rebels' forty-five-mile advance.

As they slushed through the muddy lane out of Bridgwater they saw on their left the small village of Chedzoy, whose vicar, the Reverend Andrew Paschall, was a keen observer of events and left a reliable account of them.[4] Exactly six months earlier, at dawn on 21 December 1684, he had observed in the sky above Weston Zoyland a number of parhelia or false suns – balls of fire hanging above the horizon on a clear frosty morning, resembling the rising sun, but too far south to be the real thing. Linking this in his mind with events five years earlier, when babies had been born curiously joined one to another down half of their bodies, and remembering an earthquake that had recently shaken his house, he concluded that all these were omens of impending disaster. Just three weeks before he had written a letter for the attention of King James II, entreating him to cast an eye in this direction, so certain was he of the ominous nature of these phenomena.

The ruins of Glastonbury Abbey, though in a better state of preservation than they are today, were not ideal for sheltering eight thousand men and a thousand horses, and it is not surprising that some of the troops moved on to Wells to find a more comfortable billet for the night. Those left in Glastonbury lit large fires among the ruins, but it was with relief that they resumed their journey.

The sight of Monmouth's vast army, moving with gathering strength and determination, caused the Bridgwater 'club men' (an association formed during the civil war to protect the area from plundering armies) to assemble again after forty years of tranquillity. Monmouth mistakenly thought that they were loyal to him, for one of their members rode to Glastonbury to assure him that they would fight for his cause. Whether this man was misinforming him deliberately, or was acting out of misplaced zeal, is uncertain. At any rate Monmouth officially enrolled the great 'club army' under his banner. But instead of the many thousands of reinforcements that had been promised, none appeared until the end of the rebellion, and their number was a mere 160.

The next stop was Shepton Mallet, where Monmouth spent the night at the home of Edward Strode, whose brother William was in prison for his rebellious views. While in prison he had managed to send money and horses from his estate near Ilminster to the rebels at Lyme Regis, and Edward now gave Monmouth a present of 100 guineas.

At a council of war Monmouth informed his officers of his intention to attack Bristol. Major Wade, who was a Bristol man, advised crossing the River Avon at Keynsham, and attacking the city from the Gloucestershire side. The city was rich in provisions, money and arms, and would be a most valuable prize. The overall plan was for the army to continue the march to Gloucester, cross the River Severn, then, keeping the river on their right, move through Shropshire to Cheshire, where there would be considerable reinforcements organized by Monmouth's friends Lord Delamere and Lord Macclesfield, the latter with his son Brandon. The combined force would march on London, where three thousand men were reputedly waiting to assist him, under Wildman and Danvers. In spite of his present strength, Monmouth did not contemplate an immediate march on London. In this he was sensible, for the weather was bad and was to continue so for many days. His men were averaging little more than twelve miles per day, and the feeling was growing that such slow progress could not be maintained without something decisive happening. It would probably be a fortnight before they reached the capital, and resistance would stiffen as they moved out of the friendly West Country towards an enemy whose line of communication would be shortening. A brilliant victory now could make all the difference.

It was at Shepton Mallet that Major Oglethorpe discovered them. He had left London three days before, in charge of a reconnaissance party of fifty mounted guards, whose assignment was to seek out the exact whereabouts of the rebel army and report to his chief, Lewis Duras, Earl of Feversham, who had just been appointed Lieutenant-General of all the King's forces in the West and had set out on the same day, but by a different route, from London to Bristol. On the way there Feversham, with his party of two hundred guards, had linked with the Earl of Pembroke and his Wiltshire and Hampshire militia at Chippenham. On the twenty-third they arrived at Bristol, which was guarded by the Duke of Beaufort and the Gloucester, Monmouth and Hereford militia. The next day Feversham moved back to Bath, where he found Oglethorpe, but he instantly dispatched him again to gather more certain information regarding the enemy's strength and intentions.

The Duke of Somerset was also to be found at Bath, much distressed about the number of desertions. The greater part of the Somerset militia had in fact deserted to Monmouth within a day or two of his leaving Lyme; their officers did not seem to have any control over them, and Albemarle's army, which had out-numbered Monmouth's by a thousand men, fell back on the fifteenth and refused to fight. Somerset had been left with only one regiment of foot and a troop of horse, 'which', he deplored, 'I'm afraid will hardly stand, because the others have showed them the way to run'.[5]

All the while that the rebel army had been advancing in triumph, they were being mildly harassed from behind by dragoons under Colonel John Churchill, who had arrived from London on the sixteenth. With Churchill was one Colonel Kirke, already well known as an officer of 'the Lambs' – the nickname for the Royal West Surreys, who had distinguished themselves in garrisoning Dunkirk, and later, as the 'Tangerines', in garrisoning Tangier. There was also a troop under Lord Oxford. To have such dangerous men close on Monmouth's heels, so close that they could occupy a town on the very day he had left it, and ever appearing unexpectedly for a brief exchange of gunfire, would keep him and his men alert the whole time. And there was always Albemarle a few miles to the west, and Lord Bath behind him.

. . . . . .

After one night at Shepton Mallet, Monmouth turned due north for Bristol, exactly twenty miles away. He reached Pensford towards evening. Hearing that the bridge over the Avon had been destroyed at Keynsham, he sent a party to repair it under cover of darkness, while his army rested at Pensford, within five miles of the city. The bridge, which was more or less in midway position, was successfully repaired by Captain Tyley and his men, who also defeated a company of Gloucestershire militia, taking two horses and a prisoner.

At ten the next morning Monmouth led his army, now eight thousand strong, over the bridge and then back again, as though testing its strength, but really to confuse the enemy, who were now only three miles off. He decided to pitch camp where he was, but his soldiers, who were in the process of finding quarters in the village, were surprised by the sudden appearance of Major Oglethorpe, who galloped through the narrow streets with two troops of horse, thinking he was among friends. Realizing his mistake, he charged the nearest group of soldiers, and an improvised battle began. Monmouth's cavalry dashed to the rescue, and Oglethorpe was driven off – but not before he had killed fourteen men, including Captain Brand of the rebel cavalry. He left behind only three prisoners, who informed Monmouth that Feversham was waiting outside the city gates with an army of four thousand.

This was a decisive moment in the story of the rebellion. Monmouth had to decide whether or not to fight the King's army, now concentrated round Bristol. He was very short of artillery, having only four cannon, while the Royalists had sixteen, as well as the existing city defences. If, in the ensuing battle, Feversham withdrew into the city and fortified it, could he conduct an effective siege with such a few cannon? For assaulting a fortified town, a preliminary bombardment is certainly effective. But this should not deter him, as there was very little chance of his ever obtaining superiority in artillery: from time to time promises to supply a few extra guns were made, but they came to nothing.

The other problem was the cavalry. No one wanted a repetition of the Bridport fiasco, when, through no fault of their masters, the untrained horses had taken fright at the unaccustomed sound of gunfire. Had the horses now had time to get to know their masters? And had their masters had time to accustom them to the novel situations of a military campaign? In any case, the cavalry would always be an uncertain arm, in view of the lack of training of the improvised soldiery. On the other hand, if Monmouth could defeat Feversham now, he would temporarily have defeated the whole Royalist strength. Feversham's army represented about the maximum that James II could put into the field, and though the militia could muster more than ten thousand, they had already shown how profitable to the rebels an encounter might be. If God granted Monmouth a victory now, he could march straight to London, without the weary detour through Gloucestershire, Shropshire and Cheshire.

Doubtless he and his staff considered several plans of attack, such as creating a great diversion on the south-western side of Bristol, but then assaulting it from the east. Several of his soldiers, including Colonel Wade and Captain Tyley, were Bristol men and knew the layout well. What made him decide against such a plan? There was a promise from a Mr Adlam of four hundred horses awaiting him in Wiltshire. But although this promise was never fulfilled, it was not a decisive factor, since Monmouth had plenty of horses. A more likely reason for his decision is the danger that his presence created for the inhabitants of Bristol. The Duke of Beaufort had already imprisoned seventy of the dissenting leaders, and had threatened that at the first sign of a demonstration in favour of Monmouth he would level the city to the ground by cannonade from the castle. Between 10 and 11 o'clock on the night of the twenty-fourth, while the rebel army was still at Pensford, a fire was seen in the direction of Bristol. This aroused fears that Beaufort was carrying out another of his threats: to destroy the city by fire. Monmouth is reported to have reacted by saying: 'God forbid that I shall be accessory to the ruin of my friends, or that for any consideration I should subject so great a city to the double calamity of sword and fire.'[6] The fact was that a ship in Bristol harbour, called the *Abraham and Mary*, had been fired by Monmouth's own sympathizers, who thought that they could create a diversion in so doing and thus allow the rebels to effect an entry. But Beaufort, with his twenty-one companies drawn up threateningly on Redcliffe Mead, effectively quelled the alarm that was spreading through the streets.

Like the inhabitants of Bristol themselves, Monmouth appears to have been daunted by the determined readiness to resist on the part of the Royalists – a readiness evinced by Feversham with his army of four thousand, and by the Duke of Beaufort's threatening attitude. This determination, coming sooner than Monmouth had really anticipated, demonstrates the high level of efficiency in Feversham's organization.

Monmouth now found himself in the position of volunteering to fight an army of which he had formerly been the commander-in-chief, including regiments he had personally commanded in battle over a period of seventeen years, and a great many personal friends. Daunted, he spent much time in prayer; the motto 'Fear nothing but God' was written in gold letters on his green-coloured standard, as well as being inscribed in the pocket-book he always carried with him.[7] Among the prayers, verses, strains of music, recipes, charms, itineraries, conjurings, notes on warfare and other items, this book also contains a drawing by the Abbé Pregnani of the 'Wheel of Pythagoras', an intricate device designed by a series of complicated calculations to give answers to questions on 'Life', 'Death'. 'Happiness' and 'Adversity'.[8] It seems likely that a superstitious man like Monmouth may have been influenced by an adverse answer to the question he asked 'the wheel' on Thursday, 25 June. At any rate, he must have thought that God was no longer on his side, as he crept away at midnight, moving south-east towards Bath.

Sunrise found the rebel army on the hills overlooking the city. Monmouth now sent a herald to order the citizens to surrender, but the city guards shot him dead. Making their weary way southwards, his troops arrived, after a further five miles, at the village of Norton St Philip. Monmouth put up at the Old House, posting his four cannon by the market cross outside his door and ordering his infantry to camp in two fields behind the town. They were allowed a night's sleep before the next ordeal, which they had to face the following morning, 27 June. Looking in the direction of Bath, they saw the entire Royalist army advancing steadily towards them.

The approach to the village was by a lane lined with thick hedges, and at the point where the lane joined the village Monmouth had already erected a barricade manned by fifty men under Captain Vincent. Seeing the advance guard of forty-five grenadiers under his half-brother the Duke of Grafton approach the lane a quarter of a mile off, Monmouth was able to bring up musketeers to the hedges in such a way that Grafton and his grenadiers did not see them until they had almost reached the village. They were fired on from both sides and well and truly ambushed. As they battled on into the village, a third fusillade greeted them from the barricade across their front. Cut off from the rear by a swiftly executed cavalry manoeuvre organized by Monmouth himself, some of the grenadiers managed to force their way through the thick hedges, only to die in the cornfields beyond, while those who retreated were harried by the cavalry and those who stayed in the village were killed or taken prisoner. Twice reinforcements were thrown in by Feversham to help Grafton, but Monmouth still won the day. The Royalists lost at least eighty men – a hundred by some accounts – while the rebel losses did not exceed eighteen.

For the rest of the day a cannonade was kept up between the King's forces, whose sixteen cannon were stationed five hundred yards away, and the four guns of the rebels, two of which were at the entrance to the village and two on rising ground to the right. Though this bombardment continued for many hours only one man, a rebel, was hit, which says very little for the efficiency of the artillery on either side. The rain was pouring down hard, which may have affected their accuracy, and most of Monmouth's men obviously withdrew out of Royalist range.

But as evening approached, Monmouth, showing great determination, decided to attack, and started clearing paths through the hedges for his army to pass. At this point Feversham decided to withdraw, and the great Royalist army retreated seven miles north-east, to Bradford-on-Avon. At the same time the rebels were trudging through heavy rain and mud in the small hours of the morning of 28 June until they came to Frome, six miles away.

During the two days Monmouth spent at Frome as many as two thousand men deserted him. Probably the disappointment of not having fought a decisive battle, coupled with the foul weather, made the temptation of their own homes and hearths over-mastering. Discipline, which had been excellent, now deteriorated. Several murders were committed and houses were plundered. When the news of Argyll's defeat reached the rebels at Frome, Monmouth seriously considered abandoning the whole enterprise and taking ship to Holland. Two senior officers, Colonel Venner and Major Parsons, attempted to do so, and later the paymaster, Goodenough, disappeared, with £400 out of the funds.

Argyll had been made a prisoner ten days before, after making a forlorn attempt to take Glasgow. He had lost his supply ships, and his force had also dwindled from two thousand to a mere five hundred by the time he launched his attack. Defeated and taken prisoner on the same day, he was removed to Edinburgh Castle, where he was tried and found guilty of his original crime of refusing to take the Test, and was executed on the last day of June. He behaved with great coolness throughout: riding with his hands tied behind his back from Glasgow to Edinburgh; treating the trial with unconcern; sleeping in his cell until two hours before his execution. On the scaffold he gently measured the block with a pocket rule and pointed out that it was not lying even. The executioner adjusted it and performed his office efficiently.

On the day that Argyll was executed, Monmouth turned west and returned to Shepton Mallet. He had wanted to move in the direction of London, but Feversham had marched across his intended route as far as Westbury, and this had deterred him. The path of the rebel army so far had outlined the shape of an axe – appropriately enough for an enterprise involving high treason. The four corners of the blades lay at Bristol, Bath, Frome and Shepton Mallet – this being the point at which the blade joined the handle, stretching crookedly down via Bridgwater and Taunton to the south coast.

Monmouth still had enough men to fight a decisive battle, and he had now to find a way of achieving this successfully. Bridgwater was chosen as a base, to occupy and fortify, before exploring new areas.

The Battle of Sedgemoor

THE Royalist force that we last saw marching from Bradford to Westbury had a total of about 2800 regular soldiers. The infantry consisted of one battalion of Dunbarton's Scots, two battalions of Grenadier Guards, one of Coldstream Guards, one of Trelawney's regiment and two under Colonel Kirke, making a total of 2100; the cavalry of three companies of Horse Guards, seven of the King's Regiment of Horse and three of Dragoons, making a further 700. These figures included the crews of the 16 cannon, and their horses, which were supplied from the coach-horses of Bishop Mews of Winchester, who was also there, dressed in armour, fighting alongside them. Every battalion had a company of grenadiers attached; these were bombers rather than guardsmen. There were also considerable numbers of militia on hand, though they were merely held in readiness and did not actually take part in the fighting.

Monmouth's force, which outnumbered the Royalist regulars by about 700, was divided into 5 regiments of foot and 1 of horse: the Red Regiment under Colonel Wade (800); the Blue under Colonel Basset (600); the Green under Colonel Holmes (600); the Yellow under Matthews (500); and the White under Colonel Foulkes (400). The Horse under Lord Grey amounted to 600. The total of infantry was 2900, and of cavalry 600. There were 4 cannon. Monmouth possessed very few grenades, but had collected instead 1000 scythemen, with the blades of their scythes attached to long poles, and these he allotted to his regiments to the tune of 200 apiece.

Of his regimental commanders, all had landed with Monmouth at Lyme Regis except for Colonel Basset, who had joined him at Taunton with a force of 800 which he had personally mustered. Basset had been a captain under Cromwell forty years earlier, whereas Wade, who had distinguished himself during the Bridport incident, for which he was promoted to the rank of colonel, had originally been not a soldier but a lawyer. Wade showed himself to be a most energetic and useful leader and while at Lyme had formed the 'Duke's Regiment', which became the 'Red Regiment' – the Duke himself organizing his own bodyguard of forty horsemen. Colonel Holmes had had one arm shot away three days before, at Norton St Philip, but with surpassing gallantry stayed fighting until the rebellion was over. Lord Grey was the only man present who was a friend of Monmouth's of long standing, and it must have been a comfort to have him there. He behaved with courage throughout, in what was perhaps the most difficult job of all.

Another man who, like Basset, had joined the rebels at Taunton was Colonel Perrot. He had been a lieutenant under General Harrison in the civil war, and after the Restoration had become an associate of the notorious 'Captain Blood', one of the greatest villains in history. Perrot was actually one of the five accomplices in Blood's daring attempt to steal the crown jewels in 1671.

Robert Ferguson, chief of the chaplains attending the army, had been born in Aberdeenshire and had held a living in Kent until he was dismissed under the Act of Uniformity of 1662. A thin man, with bright eyes and a Roman nose, a loud Scottish accent and an inimitable shuffling way of walking, he had an explosive manner that inspired awe in all who met him. Happiest when preaching to vast crowds from his pulpit in Moorfields, he spent the rest of his time hatching seditious plots or exposing conspiracies, writing numerous tracts in the process. A man of great personal courage (he insisted on being in the forefront of all the fighting), he belonged to the class of prelates who were as much soldiers as priests. Others included Bishop Mews of Winchester, who was nearly seventy years old when he put his armour on to fight against Monmouth, and then volunteered three years later to do the same against William of Orange. He is said to have been the last English prelate to shed blood in battle. Yet another was Nathaniel Hook, who was Monmouth's personal chaplain throughout the rebellion and later joined the army of Louis XIV, in which he rose to the high rank of lieutenant general and fought in many campaigns in many lands.

The command of the rebel cavalry would not have been chiefly in Grey's hands had not a strange incident occurred soon after their arrival at Lyme. It will be remembered that two men in Monmouth's party had been the first to land and had galloped northwards to spread the news and fetch assistance. These two men were Hayward Dare and Chamberlain. Dare had returned with forty new horses, himself riding a particularly fine mount. But Fletcher of Saltoun, who was then sharing the command of the cavalry with Grey, claimed this horse as his; when Dare protested he shot him with his pistol and killed him. Monmouth promptly put Fletcher back on board the frigate they had sailed in, and he was forced to remain on board when it sailed away to Spain.

Monmouth spent his night at Shepton Mallet at the home of Edward Strode, a mile from the town, while his men quartered themselves on almost every house in the town. Some exciting news reached them there on the morning of 1 July: some wagons had been left behind at Wells by Colonel Kirke's regiment, and were being guarded by only a few dragoons. Naturally Wells was chosen as the next stop, and the carriages were secured, with arms, ammunition and money in them. The *London Gazette* gives a lurid picture of the behaviour of Monmouth's men at this stage: 'They robbed and defaced the cathedral, drinking their villainous healths at the altar, plundered the town, ravished the women, and committed all manner of outrages.'[1] Most witnesses agree that this report was much exaggerated; Monmouth himself later attested that all that was done was the stripping of lead from the cathedral fabric, to make bullets. However, Lord Grey was seen standing at the high altar with drawn sword to protect the sanctuary from violation.

With regard to damage and compensation, there were discrepancies in the policy of the rival armies. Monmouth's policy was not to damage the homes of Royalist sympathizers or their persons unless they had actually taken up arms against him, but some of the homes of those who aided the rebels were destroyed by direct order of the King, with no compensation offered. Moreover, there is no record at all of enemies of Monmouth being ill treated or executed, while even at this early stage the King was ordering that men found publishing propaganda or even voicing the opinion that Monmouth had been born legitimate were to be hanged. On the other hand, when homes were damaged wantonly, and not as a punishment, the Royalists offered their victims generous compensation, while Monmouth was not rich enough to do the same. But then prisoners who had been taken by the rebels were not ill treated, and if wounded, were usually given the best medical treatment possible. Fear of maltreatment by the King's men compelled the rebels to carry all their wounded along with them as they marched, usually setting the fractured limbs at night and jogging the poor wretches in their carts as the army moved by day. This inevitably reduced the efficacy of the relief that had been intended, but there is no doubt that it was conscientiously administered.[2]

Of the three surgeons attending the rebel army, two, Dr Henry Pitman and Dr Oliver, wrote valuable accounts of their adventures. The third, Dr Benjamin Temple, was one of those who sailed knowing nothing of Monmouth's intention to invade England until they had been some time at sea. He and Dr Oliver were young men finishing their medical studies at Leyden when they became involved with Monmouth, while Dr Pitman happened to be in Somerset at the time of the landing and had gone to Taunton out of curiosity when his friends prevailed on him to help them with his medical skill. The sight of the sick and wounded, and the lack of surgeons, aroused his pity and caused him to throw in his lot with the rebel army.

After only one day at Wells, the rebels continued their return march to Bridgwater. Assembling at 3 am on 2 July, they took the road to Glastonbury, which they reached after journeying five miles in a southerly direction; they then marched a further five miles westwards, to Pedwell Plain, where they bivouacked. Just before this, Monmouth had sent his personal chaplain, Nathaniel Hooke, to London with an urgent message to Colonels Wildman and Danvers to raise the city in arms without delay. If only a major diversion could be organized in London or elsewhere, then the King would have to divide his army, which was anyway so small now that it was already outnumbered by Monmouth's. As we have seen, the other hope on which Monmouth pinned much of his faith was the 'club army'. Only four days before he had been told that they were massing in great numbers in the Somerset marshes, near Axbridge, and soon their supposed thousands would link up with the rebels to create a force of overwhelming strength. But as we know, only 160 materialized.

While the rebels halted for a brief while on Pedwell Plain, a deputation from Taunton arrived, with the request that Monmouth should return no more to their town, as the inhabitants were greatly alarmed at the news of his retreat. They were afraid that their buildings would be burned as a reprisal for harbouring the rebels. Though this request must have made rather depressing hearing, it in fact made little difference to Monmouth, as he had already decided to establish his base at Bridgwater, where the inhabitants were still friendly. The rebel army entered Bridgwater at 10 o'clock the next morning. The men set about finding quarters or encamping on the castle field, while the officers addressed themselves to the problems of fortification and preparing the town to withstand a siege. All available carpenters were summoned and 190 labourers were enlisted to begin the works; bread, cheese, oxen, sheep, calves, hay and oats were commandeered, 'with all speed imajonable',[3] and a certain Captain Silver, brother of the master-gunner for England, appeared with an ingenious idea for a machine that could fire twenty muskets simultaneously.

The next day being a Saturday, many hundreds of men took leave to visit their families in Taunton and the neighbouring villages, or to take advantage of this first opportunity for a brief holiday. It says much for the spirit that buoyed up Monmouth's cause that they nearly all returned the next day. In the meantime, Major Manley had arrived with his son, who had just escaped from prison in London. He carried messages from Mr 'Indenture' – the code name for Colonel Wildman – which must have relieved some of Monmouth's anxieties. Wildman wrote, for instance, that Lord Delamere was busy galvanizing Monmouth's Cheshire allies into action, but alas, this was not true: Delamere had been taken prisoner in Chester Castle ten days earlier.

On the Friday Feversham had moved his army into Somerton, the ancient capital of Somerset. Realizing that Monmouth would most probably soon be moving on, he personally reconnoitred the low moors to the north-west of Somerton to find a camp sufficiently near to anticipate any sudden move. Selecting the village of Weston Zoyland, three miles from Bridgwater, he moved there on Sunday the fifth, quartering his cavalry of 700 horses in the village, and his infantry of 2100 in the neighbouring village of Chedzoy.

On this same day Monmouth was making preparations for a move to the north, though spreading rumours that he was going to the south coast to find his ships. By the afternoon forty baggage-wagons had been loaded, and the army warned of a departure. At 3 pm one Richard Godfrey of near-by Godfrey Farm told Monmouth that he had been sent by William Sparke, a farmer of Chedzoy village (which had a tower useful for spying on the enemy), that the Royalist soldiers were drinking large quantities of cider and seemed to be in a very relaxed mood. He had also noted that all their guns were concentrated on the road from Bridgwater.

Monmouth himself climbed the spire of Bridgwater church and examined the enemy's disposition through a telescope. It occurred to him that if he could surprise them on their northern and eastern flanks, he would avoid their cannon and most of their cavalry. So confident was he as he looked through his telescope that he commented: 'We shall have no more to do than lock up the stable doors and seize the troopers in their beds.'[4]

The enemy were camped round one side of the road three and a half miles away, both in the village itself and in the field to the north of the village road. If Monmouth attacked down this road he would meet sentries posted at least a mile from the enemy, and they would give the warning. Farther on the road was covered by the enemy cannon and would have guards galore. If he attacked from the south, he would have to cross the River Parrett, which is exceptionally wide, and he would also be approaching the road on which the enemy's main defensive strength was focused. On the other hand, if he approached from the north he would outflank the cannon and the cavalry. The next question that faced him was how to get off the eastern causeway that leads to Bristol and the east and make a 90° turn across the moorland, encumbered as he was with forty heavily laden wagons, and yet preserve the secrecy that was all important. The obvious turning was the road to the village of Chedzoy about a mile up the causeway from Bridgwater, but as this was the only road in the direction of Weston Zoyland, besides being the main road from Bridgwater, it would also be closely guarded and reconnoitred.

Monmouth solved the problem by selecting a lane running off the main road about two miles away, rightly guessing that sentries would not be posted as far out as that. This lane led right by Bradney Green to Peazey Farm and the village of Bawdrip, where it circled back to the eastern causeway. (This eastern causeway connected with the main road to Bristol and the North.) If he could escape unnoticed down the lane while pretending to be evacuating Bridgwater altogether, he could leave his heavy wagons at Peazey Farm and stealthily cover the three miles of moorland so as to come up on the enemy.

But one question remained: would the weather allow him to succeed? As darkness fell the light of the full moon, which would otherwise have proved fatal to the element of surprise, was obscured by a thick mist that rolled over the moorland, giving him a real chance of victory.

While Monmouth weighed up these various problems Robert Ferguson gave a lengthy sermon in the castle field. He chose his text from the twenty-second chapter of *Joshua*: 'The Lord God of Hosts knoweth and Israel he shall know if it be in rebellion or in transgression against the Lord, save us not this day.' This was a brilliant choice of text by the rebel chaplain to remind the men once again that James II was the transgressor and that his followers were the real rebels. Many of the local people were observing events and reporting them to the rival commanders, so this sermon against rebellion would also serve to put anyone overhearing it off the scent, as he would not understand that the roles had been reversed. One Bridgwater girl did indeed get wind of the secret plan of attack and walked the three miles to Weston Zoyland to seek an interview with Feversham, but he treated her and her story with disdain.

At 7 pm the drums beat the 'assembly' and the stout-hearted followers of Monmouth assembled in the castle field. At 11 pm the long, sinuous column of more than three thousand men set off down the narrow eastern causeway, with the cavalry in front and Monmouth at their head.

Monmouth knew, from Richard Godfrey, who was by his side, that there were two obstacles to be overcome: ditches, such as are still to be found draining the reclaimed moorland of that area. Known locally as 'rhines', these ditches were not impossible to negotiate but they were awkward for horses in the darkness and might have been swollen by the recent rains; they had fords or 'plungeons', and as Godfrey knew their location, they might not prove too troublesome. What Godfrey had not told Monmouth, perhaps through a slip of memory, was that the enemy camp was half encircled by such a ditch, on its northern and western boundaries. If Monmouth had known this he might have taken the precaution of making a few portable bridges, such as were commonly used in the civil war. With his military experience he must have known of such a tactic and his very able advisers could have organized something along these lines in the few hours available for preparation.

As they moved out of Bridgwater the thunder of horses' hooves caused the rebel troops to withdraw into the shadow of the hedges to avoid a patrol under Major Oglethorpe, which came galloping on to the road ahead of them. Somehow Oglethorpe missed them and they continued their advance, scarcely daring to breathe, for two and a quarter miles, until they found the lane they were looking for and silently vanished into the shadows of the night.

When at last they found themselves on the moor, having shed their baggage-wagons at Peazey Farm, they still had two and a half miles to go. They must have felt relief when the first rhine was soon encountered; the plungeon was found, and the whole army filed over in complete silence. Richard Godfrey, without whom this could not have happened, had shown himself to be a most helpful guide. The cavalry now waited for the foot to come into line, and they all moved off over another mile of moorland. Chedzoy village on their right, though occupied by a strong Royalist guard, was quite unconscious of their proximity. When the second or Langmore rhine was reached, there was some difficulty in finding the plungeon. But soon the cavalry, followed by the four iron guns and a seemingly endless file of scythemen and musketeers, had crossed over to the other side. Unfortunately, during the temporary confusion caused by the search for the crossing-place, a disaster had occurred. Captain Tucker, who had been Monmouth's advance guard and host at Taunton, had accidentally fired his pistol, thus warning the enemy, who immediately set a close guard over the two fords across the last rhine of all.

Near where the pistol had been fired stood an imposing black boulder of marble known as 'the Devil's Upping Stock', which has since been demolished. A Royalist sentry had been posted there, about three-quarters of a mile away from the camp, but – such was the Royalists' false sense of security – he had been withdrawn at midnight. It is possible that but for that unlucky pistol shot, the marsh mist and the silent approach would have enabled Monmouth's men to take their enemy by surprise; they could have outflanked the enemy's cavalry and artillery and Grey's horsemen could have created havoc among the Royalist tents, while the infantry quickly crossed the last, or 'Bussex', rhine. Then Monmouth's thousand scythemen would have had a definite advantage over their adversaries, who would have been too close for the loading and aiming of muskets.

But as things were, when the rebels approached the camp in the fitful moonlight they saw through the mist long rows of musketeers of Dunbarton's regiment lining the far side of a ditch, at the bottom of which was mud and water not above a foot deep. The ditch itself was perhaps three and a half feet in depth, with sloping sides allowing a man to clamber up or down without difficulty, though a horse would have had to negotiate it carefully. It certainly did not present an insuperable obstacle to either infantry or cavalry. On the rebels' left the 'upper plungeon' was guarded by a strong force of the 'King's Regiment of Horse', commanded by Sir Francis Compton. On the other side of Dunbarton's men – to the right of the rebels – were battalions of Grenadier and Coldstream Guards, though most of these were too far to the flank to be immediately engaged.

Monmouth immediately told Lord Grey to attempt the upper plungeon. By giving the password 'Albemarle', a few of his horsemen succeeded. The remainder moved right across the front of Dunbarton's regiment, which was commanded by Colonel

Douglas. Challenged again, the rebels answered: 'We're for the King.' On being asked, 'Which King?', they shouted: 'King Monmouth, and God with us!', and attempted to charge. They were met by a volley of musket fire both from Dunbarton's regiment and from the Grenadiers, which effectively threw back in disorder the few rebel cavalrymen who had managed the crossing, and sent the main body of horse careering back towards Langmore Stone.

Monmouth's infantry, guided by the glowing slow matches of the opposing muskets, moved to a position more than twenty yards from the edge of the ditch. The Red, the Green and the Yellow Regiments, standing in battle order, started shooting, but they aimed too high to do any harm. Three of the rebel cannon were plied with accuracy and were able to inflict many casualties. The Royalist infantry now did not return the fire but waited for the cannon to be dragged from the Bridgwater road to face the rebels on the northern flank.

After the rebel cavalry had proved unable to effect a crossing, a second attempt was made by three hundred horsemen commanded by Captain Jones. The fighting was over for the moment; there were casualties on both sides, and Sir Francis Compton was seriously wounded, but as he had received ample reinforcements to replace his losses, he could not be dislodged.

For nearly an hour the rebel cannon bombarded the Royalists, without much fire being returned: the Royalist infantry stood meekly by while holes were torn in their ranks, and the casualties mounted. At last the sixteen guns were moved from their position on the left flank of the Royalist camp, where they were guarding the road to Bridgwater, to the northern boundary, where they could engage the enemy across the ditch. From this point the battle settled down to being an artillery duel, with the rebel muskets still aiming too high and the Royalist infantry not shooting at all. For some inexplicable reason, while Bishop Mews's carriage-horses were dragging the sixteen iron guns over a distance of four hundred yards, the infantry were never ordered to fire their muskets, even though the three rebel guns were shooting them down in their hundreds.

Soon after the arrival of the sixteen cannon, the rebels ran out of cannon-balls. 'Ammunition, ammunition, for the Lord's sake ammunition,' they shouted, but the ammunition-wagons left at Peazey Farm were being driven at breakneck speed 180° in the wrong direction, frightened by the wild careering horses of Lord Grey's cavalry.

For perhaps another hour Feversham watched his cannon firing before deciding to cross the ditch. First came the Horse Guards and Grenadiers, on his left – a total of about 150 were ordered over. These were simultaneously joined by Major Oglethorpe's troop, who had just returned from reconnoitring the eastern causeway but had somehow failed to notice the rebel army's approach. Oglethorpe now charged a party of rebel infantry but was beaten back, losing both horses and men.

Perhaps daunted by this, Feversham refused to make any new offensive moves until the first streaks of dawn appeared in the sky. It was only then that his infantry and the rest of the cavalry were ordered over the ditch and, by the light of the early sun, pursued and routed their enemies. A total of 300 of Monmouth's men were killed during the battle; 1000 were killed in the pursuit; 1200 were taken prisoner (see Appendix II). Of the Royalist force, only 400 were killed or wounded.

Flight and Execution

At approximately 3 am Lord Grey rode up to his chief and, indicating the 150 Royalist horses that had crossed the ditch, told him that in his opinion all was up, and they had best quit the battle. Monmouth was already divesting himself of his armour, having independently come to the same conclusion, and the two friends, after selecting three additional companions for the journey, rode to Chedzoy. Here Monmouth's tired horse was exchanged for a fresh one, at the house of a man called William Stradling. Monmouth unbuckled a lady's blue girdle that he wore round his neck and gave it, with its silver buckle, to a small boy who happened to be in the house, with the words: 'This may be of use to you some day, and I can have it again.'[1] Needless to say, this buckle was treasured for many years to come and was sometimes touched by people suffering from the 'king's evil'.

Without more ado, Monmouth, Grey and their three companions galloped on to the main northern road, by way of Crandon Bridge. Crossing the Polden Hills, they looked back on the battlefield, where the cannons' flash still showed. The distant murmur of many shouting voices, with the boom and crackle of gunfire, told them that the battle was not yet over. On they galloped at such a rate that by 6 am they had put twenty miles between them and the field of carnage. The general direction was Axbridge and Bristol, but they were still undecided as to whether they should turn west, north or east in their effort to escape capture.

Monmouth's and Grey's three companions were Monmouth's

servant, Williams, Dr Oliver, the physician, and a German from Brandenburg called Anthony Buyse. When they were about twelve miles from Bristol, probably in the area of Winscombe or the village of Churchill, Dr Oliver addressed the Duke: 'Sir, this is the farthest you can go without throwing yourself into the hands of your enemies, who are waiting for you all over the country eastward. Nobody has yet heard of our ill success in those dark parts; let us turn off to the sea coast over against Wales, seize one of the passage boats at Uphill, and get over to the other side, where I know you have friends among whom you will be safe till you can retire elsewhere.'[2]

This was excellent advice, and practical. They were only about ten miles from Uphill. The residents of Uphill, at the early hour of 8 am, would not have heard anything at all about a battle. Monmouth had £100 in gold on him, and this would enable him to find a boat to take him across the Bristol Channel to Wales, a sea journey of twelve miles. With luck he might find someone to take him to the coast of France, in which case he could be in Holland before his pursuers even realized that he had left the English shore.

Unfortunately, however, Lord Grey countered with the advice to go south-eastwards, over the Mendip Hills to Shepton Mallet. They could count on the loyalty of Edward Strode, he said, though they would be in the heart of enemy country. Monmouth took this advice, but now that his cause had been defeated, the £5000 reward would tempt most people to regard him as worth capturing. The Royalist soldiers, the constables, the sheriffs and the militia would be alerting everybody to the possibility of discovering them. He would have to be disguised. How was he to leave the country? The only possible help would surely come from the Mayor of Lymington, nearly a hundred miles away, who was sufficiently loyal and powerful to find him a boat.

Saying goodbye to Dr Oliver, Monmouth took his plumed hat in exchange for his own and parted with him for ever. 'God bless you sir,' Oliver said with tears in his eyes, 'I will never see you more.'[3] While the doctor rode off alone to Bristol, the other four fugitives journeyed a further twenty miles through the beautiful Mendip country to Shepton Mallet, where Edward Strode received them at his house called 'Downside', a mile or so outside the town.

After resting a short while with their kind host, who was risking his life in sheltering them, the fugitives set off on the road to Shaftesbury, yet another twenty miles away. Monmouth left his pistols behind as a gift for the friend who had given him 100 guineas only two weeks before. The four riders eventually reached Gillingham, where a guide was found to help them, a man called Holyday. With his help they went through Shaftesbury and White Street to Cranborne Chase. Where the old mail-road crosses the Chase near the junction of the three counties of Hampshire, Wiltshire and Dorset, there is a posting-house, then known as 'Woodyates Inn'. Here they disguised themselves (Monmouth as a shepherd), turned loose their horses and hid the bridles and saddles.

Walking southwards a further five miles, they came to Cranborne, near which is St Giles, the country seat of Lord Shaftesbury, where they separated into two groups. How Monmouth must have wished that the great Whig was still alive: he would have helped them more than anyone.

At 5am on the morning of 7 July some Royalist soldiers belonging to a force commanded by Lord Lumley saw two yokels at a crossroads near Holt Lodge, four miles west of Ringwood. They detained them for questioning and found them to be Lord Grey and the guide. Grey had travelled between eighty and a hundred miles since leaving the battlefield twenty-four hours earlier, and, considering the long battle with its difficult approach march, the endless attempts to control the disorderly cavalry and the continual imminent peril in which he had existed, it is amazing that he proved to be so calm and coherent.

Lord Lumley himself soon appeared and inaugurated a detailed search of the cottages, woods and fields. A woman called Amy

Farrant, who lived in one of the cottages, showed him a hedge over which she had seen two men climb. The fields enclosed by the hedge were searched, and the boundary was guarded by militiamen, but all that day the remaining fugitives eluded the pursuers. At about 5 am on the eighth the Brandenburger was discovered, having parted from Monmouth four hours earlier. Stimulated by the reward of £5000, which Lord Lumley promised would be divided between all those involved in the capture, the troops intensified the search until, at 7 am, Henry Parkin, servant to a man called Samuel Rolles, discovered Monmouth lying in a ditch of brambles and bracken, in the shade of an ash tree, near the manor of Woodlands, on the estate of Lord Shaftesbury.

Poor Monmouth was in a state of utter exhaustion. He could not stand and was almost unrecognizable, so haggard was his appearance. Sir William Portman, who happened to be near the scene of the discovery, rode up and ordered Parkin and two other militiamen who were holding him not to shoot but to hold him for searching, as he was uncertain as to the identity of the strange vagrant. When his pocket-book was found, his 'George' medal and other notebooks, he was identified, and taken to Holt Lodge, about a mile from the spot. There he was interviewed by a magistrate who lived there, named Anthony Etterick. The George was entrusted to two officers to take to James II. They reached the King at midnight on the same day, 8 July.

Monmouth wrote to his uncle: '. . . I am sure, Sir, when you hear me, you will be convinced of the zeale I have for your preservation, and how heartily I repent of what I have done. . . . I hope, Sir, God Almighty will strike your heart with mercy and compassion for me, as he has done mine with the abhorrence of what I have done.' He further begged to be seen in a private audience, and signed the letter with the words: '. . . you will be convinced, how much I shall ever be, Your Majesties most humble and dutifull Monmouth.'[4]

That very night the order came for his removal to London.

Though his hands were tied behind his back, he sprang into the saddle of his horse, refusing all assistance. Then, under strong guard, he and Lord Grey were escorted to Winchester, and thence, their guard reinforced, to London.

It was Charles II's widow, the Dowager Queen Catherine, who urgently pressed James II to grant Monmouth an audience. Monmouth had addressed a letter to her begging her to persuade the King to see him, and she was so successful in her petition that many thought that, after seeing Monmouth, James was somehow defaulting in not pardoning his nephew.

Monmouth and Grey were brought to Whitehall, and both had an interview with the King. Bishop Kennet wrote that Monmouth collapsed on his knees in the King's presence and, with tears in his eyes, reminded James: 'I am your brother's son, and if you take my life, it is your blood that you shed.'[5] He did, however, sign a declaration attesting that his father had assured him of his illegitimacy, and then whispered his sorrow for his own misfortunes.

The King, after these concessions, expressed his own sorrow, but insisted that the crime was of such consequence that it could not go unpunished. Queen Mary is said to have been more insulting and arrogant than her husband, causing Monmouth swiftly to compose himself and rise, before being carried off to the Tower. Lord Grey, by contrast, never once begged for his life.

The bill of attainder, lately passed by Parliament, superseded the necessity for a trial. Monmouth's execution was fixed for the following morning. He begged for a delay, but this was denied him.

Four bishops visited Monmouth in his cell – but only to argue heatedly about his crime rather than consoling him in his sorrow. Lady Henrietta Wentworth was specifically reviled as an object of his sins. Nevertheless, they were all impressed by Monmouth's devotion to his prayers on that day before his execution.

.   .   .   .   .   .

The Duchess of Monmouth and Buccleuch had gone with her children to the Tower when news came that Monmouth had proclaimed himself king at Taunton. This was a shrewd move, to show her reverence for the King and to protect herself and her children in case of civil war. A contemporary of the period wrote: 'The Duchess of Monmouth has demained herself dureing this severe tryall and dispensatione of providence with all the Christian temper and compositione of spirit that possibly would not appeir in a soule soue great and virtuous as hers. His Majestie is exceedingly satisfied with her conduct and deportment alonge, and has assured her that he will take a cair of her and her children.'[6] (Lady Anne Scott, the ten-year-old daughter of the Duke and Duchess, died in the Tower. She was buried in Westminster Abbey on 13 August 1685.) While with her husband, the Duchess

. . . asked him if ever she had the least notice and correspondence with him about these matters, or had ever assented to or approved of his conduct during these four or five years; if ever she had done anything in the whole course of her life to displease or disoblige him, or ever was uneasie to him in anything but two, one as to his women and the other for his disobedience to the King, whom she always took the liberty to advise him to obey, and never was pleased with the disobedient course of life he lived in towards him. If in anything else she had failed of the duty and obedience that became her as his wife, she humbly begged the favour to disclaim it, and would fall down on her knees and beg his pardon for it. To which moveing discourse he answered that she had always shown herself a very kind, loving, and dutiful wife toward him and had nothing imaginable to charge her with, either against her virtue and duty to him, her steady loyalty and affection toward the late King, or kindness and affection towards his children; that she was always averse to the practice of life and behaviour towards the late King, and advised to great compliance and obedience towards his commands.[7]

On one point no reasoning or exhortation could move him, and that was the opinion he held as to his connection with Lady Henrietta Wentworth. Admitting their intimacy, he persisted in asserting its blamelessness: 'He knew her,' he said, 'to be a virtuous and godly lady' – these were his own words – 'and far from deserving the unkind censure she lies under on his account.'[8]

The last meeting and farewell with his wife and children took place on the morning of his execution. His behaviour all the time was so brave and unmoved that no bystander could see it without melting in tears.

When the moment of Monmouth's death came he was asked to pray for the King, so that his children and wife might be spared any undue punishment. He turned upon the bishops to ask: 'What harm have they done? Do it, if you please. I pray for him and for all men.' The clergy commenced with the prayers: 'O Lord, shew thy mercy upon us.' Monmouth answered: 'And grant us thy salvation.' 'And mercifully hear us,' he responded, 'when we call upon thee.' The bishops were not content with these prayers, and implored Monmouth to pray with more devotion for the King. Again the prayers were begun, but they were interrupted by Monmouth's abrupt 'Amen'. He was then asked to make some declaration to the people concerning the loyalty of subjects to their monarch. But he was beyond quibbling: 'I have said I will make no speeches. I will make no speeches. I come to die.'[9]

Before the bishops could entreat him further, he sent for a friend's servant and gave him a toothpick case to be delivered along with a ring to Lady Henrietta (see Appendix III). He then gave his executioner six guineas, imploring him not to serve him as he had served Lord Russell, who, it was rumoured, took three or four chops from the axe before being killed. Turning to the servant, he gave him more guineas, to be paid to the executioner if the work had been done as promised. He was quite calm. He whispered again to the executioner: 'If you strike twice, I can't promise you not to stir.'

Neither blindfolded nor bound, Monmouth patiently knelt before the block and fitted in his neck. He then rose on one elbow and ran his thumb along the edge of the axe. 'It's not sharp enough,' he said. 'It's sharp enough and heavy enough,' the executioner answered.[10] He lay down again. The first chop only wounded his neck. He did not cry out but only turned to stare at the executioner. After the second chop he crossed his legs. With the third unsuccessful effort, the executioner flung down the axe and cried, 'God damn me, I can do no more. My heart fails me.' The sheriffs begged him to return to his duty, and the crowd swayed forward in a rage. Many were yelling vengeance. The executioner returned and dealt the final chop. Many came forward to dip their handkerchiefs into Monmouth's blood and carry them away as precious relics, for in years to come he was to be remembered with reverence.

On the scaffold, close to the block, lay a coffin covered in black velvet. In this the body of the Duke of Monmouth was placed, and a hearse, drawn by six horses with funereal trappings, conveyed the remains to the Tower, followed by a mourning-coach, also drawn by six horses. On arrival at the Tower the head was sewn to the body, which was buried under the altar of the chapel of St Peter ad Vincula.

Appendix I

THE Reverend Peter Bell was imprisoned in Newgate Gaol on a charge of being implicated with Shaftesbury when he wrote the following letter to Dr Lake, Chaplain to the Duke of York:

Reverend Sir, I was glad of this opportunity . . . of hearing from Mr Werden of Preston in Lancashire, that hee could prove that my Friend, ye Duke of Monmouth, was ye rightfull Heire of ye Crowne of England, and foreseeing yt 'twould bee noe less a gratefull peace of servise to my dear friend Lord Shaftesbury then in process of time beneficiall to my selfe, I writ his Lorship this short Narrative, viz that Mr Werden of Preston having beene some yeares resident at Durham in ye quality of Clerke to his Uncle an Attorney there, had in that time understood of one Mr Forder of Houghton in le-Spring, a Gentleman of 4 or £500 per annum, quondam Stuard of ye late Bishop of Durham [John Gosin, who died in 1672], and his servant abroad when hee waited on ye King in his Exile; had severall times declar'd in Public company, that to his knowledge ye Duke of Monmouth was ye lawfull Heire of ye Crowne of England: for hee was present at ye Marriage of his Grace's mother to ye King, a competent time before ye birth of ye Duke of Monmouth; of which, he was, *to ye discharge of a good Conscience*, ready to make affidavit, before legall authority; in soe much *afterwards* that the saide Mr Werden being once drinking a glass of Wine in a Taverne in Durham amongst some Gentlemen that were Popishly Affected, and refus'd to drinke ye Duke of Monmouth's Health, calling him Sone of a Whore, and in other opprobrious language *reflecting on his Grace*; so incens't a Gentman . . . that though a stranger, hee came into theire Roome, and draw'd his Sword and demanded satisfaction, or ye blood of any that should dare to call ye

Duke of M. a Bastard, for to ye knowledge of his friend the afore-saide Mr Forder his Grace's Mother was lawfully married to ye King, and hee would justifie it with his life; I haveing first acquainted Mr Spencer of Ashton in Lancashire whoe offer'd to bee one of ye Justices of ye Peace, to take Mr Forder's oath, and preserve it till their should bee either a House of Commons or till ye death of his sacred Majesty; My Lord S. [Shaftesbury] sent downe one Mr Williams, or Mr Spencer, a Barrister of Gray's Inn, aboute a month after, to over-heare ye truth of ye premises, from Mr Werden's owne Mouth . . . and alsoe to prepare mee for my Defence at my Tryall; and that I should by noe means submit to ye mearcy of ye King till after sentence; *that* if I was fin'd I had Mony, and my Lord S. [Shaftesbury] would doe mee right: that I should bee reimbursed if I printed ye Tryall: and be rewarded *for ye hazzard of ye King and Duke's* [York's] *displeasure* with great Preferment; *But Dear Sir Uppon ye word of Truth* I cannot say that ye Duke of Monmouth knew anything or yet know anything of ye Premises; *for really* I thinke his Grace is too good a subject, ihn [*sic*] to converse with ye Company hee is to frequently manaijd with-all.

Sir, Yours Eternally oblig'd etc.

Peter Bell[1]

Shaftesbury may have had other sources of information: his friend Lord Russell had married the widow of Lord Vaughan, who as Lucy Walter's second cousin must have heard frequent discussions as to what were the true relations between Charles II and Lucy in 1648. In this respect, unless conclusive evidence comes to light, the mystery will remain.

Appendix II

In the latter part of August 1685, when the prisons of the West Country were crowded to suffocation with the captured rebels, five judges went forth to hear their cases. At their head was the terrible Judge Jeffreys, Lord Chief Justice, who also had the authority of Lieutenant General.

The 'Bloody Assizes' began at Winchester and resulted in sentences of whipping, fines, hanging, drawing and quartering. Many of the rebel prisoners were transported to the West Indies as slaves – some for as long as ten years. Those who survived the appalling conditions of the voyage were generally well treated by the West Indian merchants. Their exile accounts for the Somerset accent that, to the surprise of visitors to the island of Barbados, is to be heard in the speech of its inhabitants to this day.

Appendix III

THE Duke of Monmouth's six children by the Duchess were:
Charles, Earl of Doncaster (born 24 August 1672, died 1673).
James, Earl of Doncaster and Dalkeith (1674–1705).
Lord Henry Scott, who became Earl of Deloraine, a dignity that
has recently become extinct (1677–1703).
Lord Francis Scott.
Lady Charlotte Scott (died in infancy).
Lady Anne Scott (died in infancy).

After Monmouth's death his English peerages of Monmouth,
Doncaster and Tindale were forfeited by an Act of Parliament
(1685) and it was considered necessary to obtain a Sentence of
Forfeiture against him and his descendants by the court of
Edinburgh judiciary in Scotland. By proclamation at the market
cross of Edinburgh, in June 1685, he was cited to appear within
sixty days to answer a charge of high treason.

In September of the same year his heirs were cited to appear,
also within sixty days, at Edinburgh. A secret committee
deliberated on 4 January 1686, and the king's advocate decreed
that it was not safe to set the children at liberty, because it might
prove pernicious to the government if they were later used to head
a faction or rebellion.

Collins, in his *Peerage*, states that the attainder of Monmouth
did not take place in Scotland, though his posterity did not
inherit the dukedom of Buccleuch until after the death of the
duchess in 1732. Sir Walter Scott was of the opinion that the
dukedom was inherited under the operation of an act passed in

Edinburgh on 25 April 1690 and entitled 'A rescinding the For-feitures and Fines passed since the year 1665'. Monmouth's grandson, Francis, Duke of Buccleuch, was, by an Act of Parliament of 23 March 1743, restored to the titles of Earl of Doncaster and Baron Scott of Tindale, with all rights according to the grant of those honours to his grandfather.

James, the second and eldest surviving son of the Duke and Duchess of Buccleuch and Monmouth, was born in May 1674. During the lifetime of his father his courtesy title was Earl of Doncaster: later he was styled Earl of Dalkeith. It would appear that in 1692 some at least of the party that had supported the Duke of Monmouth in his attempt to seize the English throne still maintained a lingering enthusiasm for the defeated cause. In that way, in the very district of Scotland where the Covenanting spirit had been most zealously displayed, the young earl was proclaimed king. An old memorandum book, originally the property of Mr David Scrimgeour of Cartmore, and now in the Buccleuch Charter Room, supplies the following note on this apparently hitherto unknown event: 'October 31st 1692 – In the end of July, or the beginning of August, thirty or forty wyld people came to the cross and proclaimed the Earl of Dalkeith King, and then in September thereafter, Robert Hamilton [his chief sponsor], who was commander at Bothwell Bridge [where Monmouth had distinguished himself so greatly] was taken at Earlstown House, and after he was examined before the Council, was sent to Hadding-town tolbooth.'

On 2 January 1694 the Earl of Dalkeith married the Lady Henrietta Hyde, eldest daughter of Lawrence, Earl of Rochester. The Duchess of Buccleuch, writing to the Earl of Cromarty from Mews on 25 April 1693, thus expresses her satisfaction with the choice made by her son: 'At the readjusting of all my accounts with my son, this will be the proper time for the business is resolved on all hands concerning the fair lady, and the only one can be to my mind, and, which is better, the only one to my son's mind, which makes me resolved to make a better compliment to Jeams [James] than Harry.'[1] The Earl died in his house in Albemarle Street, London, on 14 March 1705, at the age of thirty-one, and was much lamented on account of his many amicable qualities. His wife survived him to the year 1730. They were both buried in Westminster Abbey. There were four sons and two daughters of the marriage. The eldest son, Francis, succeeded to the dukedom on the death of his grandmother in 1732.

In January 1686 a grant was made to Anna, Duchess of Buccleuch, the widow of the Duke of Monmouth, and his heirs, of Moor Park and lands lying in Rickmansworth, Hertfordshire, forfeited to James II by the attainder of the Duke. It is said that the widowed Duchess showed her feelings of abhorrence at the murder of her husband by pollarding the young oaks at Moor Park and the limes at Dalkeith.

Three years after Monmouth's death Anna married Charles, third Lord Cornwallis, one of the most accomplished gentlemen of the age (though extravagant and a gambler), who was later to be a special favourite of King William. The Duchess bore him a son and two daughters. She survived Cornwallis, was married a third time – to the Earl of Selkirk – died on 6 February 1732, aged eighty-one, and was buried at Dalkeith.

The Duchess was a distinguished patroness of poets, a friend of Dryden and Gay. According to Dr Johnson's *Life of Gay*, she took him into her service as secretary in 1712, and it is probable that he accompanied her for a few weeks when, aged seventy-four, she leased Monmouth House in Lawrence Street, Chelsea. The building, in the late-Elizabethan style, consisted of four houses, of which the Duchess occupied two on the western side. Monmouth House was demolished in 1835, and the small houses of Upper Cheyne Row now stand on its site.

'The Duchess of Monmouth [was] remarkable for inflexible perseverance to be treated as a princess,'[2] wrote Johnson, and his opinion was reinforced by Sir Walter Scott, in his notes on Dryden: 'The Duchess of Buccleuch and Monmouth survived the catastrophe of her husband for many years, during which she was resolute in asserting her rights to be treated as a Princess.'³ In several of the charters granted by the Duchess as Superior of the town of Dalkeith, she went so far as to adopt the style of 'Mighty Princess'. Her cousin Lady Margaret Montgomerie related that when dining with the Duchess at Dalkeith Castle (subsequently known as Dalkeith House or, locally, as Dalkeith Palace) she was permitted, being a relative, to be seated, but all the rest of the guests stood during the repast. The Duchess was attended by pages, who served her on bended knee.

In her later years the Duchess was a welcome *habituée* of the court of the Hanoverian kings of England, and a friend of Caroline of Anspach, wife of the future King George II. In the diary of Lady Cowper, a lady-in-waiting to Princess Caroline, appears the following entry: 'London, 10th March, 1716. After the evening service went to Court. The Princess [Caroline] bid me to stay to sup with her. There were the Duchesses of Monmouth and Roxburgh . . . the Duchess of Monmouth entertained us with stories of King Charles's Court and death.' The diary proceeds: 'The Duchess of Monmouth used often to be there. The Princess loved her mightily and certainly no woman of her years ever deserved it so well. She had all the life and fire of youth, and it was marvellous to see that the many afflictions she had suffered had not touched her wit and good nature but at upwards of three score she had both in their full perfection.'⁴

Monmouth denied at the time of his death that he had had any children by Henrietta Wentworth, who died of grief shortly after his execution. But Allan Fea tells us in his *King Monmouth* that a child said to be theirs was brought up in Paris by a certain Colonel Smyth and was known as R. Wentworth-Smyth-Stuart. In 1739 he married Maria Julia Crofts, then aged fifteen, who was also descended from Monmouth.

Monmouth left four illegitimate children, two sons and two daughters, by Eleanor, a daughter of Sir Robert Needham; and by Elizabeth, daughter of the poet Edmund Waller, he left a daughter.

Appendix IV

AN appreciation of Monmouth, published only twenty years after his death, when Queen Anne was on the throne, describes him thus:

One, indeed, who if he had been a little less might have been at this time one of the greatest men both in England and the world . . . none can deny but he was a great general, a man of courage and conduct and great personal valour, having signaliz'd himself both at Mons and Maestricht, so as to gain an high and just reputation. He was all along true and firm to the Protestant interest in an our of Parliament though abhorring any base way of promoting it, as well as his friend, My Lord Russell. . . . He was all along the people's darling whose hearts were entirely his by his courtesie and affability as other persons lost 'em by their soreness and haughty pride. After Russell's death he went into Flanders, whence had he prosecuted his design and gone, as it is said he intended, into the Emperor's service, how many laurels might he have won and how many more would now have been growing for him? But his fate was otherwise. . . . Providence had designed other things that our deliverance should be more just, and peaceable and wonderful.[1]

Genealogical Table

Charles I
King of England
(1625-49)
=
Henrietta Maria
of France
(d. 1669)

Charles II
King of England
(1649-85)
= Catherine
of Braganza
(d. 1705)

Mary
(d. 1660)
= William
Prince of
Orange
(d. 1650)

James II
King of England
(1685-9)
(d. 1701)
= Anne Hyde
(d. 1671)

= Mary of
Modena
(d. 1718)

Henrietta Anne
(d: 1670)
=
Philip
Duke of Orleans

Lucy Walter
(d. 1658)

James
Duke of Monmouth
(d. 1685)
= Anna Scott
Duchess of Buccleuch
(d. 1732)

William III
King of England
(1688-1702)

Mary II
Queen of England
(1688-94)

Anne
Queen of England
(1702-14)
= George of Denmark
(d. 1708)

References

Full details of works referred to will be found in the bibliography.

Chapter 1

1 Elizabeth D'Oyley, *James Duke of Monmouth*, p. 10.
2 E. Clarendon, *Life of Edward Hyde*, I, pp. 284–5.
3 D'Oyley, *Duke of Monmouth*, p. 3.
4 Lord George Scott, *Lucy Walter. Wife or Mistress?*, p. 35.
5 Thomas Harriot, *Mathematical Papers* (British Museum).
6 William P. F. Ryan, *Stuart Life and Manners*, p. 272.
7 Baronne D'Aulnoy, *Memoirs of the Court of England in 1675*, p. 366.
8 John Evelyn, *Diary*, 18 August 1649.
9 Sophia of Hanover, *Memoirs*, p. 38.
10 Scott, *Lucy Walter*, p. 111.
11 Lambeth Palace Mss, ff. 675–6.
12 Lord George Scott, 'The Life of the Duke of Monmouth', f. 111.
13 Thurloe State Papers, v, p. 161, quoted by Scott in *Lucy Walter*, p. 133.
14 J. W. Shirley, *Thomas Harriot*, p. 291.
15 Allan Fea, *King Monmouth*, p. 16.
16 Flanders Papers, 25 March/14 April 1658, quoted in D'Oyley, *Duke of Monmouth*.
17 Ruth Clark, *Strangers and Sojourners at Port Royal*, p. 61.

Chapter 2
1 Arthur Bryant, *King Charles II*, p. 69.
2 F. W. Walter, *Great Deeds of the Coldstream Guards*, p. 11.
3 Bryant, *Charles II*, p. 69.
4 Clarendon, *Edward Hyde*, I, p. 239.
5 Agnes Strickland, *Lives of the Queens of England*, IV, p. 359.
6 Bryant, *Charles II*, p. 138.
7 D'Oyley, *Duke of Monmouth*, p. 33.
8 Arthur Bryant, *Restoration England*, p. 35.
9 Samuel Pepys, *Diary*, 26 July 1665.
10 *Memoirs of Sir John Reresby*, p. 182.
11 Clarendon, *Edward Hyde*, p. 239.
12 J. Cartwright, *Madame*, p. 138.
13 Pepys, *Diary*, 20 April 1663.
14 Pepys, *Diary*, 20 April 1663.
15 Pepys, *Diary*, 8 April 1663.
16 Original letter retained at Wemyss Castle.
17 D'Oyley, *Duke of Monmouth*, p. 161.
18 Pepys, *Diary*, 20 April 1663.
19 Samuel Pepys, *Diary*, 26 April 1667.

Chapter 3
1 Bryant, *Charles II*, p. 184.
2 D'Oyley, *Duke of Monmouth*, p. 39.
3 Clarendon, *Edward Hyde*, I, p. 239.
4 Lady Burghclere, *George Villiers*, p. 243.
5 George Bevan, *James Duke of Monmouth*, p. 83.
6 Burghclere, *Villiers*, p. 243.
7 D'Oyley, *Duke of Monmouth*, p. 28.
8 Fea, *King Monmouth*, p. 49.
9 C. H. Hartman, *Charles II and Madame*, p. 193.
10 Cartwright, *Madame*, p. 261.
11 Cartwright, *Madame*, p. 261.
12 Bryant, *Charles II*, p. 356n.
13 R. Cannon, *Historical Records of the British Army*, pp. 42–3.

14 George Roberts, *The Life, Progress and Rebellion of James Duke of Monmouth*, p. 56.
15 Roberts, *Life*, p. 35.

Chapter 4

1 Scott, *Lucy*, p. 139.
2 D'Oyley, Duke of Monmouth, p. 80.
3 S. Fraser, *The Scotts of Buccleuch*, II, p. 433.
4 Fraser, *Buccleuch*, II, p. 433.
5 Fraser, *Buccleuch*, II, p. 433.
6 From the *Collected Poems of Lord Rochester*, quoted by Graham Greene in *Lord Rochester's Monkey*.
7 Fraser, *Buccleuch*, II, p. 433.
8 D'Oyley, *Duke of Monmouth*, p. 91.
9 D. Miller, *Popery and Politics in England 1660–80*, p. 123.
10 D'Oyley, *Duke of Monmouth*, p. 91.
11 Bevan, *Duke of Monmouth*, p. 69.
12 D'Oyley, *Duke of Monmouth*, p. 98.
13 D'Oyley, *Duke of Monmouth*, p. 102.
14 E. Boswell, *Restoration Court Stage*, p. 196.
15 D'Oyley, *Duke of Monmouth*, pp. 93–4.

Chapter 5

1 D'Oyley, *Duke of Monmouth*, p. 93.
2 Bryant, *Restoration England*, p. 82.
3 G. Trevelyan, *Social History of England*, p. 218.
4 D'Oyley, *Duke of Monmouth*, p. 93.
5 D'Oyley, *Duke of Monmouth*, p. 228.
6 HMC Reports, v, p. 314.
7 Miller, *Popery*, p. 153.
8 D'Oyley, *Duke of Monmouth*, p. 120.
9 J. S. Clarke, *Life of James II*, I, p. 148.
10 Clarke, *James II*, I, p. 148.
11 Bevan, *Duke of Monmouth*, p. 93.

Chapter 6

1   Miller, *Popery*, p. 185.
2   Miller, *Popery*, p. 158.
3   Miller, *Popery*, p. 158.
4   D'Oyley, *Duke of Monmouth*, p. 132.
5   Clarke, *James II*.
6   Clarke, *James II*.
7   D'Oyley, *Duke of Monmouth*, p. 128.
8   Miller, *Popery*, p. 184.
9   Miller, *Popery*, p. 184.
10 D'Oyley, *Duke of Monmouth*, p. 113.
11 Fea, *King Monmouth*, p. 70.
12 Fea, *King Monmouth*, p. 70.
13 The Diaries of Algernon Sydney, quoted in Fea, *King Monmouth*, p. 90.
14 D'Oyley, *Duke of Monmouth*, p. 101.
15 Scott, 'Life', f. 91.
16 Fea, *King Monmouth*, p. 75.
17 Calendar of State Papers, Domestic Series 1679–80, XXIII, preface, ch. 2.
18 HMC Report VII, appendix for 15 May 1679.
19 Bevan, *Duke of Monmouth*, p. 145.
20 Trevelyan, *England under the Stuarts*, p. 408.
21 Bevan, *Duke of Monmouth*, p. 146.
22 Scott, 'Life', ff. 131–1a.

Chapter 7

1   Henry Sidney, *Diary of the Times of Charles II*, p. 154.
2   Sydney, *Diary*, p. 143.
3   Lady Verney, *Memoirs of the Verney Family*, p. 284.
4   Miller, *Popery*, p. 176.
5   From documents in Weymss Castle, quoted by Fraser.
6   Bevan, *Duke of Monmouth*, p. 114.
7   Bevan, *Duke of Monmouth*, p. 115.

8 Bryant, *Charles II*, p. 285.
9 Roberts, *Life*, I, p. 46.
10 Scott, 'Life', quoting from *Burnett Letters*, XIV, p. 31.
11 Sydney, *Diary*, I, 6 January 1680.
12 Scott, 'Life', f. 194.
13 D'Oyley, *Duke of Monmouth*, p. 169.
14 Scott, 'Life', f. 193.
15 Scott, 'Life', f. 197.
16 Scott, 'Life', f. 197.
17 D'Oyley, *Duke of Monmouth*, p. 172.
18 D'Oyley, *Duke of Monmouth*, p. 172.
19 Scott, 'Life', f. 197.
20 Scott, 'Life', f. 193.

Chapter 8
1 Scott, 'Life', quoting from a pamphlet on the Succession of the Crown of England Considered, 1701, p. 212.
2 Cartwright, *Sacharisa*, p. 294.
3 Cartwright, *Sacharisa*, p. 294.
4 Cartwright, *Sacharisa*, p. 294.
5 D'Oyley, *Duke of Monmouth*, p. 176.
6 D'Oyley, *Duke of Monmouth*, p. 176.
7 Scott, 'Life', f. 197.
8 Scott, 'Life', f. 138c.
9 Bevan, *Duke of Monmouth*, p. 146.
10 D'Oyley, *Duke of Monmouth*, p. 195.
11 Scott, 'Life', f. 242.
12 Scott, 'Life', f. 244.
13 R. Ferguson, *Ferguson the Plotter*, p. 71.
14 State Trials, IX, p. 605.

Chapter 9
1 Scott, 'Life', f. 249.
2 Scott, 'Life', p. 250.
3 Scott, 'Life', p. 252.

4 Ferguson, *Plotter*, p. 65.
5 Scott, 'Life', f. 251.
6 W. D. Christie, *A Life of Anthony Ashley Cooper*, p. 458.
7 Scott, 'Life', f. 255.
8 Scott, 'Life', f. 261.
9 H. C. Barnard, *The Little Schools of Port Royal*, p. 102.
10 From here until p. 117 the quotations from the Halifax correspondence are taken verbatim from Allan Fea's biography of the Duke of Monmouth. In His chapter on the Duke in disgrace and hiding is particularly rewarding, as he has drawn upon numerous state papers, trial records and various memoirs unavailable to the present biographer.
11 Scott, 'Life', f. 262.
12 Scott, 'Life'.

Chapter 10
1 Scott, 'Life'.
2 Scott, 'Life'.
3 Scott, 'Life'.
4 Scott, 'Life', f. 350.
5 Scott, 'Life'.
6 Scott, 'Life', f. 351.
7 Scott, 'Life'.
8 Scott, 'Life', f. 352.
9 Scott, 'Life'.
10 Scott, 'Life', f. 350.
11 Scott, 'Life', f. 356.
12 Scott, 'Life'.
13 Scott, 'Life'.
14 Scott, 'Life', f. 357.
15 Scott, 'Life'.
16 Scott, 'Life', f. 358.
17 Scott, 'Life'.
18 Scott, 'Life', f. 368.
19 Scott, 'Life'.

20 Scott, 'Life', f. 359.
21 Scott, 'Life', f. 368.
22 Scott, 'Life', f. 369.
23 Scott, 'Life'.
24 Scott, 'Life'.
25 Scott, 'Life', f. 370.
26 Scott, 'Life'.
27 Scott, 'Life', f. 371.
28 Scott, 'Life', f. 372.
29 Scott, 'Life'.
30 Scott, 'Life'.
31 Scott, 'Life'.
32 Scott, 'Life'.
33 Scott, 'Life'.
34 Scott, 'Life'.
35 Scott, 'Life'.
36 Scott, 'Life'.
37 Scott, 'Life'.
38 Cartwright, *Sacharisa*, p. 233.

Chapter 11
1 Lansdowne Mss, 152ff (British Museum).
2 Lansdowne Mss, 152ff.
3 Harleian Mss 7006 (Sir Henry Elliss's original letters).
4 Paschall's account in the appendix to Heywood's *Vindication*.
5 Historical Manuscripts Commission: Stopford-Sackville Papers, 1, p. 3.
6 Ralph, *History of England*, p. 879.
7 Egerton Mss 1527 (British Museum).
8 See Louis Macneice, *Astrology*, p. 187.

Chapter 12
1 See *London Gazette* for July 1685 (British Museum).
2 See *Relation of the great sufferings and strange adventures of Henry Pitman Chyrugion to the late Duke of Monmouth*, published by

Andrew Sowle, sold at 'The Sign of the Ship', St Paul's Church-yard 1689 (Jackdaw, No. 34).

3 Historical Manuscripts Commission: Stopford-Sackville Mss, p. 12.

4 John Oldmixon, *History of England during the reign of the Royal House of Stuart*, p. 554. Also Roberts, *Life*, II, p. 58.

Chapter 13

1 William Stradling, *A Description of the Priory of Chilton Super Polden*, p. 80.

2 Oldmixon, *History of England*, p. 704.

3 Oldmixon, *History of England*, p. 704.

4 Rawlinson Mss A 139b (Bodleian Library).

5 William Kennet, *History of England*, III, p. 432.

6 Fraser, *Buccleuch*, I, p. 452. Quoted from a contemporary manu-script signed 'J.F.'.

7 Fraser, *Buccleuch*, I, p. 448.

8 Fraser, *Buccleuch*, I, p. 449.

9 From the official account of the execution: Historical Manuscripts Commission, Report XII, Appendix V, p. 1193.

10 From the official account of the execution: Historical Manuscripts Commission, Report XII, Appendix V, p. 1193.

Appendix I

1 *Calendar of State Papers (Domestic)*, September 1973.

Appendix III

1 Fraser, *Buccleuch*, I, p. 484.

2 Fraser, *Buccleuch*, I, p. 456, quoted from Johnson, *Life of Gay*.

3 See diary of Lady Cowper (British Museum).

4 See diary of Lady Cowper.
   Court, III, p. 212.

Appendix IV

1 Roberts, *Life*.

Bibliography

Barnard, H. C., *The Little Schools of Port Royal* (London 1913).

Bevan, Bryan, *James Duke of Monmouth* (Robert Hale 1973).

Bryant, Sir Arthur, *King Charles II* (Longmans Green 1932).

Bryant, Sir Arthur, *Restoration England* (Collins 1960).

Burghclere, Lady, *George Villiers* (John Murray 1903).

Burnet, Bishop G., *History of My Own Time* (1724).

Boswell, E., *Restoration Court Stage*.

Cannon, R., *Historical Records of the British Army* (London 1935).

Cartwright, J., *Madame* (Seeley 1900).

Cartwright, J., *Sacharisa* (Seeley 1893).

Christie, W. D., *A Life of Anthony Ashley Cooper* (1871).

Clarendon, E., *Life of Edward Hyde* (Clarendon 1837), vols.

Clark, R., *Strangers and Sojourners at Port Royal* (London 1932).

Clarke, J. S., *Life of James II* (London 1816).

D'Aulnoy, Baronne, *Memoirs of the Court of England in 1675* (London 1913).

D'Oyley, Elizabeth, *James Duke of Monmouth* (Bles 1938).

Emerson, W. R., *Monmouth Rebellion* (Yale UP 1951).

Evelyn, John, *Diary*, ed. H. B. Wheatley (London 1897).

Falkus, Christopher, *The Life and Times of Charles II* (Weidenfeld & Nicolson 1972).

Fea, Allan, *King Monmouth* (Bodley Head 1902).

Fraser, Sir W., *The Scotts of Buccleuch* (Edinburgh 1878), 5 vols.

Greene, Graham, *Lord Rochester's Monkey* (Bodley Head 1974).

Hartmann, C. H., *Charles II and Madame* (Heinemann 1937).

Macpherson, J., *Original Papers containing the Secret History of Great*

Britain from the Restoration to the Accession of the House of Hanover, vol. II (1775).

Melville, L., *Mr Crofts the King's Bastard* (Hutchinson 1929).

Miller, J., *Popery and Politics in England 1660–88* (Cambridge UP 1973).

Orleans, A. M. L., *Memoirs of La Grande Mademoiselle* (Eveleigh Nash & Grayson 1928).

Pepys, Samuel, *Diary*, ed. H. B. Whealey (Ladbridge 1893).

Roberts, George, *The Life, Progress and Rebellion of James Duke of Monmouth* (Longmans 1844).

Scott, Lord George, *Lucy Walter. Wife or Mistress?* (Harrap 1947).

Scott, Lord George, 'The Life of the Duke of Monmouth' (unpublished).

Shirley, J. W., *Thomas Harriot Renaissance Scientist* (Clarendon 1974).

Sidney, Henry, *Diary of the Times of Charles II* (London 1834).

Strickland, A., *Lives of the Queens of England* (Bell 1888).

Toulmin, J., *History of Taunton* (John Poole 1822).

Trevelyan, Sir G., *England under the Stuarts* (Methuen 1949).

Trevelyan, Sir G., *Social History of England* (Longmans 1946).

Verney, Lady, *Memoirs of the Verney Family* (London 1892).

Index

187